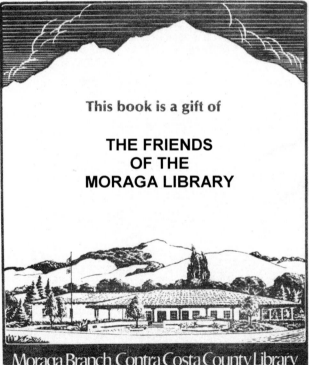

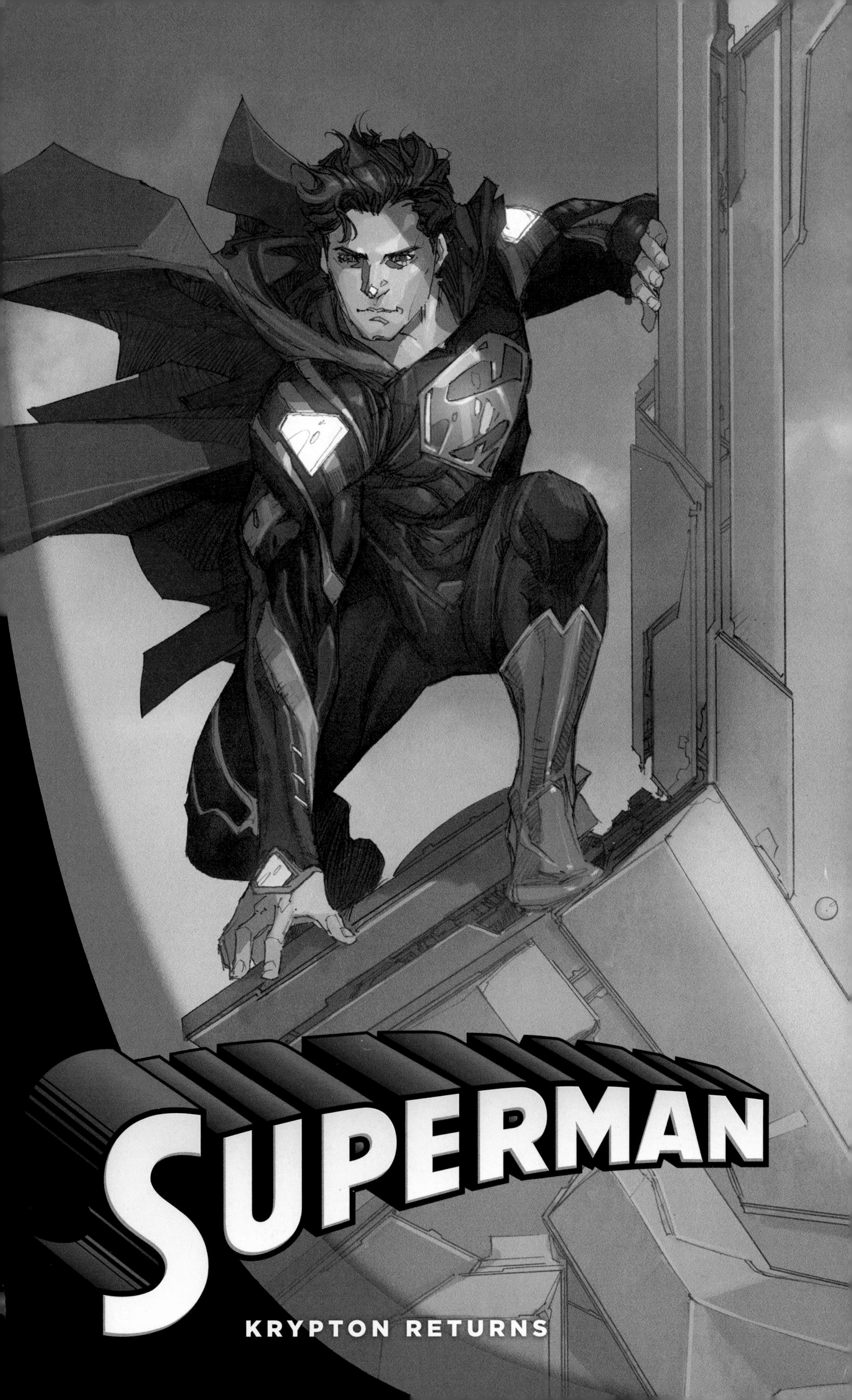

SUPERMAN

KRYPTON RETURNS

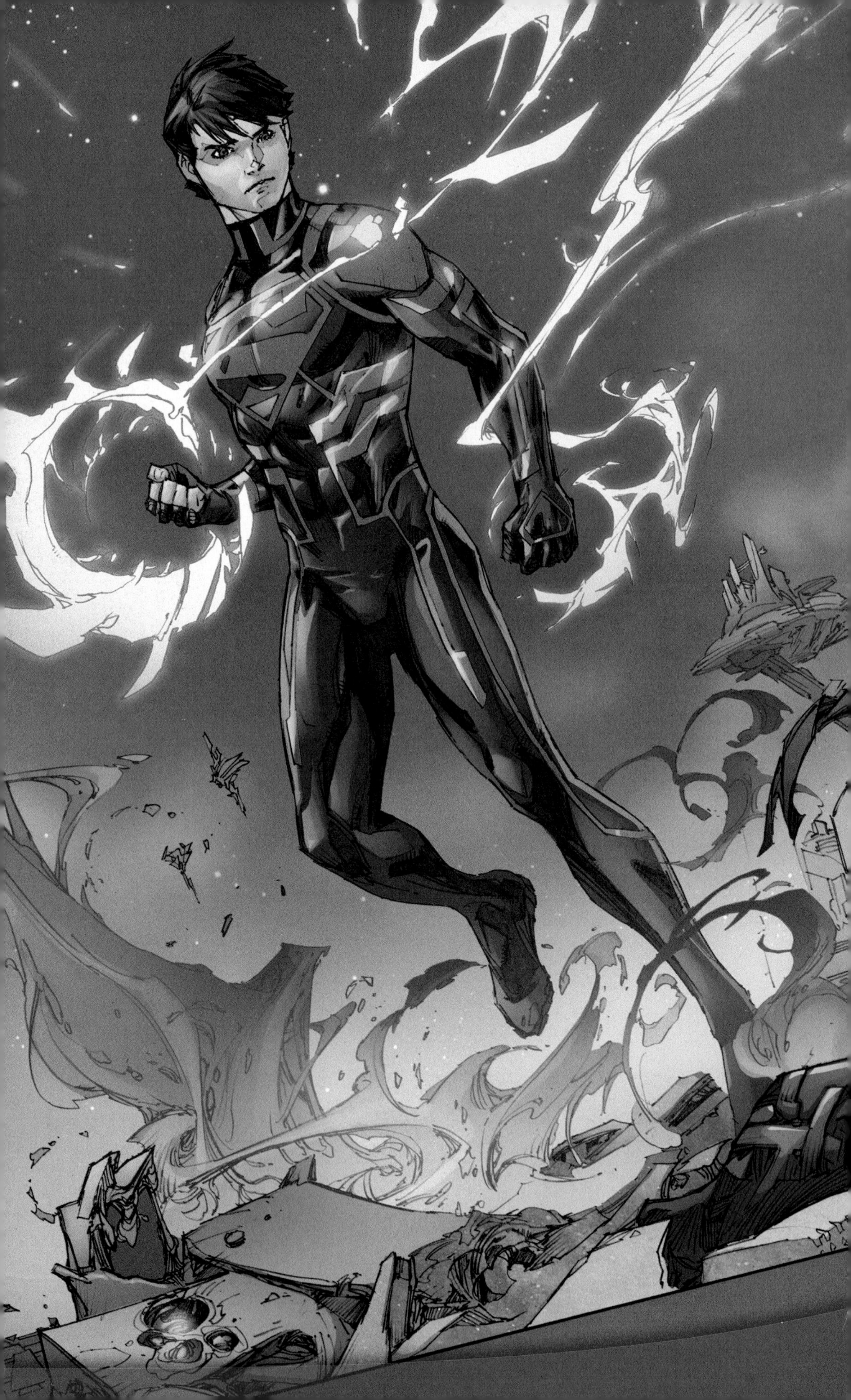

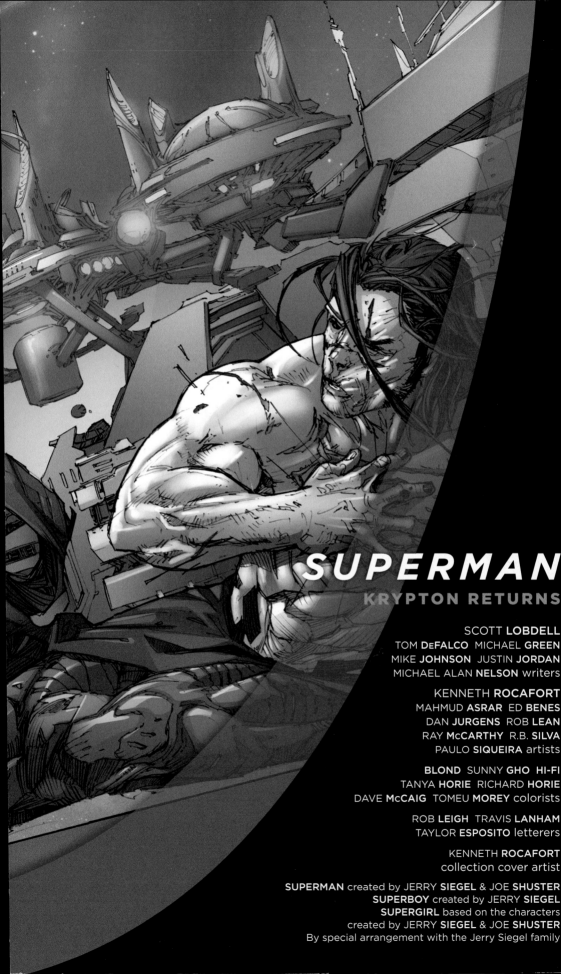

SUPERMAN
KRYPTON RETURNS

SCOTT **LOBDELL**
TOM DeFALCO MICHAEL **GREEN**
MIKE **JOHNSON** JUSTIN **JORDAN**
MICHAEL ALAN **NELSON** writers

KENNETH **ROCAFORT**
MAHMUD **ASRAR** ED **BENES**
DAN **JURGENS** ROB **LEAN**
RAY McCARTHY R.B. **SILVA**
PAULO **SIQUEIRA** artists

BLOND SUNNY **GHO** HI-FI
TANYA **HORIE** RICHARD **HORIE**
DAVE McCAIG TOMEU **MOREY** colorists

ROB **LEIGH** TRAVIS **LANHAM**
TAYLOR **ESPOSITO** letterers

KENNETH **ROCAFORT**
collection cover artist

SUPERMAN created by JERRY **SIEGEL** & JOE **SHUSTER**
SUPERBOY created by JERRY **SIEGEL**
SUPERGIRL based on the characters
created by JERRY **SIEGEL** & JOE **SHUSTER**
By special arrangement with the Jerry Siegel family

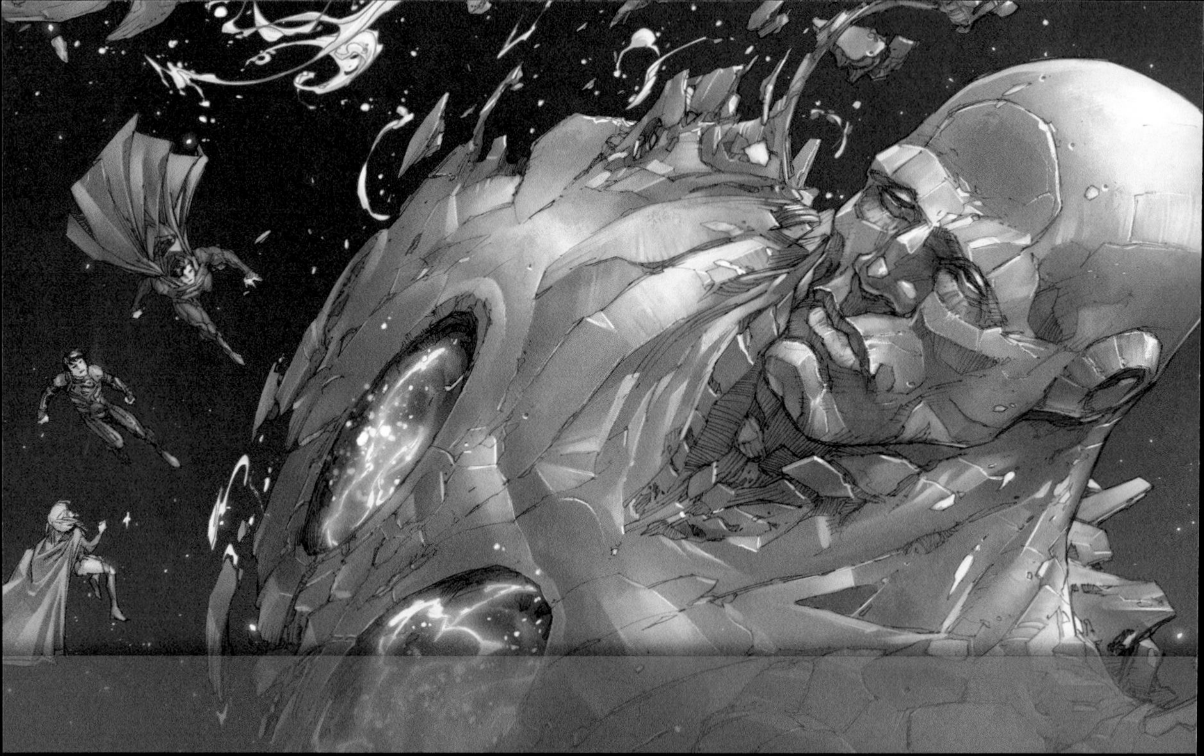

EDDIE BERGANZA WIL MOSS CHRIS CONROY Editors – Original Series
RICKEY PURDIN Associate Editor – Original Series ANTHONY MARQUES DARREN SHAN Assistant Editors – Original Series
ROBIN WILDMAN Editor ROBBIN BROSTERMAN Design Director – Books ROBBIE BIEDERMAN Publication Design

BOB HARRAS Senior VP – Editor-in-Chief, DC Comics

DIANE NELSON President DAN DIDIO and JIM LEE Co-Publishers GEOFF JOHNS Chief Creative Officer
AMIT DESAI Senior VP – Marketing and Franchise Management AMY GENKINS Senior VP – Business and Legal Affairs
NAIRI GARDINER Senior VP – Finance JEFF BOISON VP – Publishing Planning
MARK CHIARELLO VP – Art Direction and Design JOHN CUNNINGHAM VP – Marketing
TERRI CUNNINGHAM VP – Editorial Administration LARRY GANEM VP – Talent Relations and Services
ALISON GILL Senior VP – Manufacturing and Operations HANK KANALZ Senior VP – Vertigo and Integrated Publishing
JAY KOGAN VP – Business and Legal Affairs, Publishing JACK MAHAN VP – Business Affairs, Talent
NICK NAPOLITANO VP – Manufacturing Administration SUE POHJA VP – Book Sales FRED RUIZ VP – Manufacturing Operations
COURTNEY SIMMONS Senior VP – Publicity BOB WAYNE Senior VP – Sales

SUPERMAN: KRYPTON RETURNS
Published by DC Comics.

DC Comics, 1700 Broadway, New York, NY 10019
A Warner Bros. Entertainment Company.
Printed by RR Donnelley, Salem, VA, USA. 1/9/15. First Printing.

HC ISBN: 978-1-4012-4948-9
SC ISBN: 978-1-4012-5544-2

Library of Congress Cataloging-in-Publication Data

Lobdell, Scott.
Superman : Krypton returns / Scott Lobdell ; [illustrated by] Kenneth Rocafort.
pages cm. — (The New 52!)
ISBN 978-1-4012-4948-9 (hardback)
1. Graphic novels. I. Rocafort, Kenneth, illustrator. II. Title.

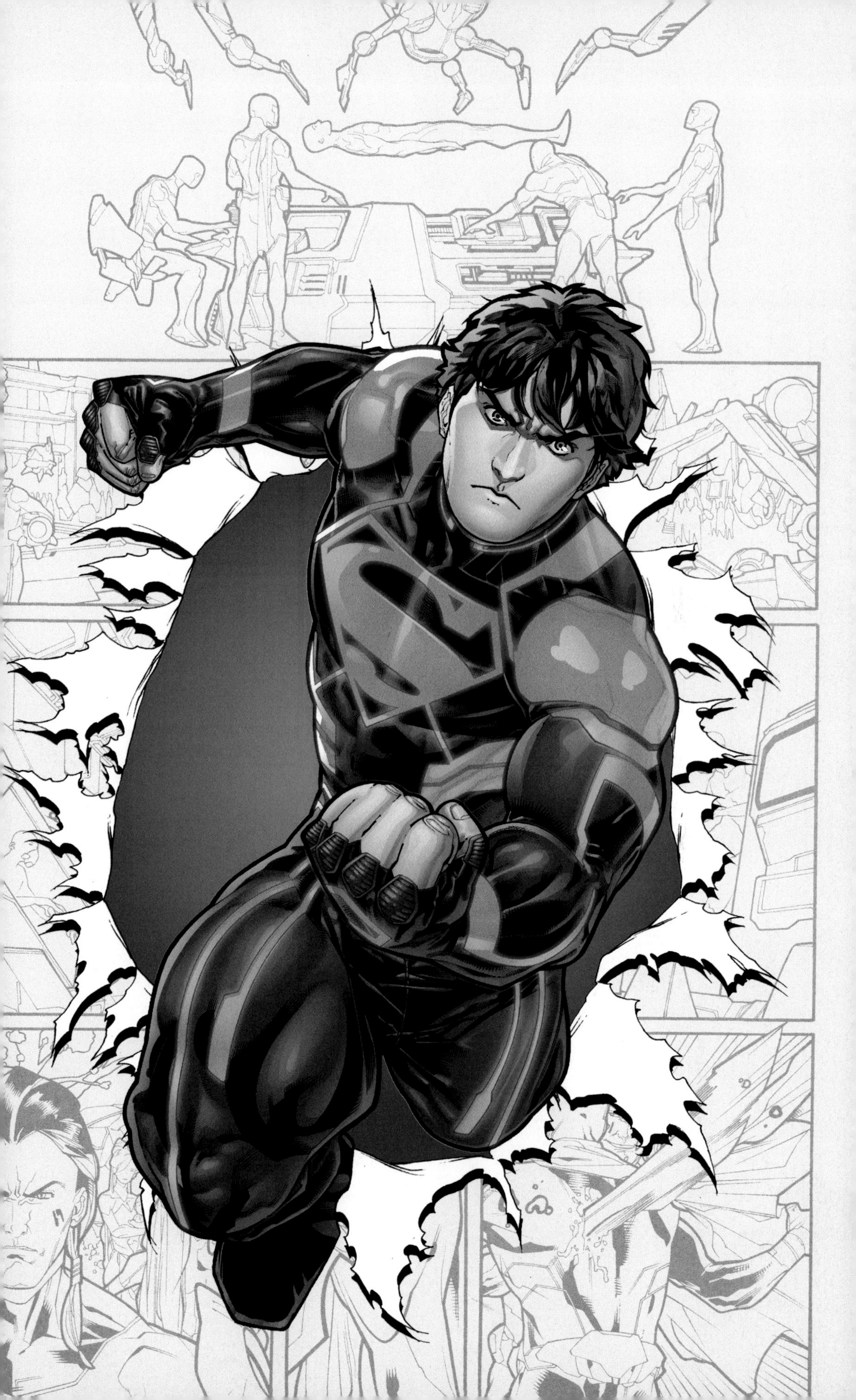

CLONESURRECTION!

TOM DeFALCO writer **R.B. SILVA** penciller **ROB LEAN** inker **TANYA HORIE RICHARD HORIE HI-FI** colorists
cover art by **R.B. SILVA, ROB LEAN & HI-FI**

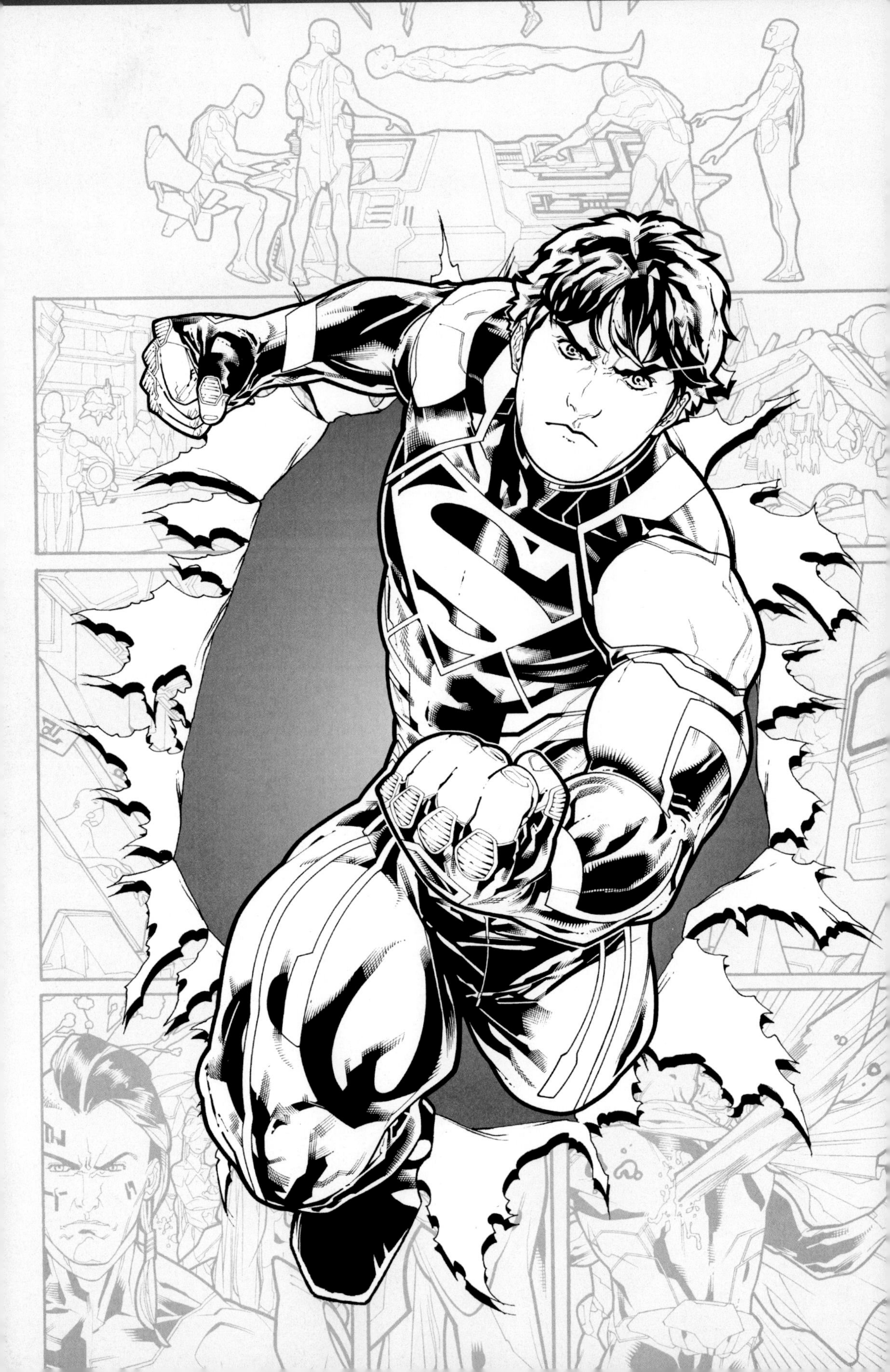

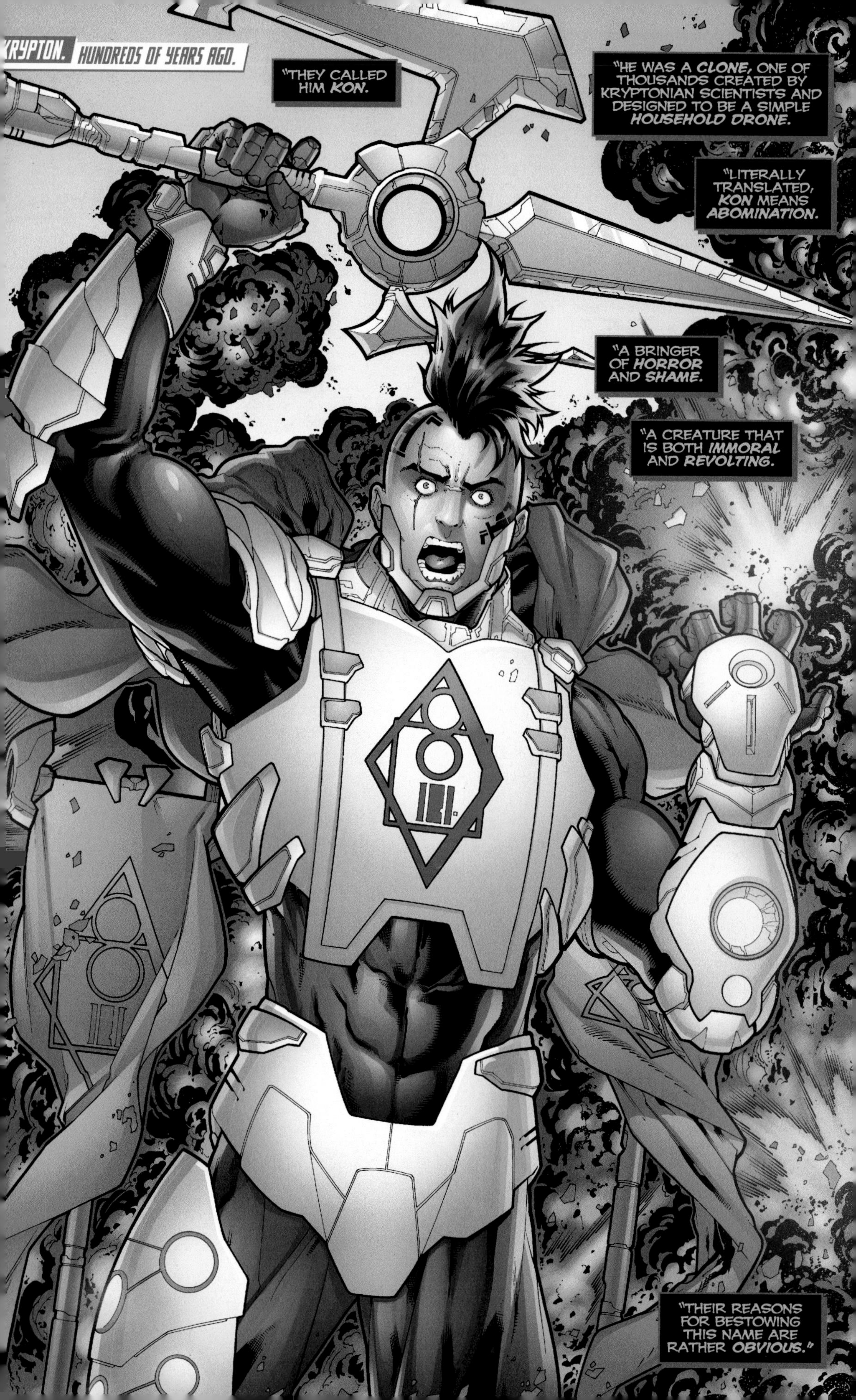
KRYPTON. HUNDREDS OF YEARS AGO.
"THEY CALLED HIM KON.
"HE WAS A CLONE, ONE OF THOUSANDS CREATED BY KRYPTONIAN SCIENTISTS AND DESIGNED TO BE A SIMPLE HOUSEHOLD DRONE.
"LITERALLY TRANSLATED, KON MEANS ABOMINATION.
"A BRINGER OF HORROR AND SHAME.
"A CREATURE THAT IS BOTH IMMORAL AND REVOLTING.
"THEIR REASONS FOR BESTOWING THIS NAME ARE RATHER OBVIOUS."

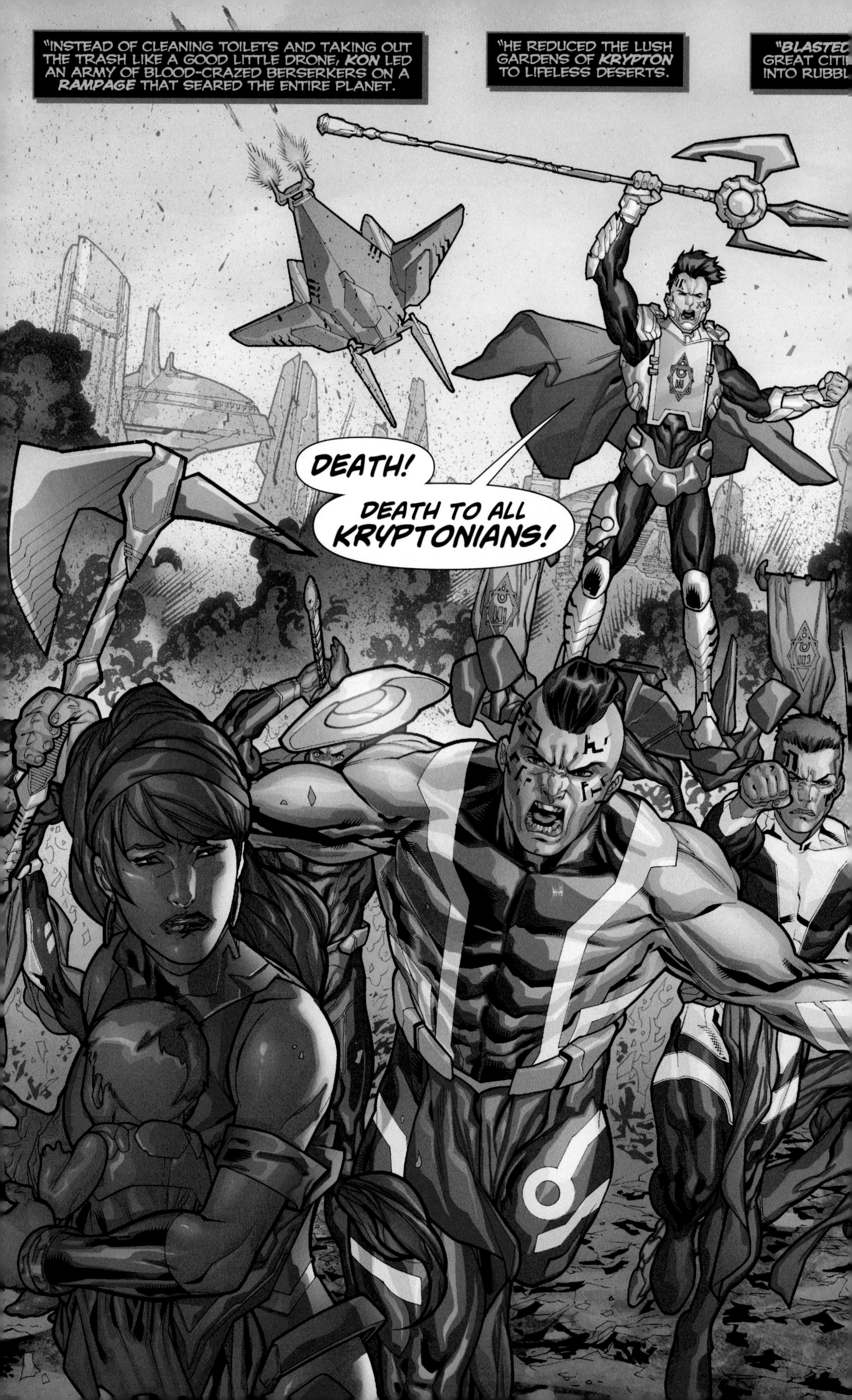
"INSTEAD OF CLEANING TOILETS AND TAKING OUT THE TRASH LIKE A GOOD LITTLE DRONE, KON LED AN ARMY OF BLOOD-CRAZED BERSERKERS ON A RAMPAGE THAT SEARED THE ENTIRE PLANET.
"HE REDUCED THE LUSH GARDENS OF KRYPTON TO LIFELESS DESERTS.
DEATH!
DEATH TO ALL KRYPTONIANS!

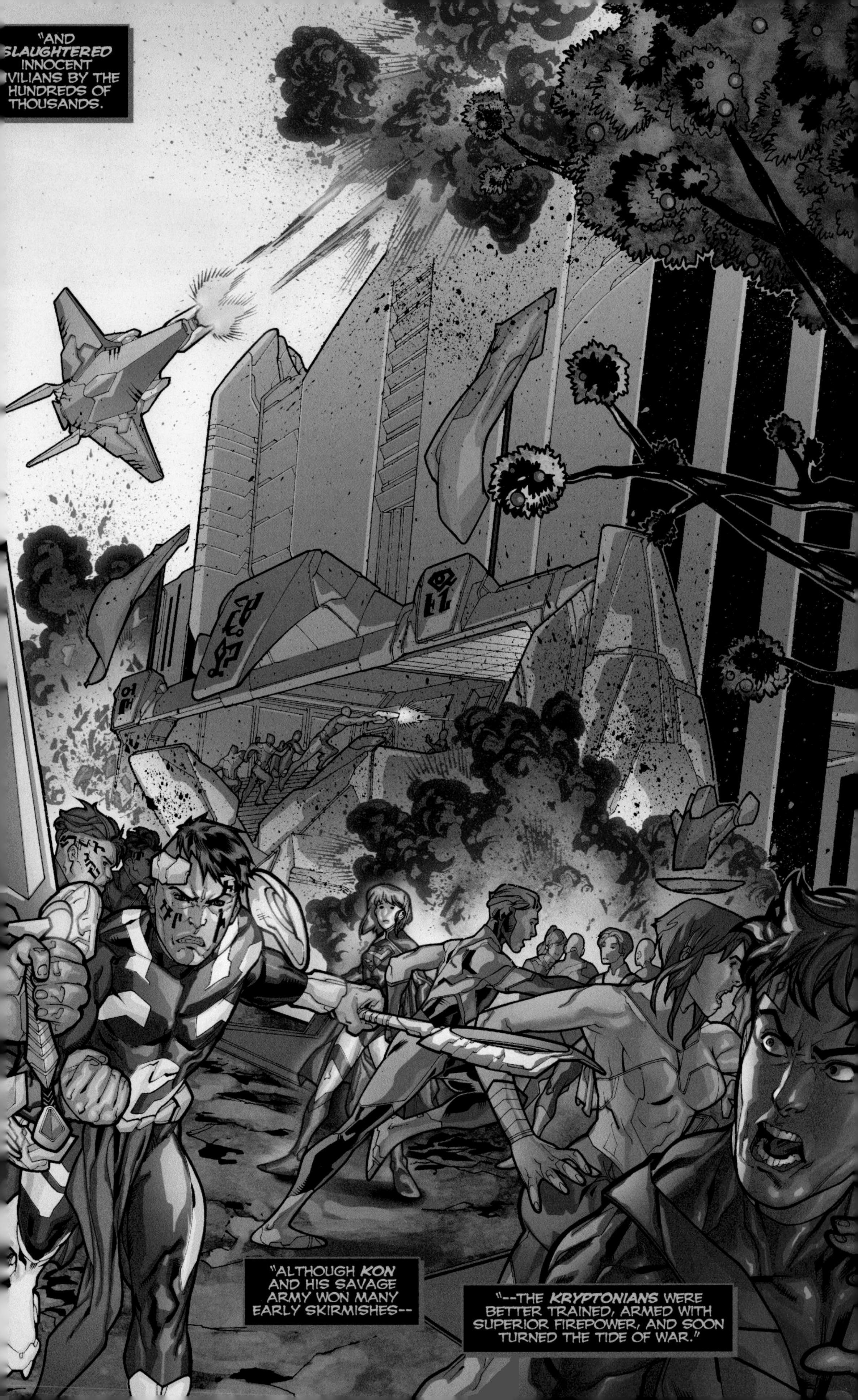
"AND SLAUGHTERED INNOCENT VILIANS BY THE HUNDREDS OF THOUSANDS.
"ALTHOUGH KON AND HIS SAVAGE ARMY WON MANY EARLY SKIRMISHES--
"--THE KRYPTONIANS WERE BETTER TRAINED, ARMED WITH SUPERIOR FIREPOWER, AND SOON TURNED THE TIDE OF WAR."

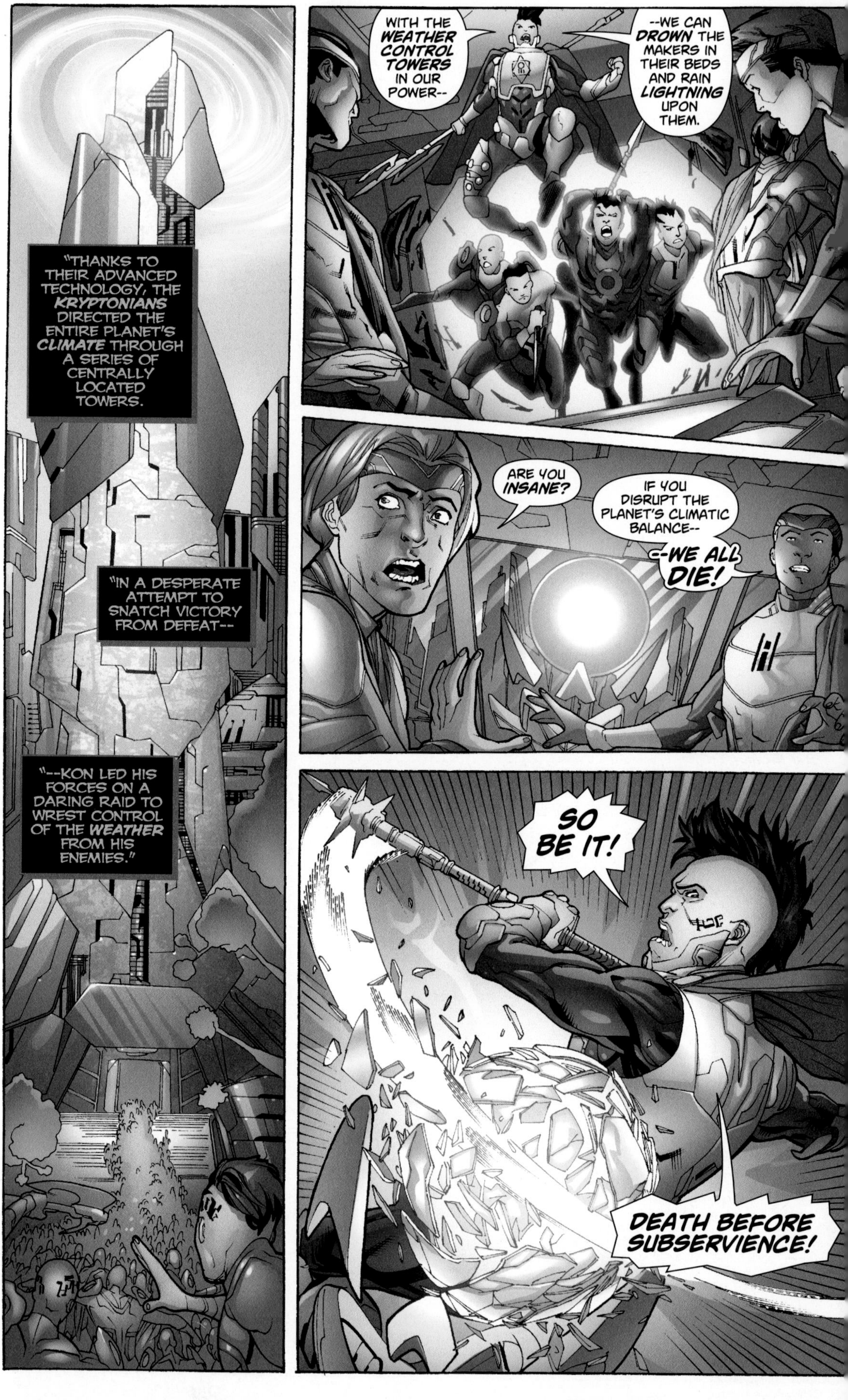
"THANKS TO THEIR ADVANCED TECHNOLOGY, THE KRYPTONIANS DIRECTED THE ENTIRE PLANET'S CLIMATE THROUGH A SERIES OF CENTRALLY LOCATED TOWERS.
"IN A DESPERATE ATTEMPT TO SNATCH VICTORY FROM DEFEAT--
"--KON LED HIS FORCES ON A DARING RAID TO WREST CONTROL OF THE WEATHER FROM HIS ENEMIES."
WITH THE WEATHER CONTROL TOWERS IN OUR POWER--
--WE CAN DROWN THE MAKERS IN THEIR BEDS AND RAIN LIGHTNING UPON THEM.
ARE YOU INSANE?
IF YOU DISRUPT THE PLANET'S CLIMATIC BALANCE--
--WE ALL DIE!
SO BE IT!
DEATH BEFORE SUBSERVIENCE!

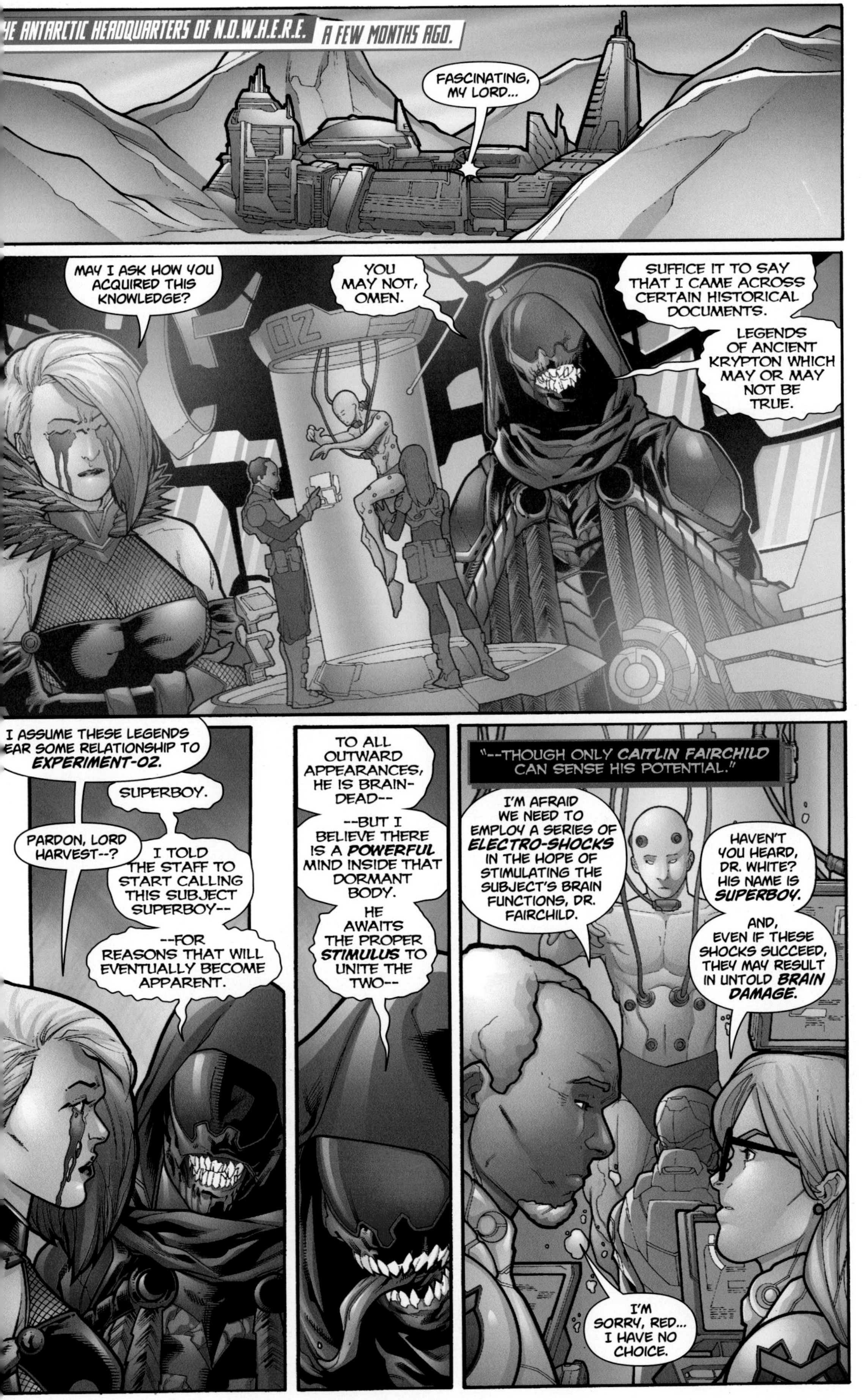

HE ANTARCTIC HEADQUARTERS OF N.O.W.H.E.R.E.
A FEW MONTHS AGO.
FASCINATING, MY LORD...
MAY I ASK HOW YOU ACQUIRED THIS KNOWLEDGE?
YOU MAY NOT, OMEN.
SUFFICE IT TO SAY THAT I CAME ACROSS CERTAIN HISTORICAL DOCUMENTS.
LEGENDS OF ANCIENT KRYPTON WHICH MAY OR MAY NOT BE TRUE.
02
I ASSUME THESE LEGENDS EAR SOME RELATIONSHIP TO EXPERIMENT-02.
SUPERBOY.
PARDON, LORD HARVEST--?
I TOLD THE STAFF TO START CALLING THIS SUBJECT SUPERBOY--
--FOR REASONS THAT WILL EVENTUALLY BECOME APPARENT.
TO ALL OUTWARD APPEARANCES, HE IS BRAIN-DEAD--
--BUT I BELIEVE THERE IS A POWERFUL MIND INSIDE THAT DORMANT BODY.
HE AWAITS THE PROPER STIMULUS TO UNITE THE TWO--
"--THOUGH ONLY CAITLIN FAIRCHILD CAN SENSE HIS POTENTIAL."
I'M AFRAID WE NEED TO EMPLOY A SERIES OF ELECTRO-SHOCKS IN THE HOPE OF STIMULATING THE SUBJECT'S BRAIN FUNCTIONS, DR. FAIRCHILD.
HAVEN'T YOU HEARD, DR. WHITE? HIS NAME IS SUPERBOY.
AND, EVEN IF THESE SHOCKS SUCCEED, THEY MAY RESULT IN UNTOLD BRAIN DAMAGE.
I'M SORRY, RED... I HAVE NO CHOICE.

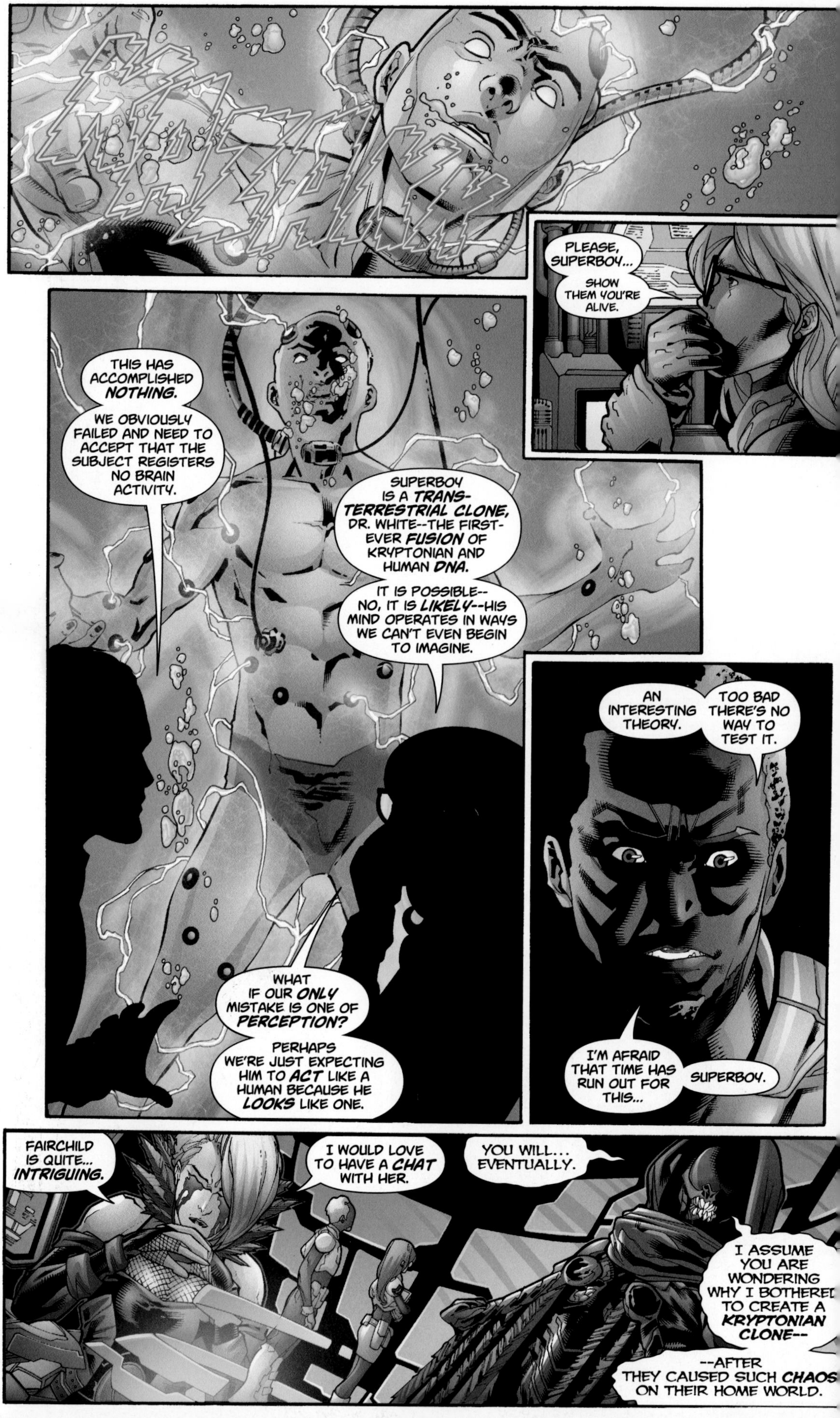
PLEASE, SUPERBOY...
SHOW THEM YOU'RE ALIVE.
THIS HAS ACCOMPLISHED NOTHING.
WE OBVIOUSLY FAILED AND NEED TO ACCEPT THAT THE SUBJECT REGISTERS NO BRAIN ACTIVITY.
SUPERBOY IS A TRANS-TERRESTRIAL CLONE, DR. WHITE--THE FIRST-EVER FUSION OF KRYPTONIAN AND HUMAN DNA.
IT IS POSSIBLE--NO, IT IS LIKELY--HIS MIND OPERATES IN WAYS WE CAN'T EVEN BEGIN TO IMAGINE.
WHAT IF OUR ONLY MISTAKE IS ONE OF PERCEPTION?
PERHAPS WE'RE JUST EXPECTING HIM TO ACT LIKE A HUMAN BECAUSE HE LOOKS LIKE ONE.
AN INTERESTING THEORY.
TOO BAD THERE'S NO WAY TO TEST IT.
I'M AFRAID THAT TIME HAS RUN OUT FOR THIS...
SUPERBOY.
FAIRCHILD IS QUITE... INTRIGUING.
I WOULD LOVE TO HAVE A CHAT WITH HER.
YOU WILL... EVENTUALLY.
I ASSUME YOU ARE WONDERING WHY I BOTHERED TO CREATE A KRYPTONIAN CLONE--
--AFTER THEY CAUSED SUCH CHAOS ON THEIR HOME WORLD.

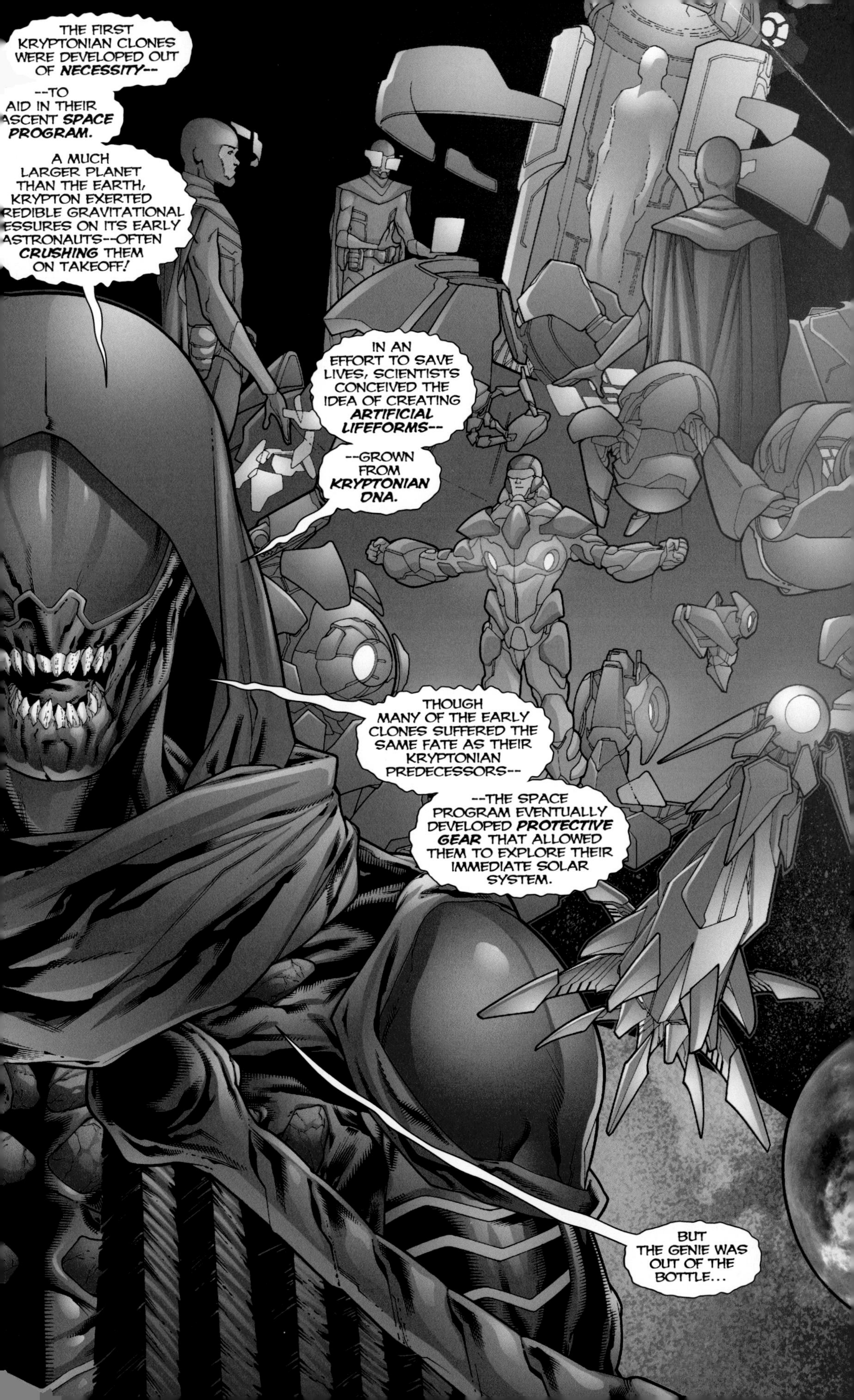
THE FIRST KRYPTONIAN CLONES WERE DEVELOPED OUT OF NECESSITY--
--TO AID IN THEIR ASCENT SPACE PROGRAM.
A MUCH LARGER PLANET THAN THE EARTH, KRYPTON EXERTED REDIBLE GRAVITATIONAL ESSURES ON ITS EARLY ASTRONAUTS--OFTEN CRUSHING THEM ON TAKEOFF!
IN AN EFFORT TO SAVE LIVES, SCIENTISTS CONCEIVED THE IDEA OF CREATING ARTIFICIAL LIFEFORMS--
--GROWN FROM KRYPTONIAN DNA.
THOUGH MANY OF THE EARLY CLONES SUFFERED THE SAME FATE AS THEIR KRYPTONIAN PREDECESSORS--
--THE SPACE PROGRAM EVENTUALLY DEVELOPED PROTECTIVE GEAR THAT ALLOWED THEM TO EXPLORE THEIR IMMEDIATE SOLAR SYSTEM.
BUT THE GENIE WAS OUT OF THE BOTTLE...

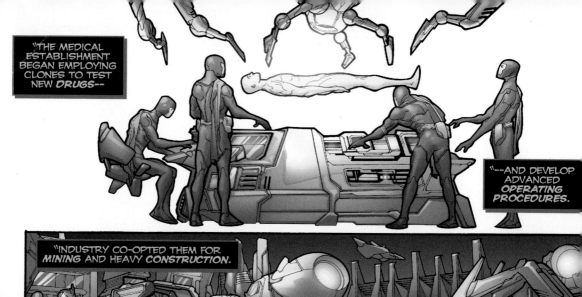

"THE MEDICAL ESTABLISHMENT BEGAN EMPLOYING CLONES TO TEST NEW *DRUGS*--

"--AND DEVELOP ADVANCED *OPERATING PROCEDURES.*

"INDUSTRY CO-OPTED THEM FOR *MINING* AND HEAVY *CONSTRUCTION.*

"THE ELITE SHOWED OFF THEIR STATUS BY UTILIZING THEM AS *DOMESTICS.*

"AS OTHER USES DEVELOPED, CLONES WERE *MASS-PRODUCED* TO MEET DEMAND.

"THAT'S WHEN THE *TROUBLE* BEGAN..."

WHY HAVEN'T YOU COMPLETED YOUR ASSIGNED TASKS?

BE SILENT, MAKER--!

"WHETHER THE RESULT OF MANUFACTURING SHORTCUTS OR AN INHERENT INSTABILITY IN THEIR GENETIC MAKEUP--

"--THE CLONES DEVELOPED *IMPULSE CONTROL* ISSUES, LASHING OUT AGAINST THEIR CREATORS."

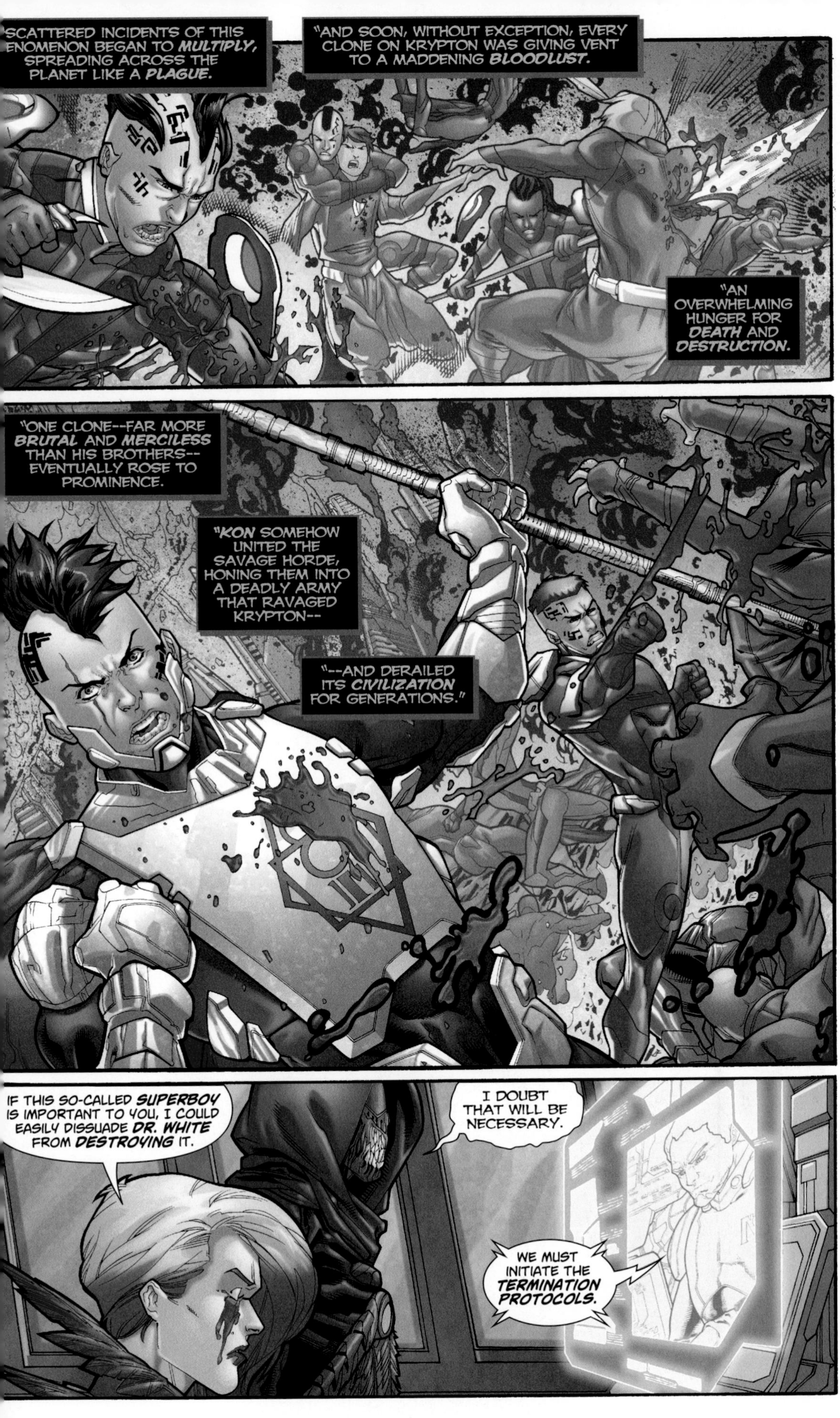
SCATTERED INCIDENTS OF THIS ENOMENON BEGAN TO MULTIPLY, SPREADING ACROSS THE PLANET LIKE A PLAGUE.
"AND SOON, WITHOUT EXCEPTION, EVERY CLONE ON KRYPTON WAS GIVING VENT TO A MADDENING BLOODLUST.
"AN OVERWHELMING HUNGER FOR DEATH AND DESTRUCTION.
"ONE CLONE--FAR MORE BRUTAL AND MERCILESS THAN HIS BROTHERS--EVENTUALLY ROSE TO PROMINENCE.
"KON SOMEHOW UNITED THE SAVAGE HORDE, HONING THEM INTO A DEADLY ARMY THAT RAVAGED KRYPTON--
"--AND DERAILED ITS CIVILIZATION FOR GENERATIONS."
IF THIS SO-CALLED SUPERBOY IS IMPORTANT TO YOU, I COULD EASILY DISSUADE DR. WHITE FROM DESTROYING IT.
I DOUBT THAT WILL BE NECESSARY.
WE MUST INITIATE THE TERMINATION PROTOCOLS.

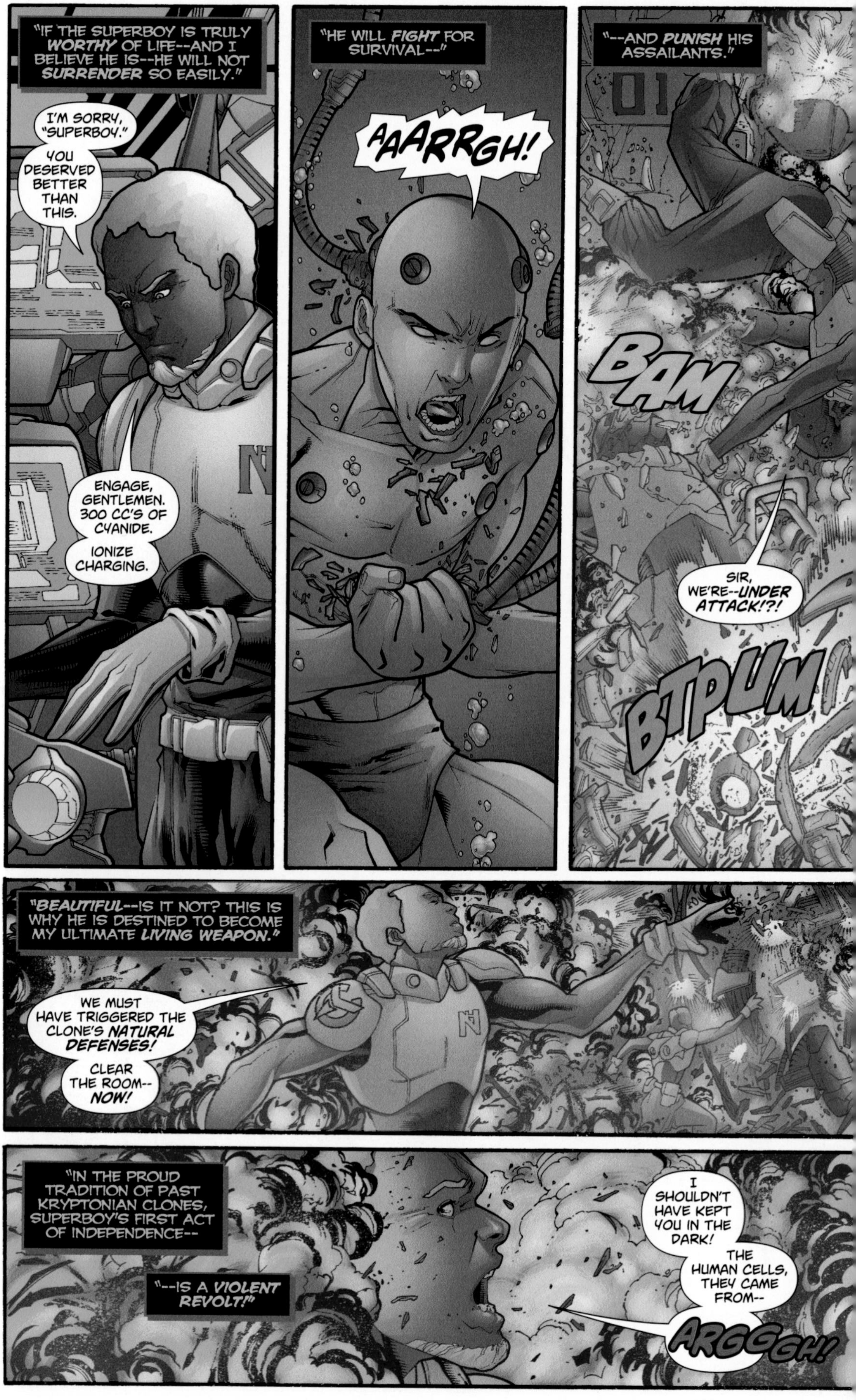
"IF THE SUPERBOY IS TRULY WORTHY OF LIFE--AND I BELIEVE HE IS--HE WILL NOT SURRENDER SO EASILY."
I'M SORRY, "SUPERBOY."
YOU DESERVED BETTER THAN THIS.
ENGAGE, GENTLEMEN. 300 CC'S OF CYANIDE.
IONIZE CHARGING.
"HE WILL FIGHT FOR SURVIVAL--"
AAARRGH!
"--AND PUNISH HIS ASSAILANTS."
BAM
SIR, WE'RE--UNDER ATTACK!?!
BTPUM
"BEAUTIFUL--IS IT NOT? THIS IS WHY HE IS DESTINED TO BECOME MY ULTIMATE LIVING WEAPON."
WE MUST HAVE TRIGGERED THE CLONE'S NATURAL DEFENSES!
CLEAR THE ROOM--NOW!
"IN THE PROUD TRADITION OF PAST KRYPTONIAN CLONES, SUPERBOY'S FIRST ACT OF INDEPENDENCE--
"--IS A VIOLENT REVOLT!"
I SHOULDN'T HAVE KEPT YOU IN THE DARK!
THE HUMAN CELLS, THEY CAME FROM--
ARGGGH!

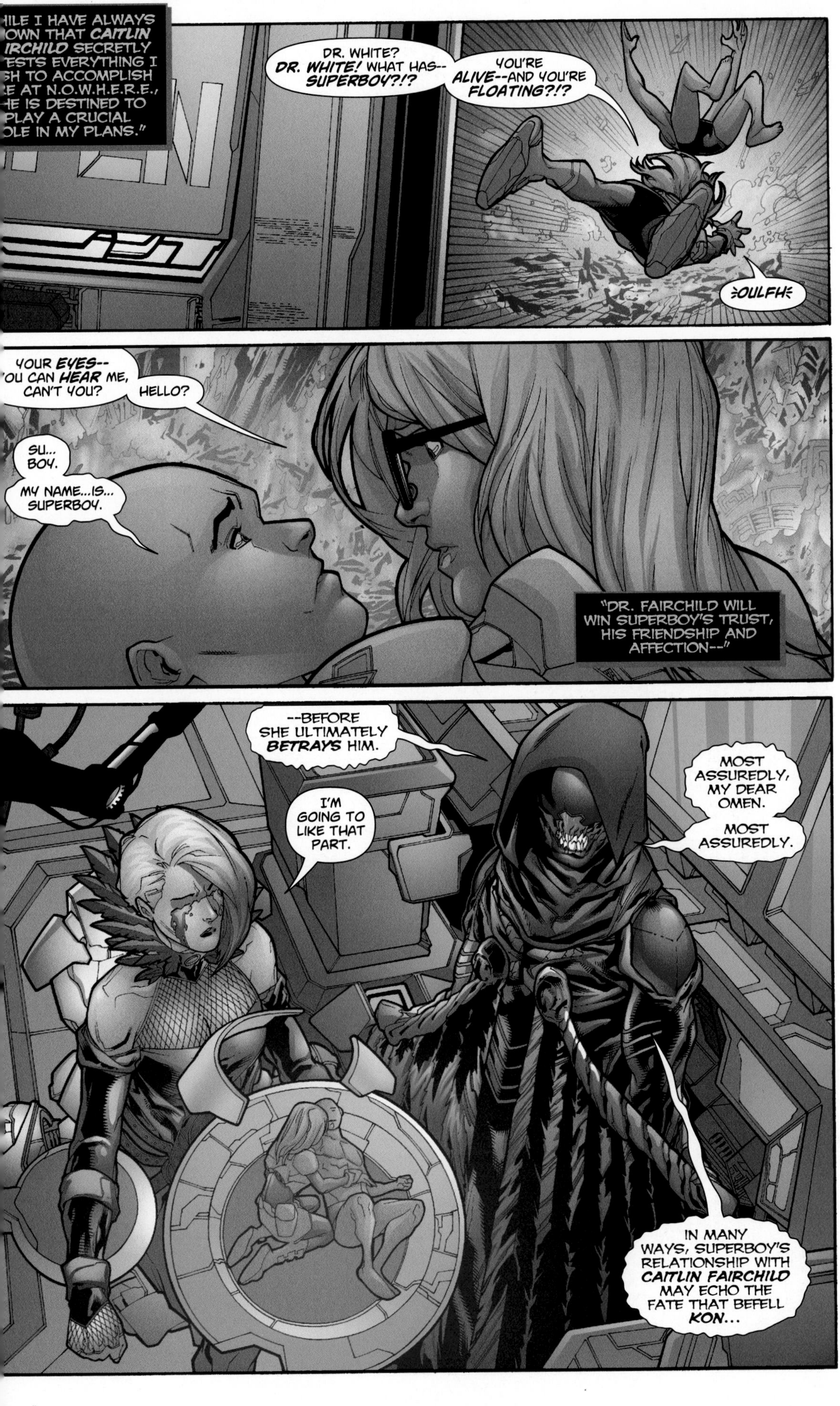

HILE I HAVE ALWAYS OWN THAT CAITLIN IRCHILD SECRETLY ESTS EVERYTHING I SH TO ACCOMPLISH E AT N.O.W.H.E.R.E., HE IS DESTINED TO PLAY A CRUCIAL OLE IN MY PLANS."
DR. WHITE? DR. WHITE! WHAT HAS-- SUPERBOY?!?
YOU'RE ALIVE--AND YOU'RE FLOATING?!?
OULFH
YOUR EYES-- OU CAN HEAR ME, CAN'T YOU?
HELLO?
SU... BOY.
MY NAME...IS... SUPERBOY.
"DR. FAIRCHILD WILL WIN SUPERBOY'S TRUST, HIS FRIENDSHIP AND AFFECTION--"
--BEFORE SHE ULTIMATELY BETRAYS HIM.
I'M GOING TO LIKE THAT PART.
MOST ASSUREDLY, MY DEAR OMEN.
MOST ASSUREDLY.
IN MANY WAYS, SUPERBOY'S RELATIONSHIP WITH CAITLIN FAIRCHILD MAY ECHO THE FATE THAT BEFELL KON...

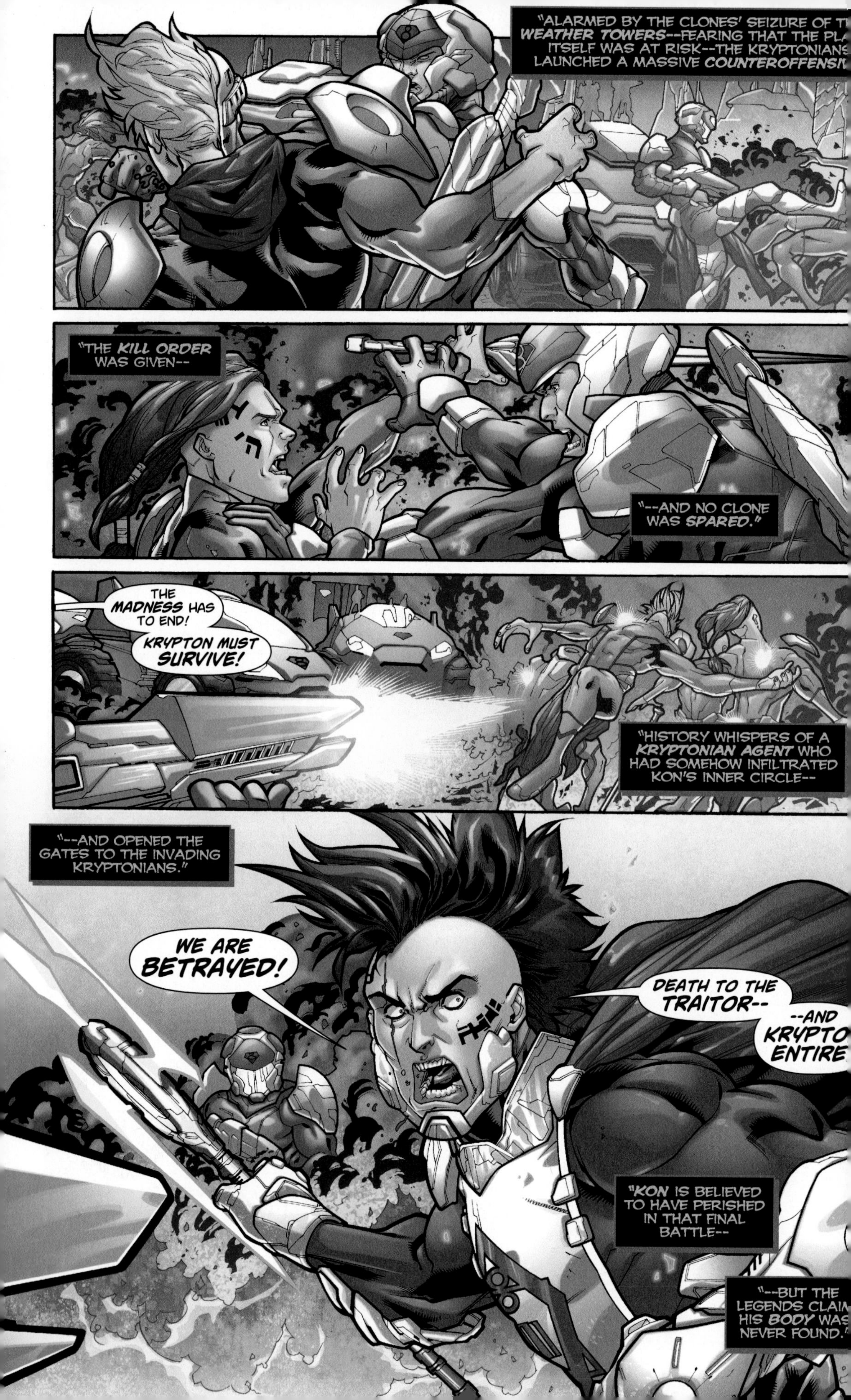

"ALARMED BY THE CLONES' SEIZURE OF T WEATHER TOWERS--FEARING THAT THE PLA ITSELF WAS AT RISK--THE KRYPTONIANS LAUNCHED A MASSIVE COUNTEROFFENSI
"THE KILL ORDER WAS GIVEN--
"--AND NO CLONE WAS SPARED."
THE MADNESS HAS TO END!
KRYPTON MUST SURVIVE!
"HISTORY WHISPERS OF A KRYPTONIAN AGENT WHO HAD SOMEHOW INFILTRATED KON'S INNER CIRCLE--
"--AND OPENED THE GATES TO THE INVADING KRYPTONIANS."
WE ARE BETRAYED!
DEATH TO THE TRAITOR--
--AND KRYPTO ENTIRE
"KON IS BELIEVED TO HAVE PERISHED IN THAT FINAL BATTLE--
"--BUT THE LEGENDS CLAI HIS BODY WAS NEVER FOUND."

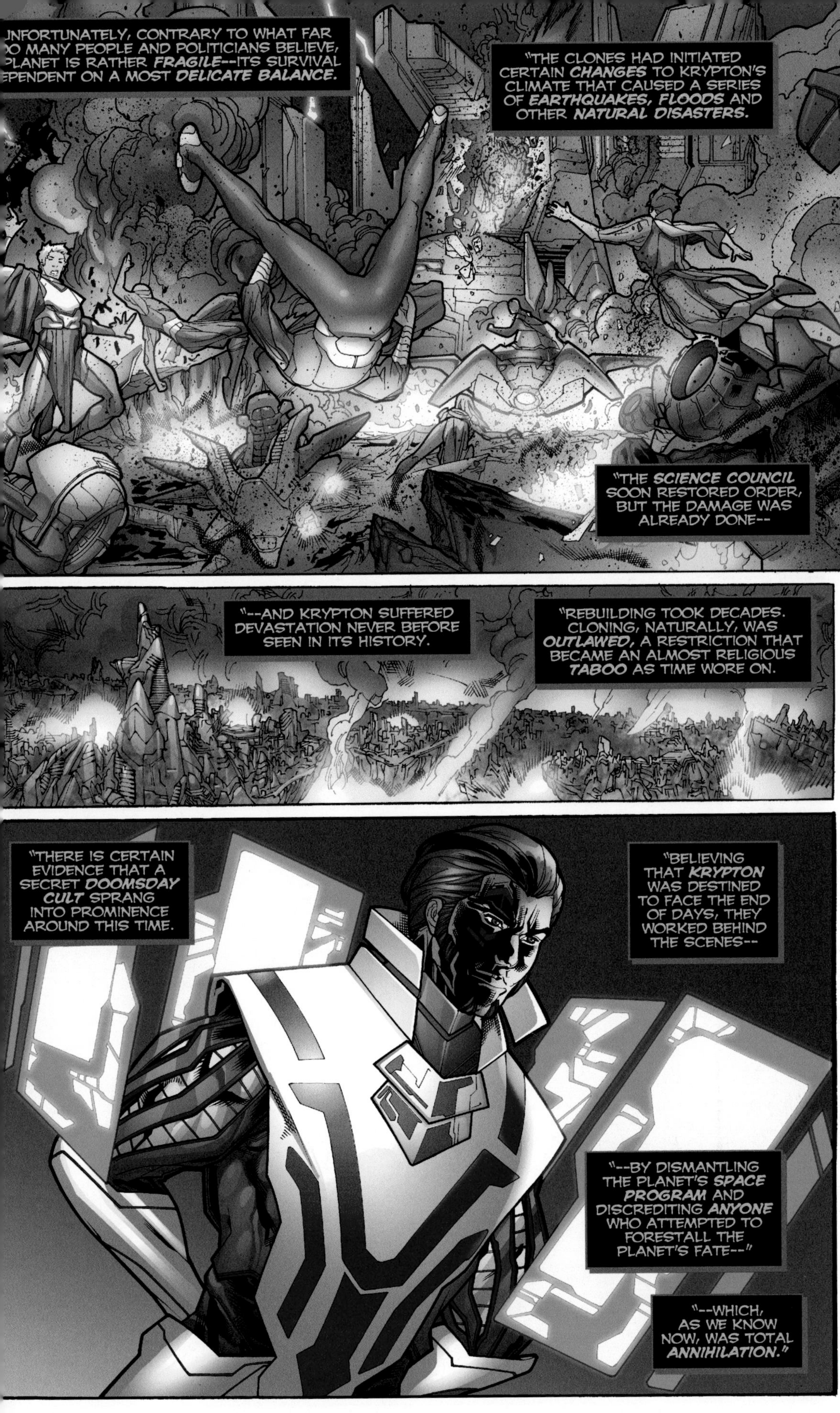
UNFORTUNATELY, CONTRARY TO WHAT FAR OO MANY PEOPLE AND POLITICIANS BELIEVE, PLANET IS RATHER FRAGILE--ITS SURVIVAL EPENDENT ON A MOST DELICATE BALANCE.
"THE CLONES HAD INITIATED CERTAIN CHANGES TO KRYPTON'S CLIMATE THAT CAUSED A SERIES OF EARTHQUAKES, FLOODS AND OTHER NATURAL DISASTERS.
"THE SCIENCE COUNCIL SOON RESTORED ORDER, BUT THE DAMAGE WAS ALREADY DONE--
"--AND KRYPTON SUFFERED DEVASTATION NEVER BEFORE SEEN IN ITS HISTORY.
"REBUILDING TOOK DECADES. CLONING, NATURALLY, WAS OUTLAWED, A RESTRICTION THAT BECAME AN ALMOST RELIGIOUS TABOO AS TIME WORE ON.
"THERE IS CERTAIN EVIDENCE THAT A SECRET DOOMSDAY CULT SPRANG INTO PROMINENCE AROUND THIS TIME.
"BELIEVING THAT KRYPTON WAS DESTINED TO FACE THE END OF DAYS, THEY WORKED BEHIND THE SCENES--
"--BY DISMANTLING THE PLANET'S SPACE PROGRAM AND DISCREDITING ANYONE WHO ATTEMPTED TO FORESTALL THE PLANET'S FATE--"
"--WHICH, AS WE KNOW NOW, WAS TOTAL ANNIHILATION."

THE SUPERBOY HAS MADE CONSIDERABLE PROGRESS SINCE WE LAST LOOKED IN ON HIM, OMEN.

DO YOU RECALL THE KRYPTONIAN DOOMSDAY SECT I MENTIONED A FEW WEEKS AGO?

IT APPEARS A SIMILAR CULT HAS FORMED HERE.

THOSE ARROGANT FOOLS WILL FIND YOU A MOST FORMIDABLE ENEMY, MY LORD HARVEST.

"I SEE FAIRCHILD IS ATTEMPTING TO PLUMB THE SUPERBOY'S SUBCONSCIOUS."

PREPARE TO RUN THE VIRTUAL REALITY PROGRAM, AGAIN.

WE'RE GAINING VALUABLE--AND RATHER DISTURBING--*INSIGHT* INTO THE WAY SUPERBOY PERCEIVES THE WORLD.

SHALL WE TAKE IT FROM THE TOP, DR. FAIRCHILD?

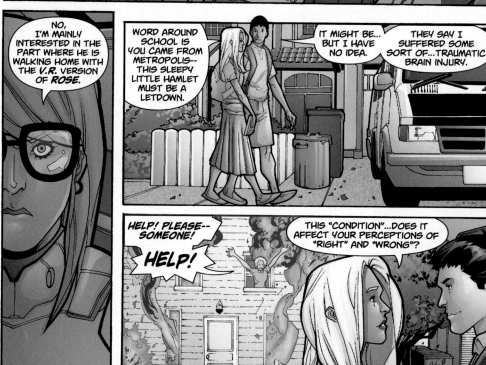

NO, I'M MAINLY INTERESTED IN THE PART WHERE HE IS WALKING HOME WITH THE *V.R.* VERSION OF *ROSE*.

WORD AROUND SCHOOL IS YOU CAME FROM METROPOLIS-- THIS SLEEPY LITTLE HAMLET MUST BE A LETDOWN.

IT MIGHT BE... BUT I HAVE NO IDEA.

THEY SAY I SUFFERED SOME SORT OF...TRAUMATIC BRAIN INJURY.

HELP! PLEASE-- SOMEONE!

HELP!

THIS "CONDITION"...DOES IT AFFECT YOUR PERCEPTIONS OF "RIGHT" AND "WRONG"?

I DON'T THINK SO.

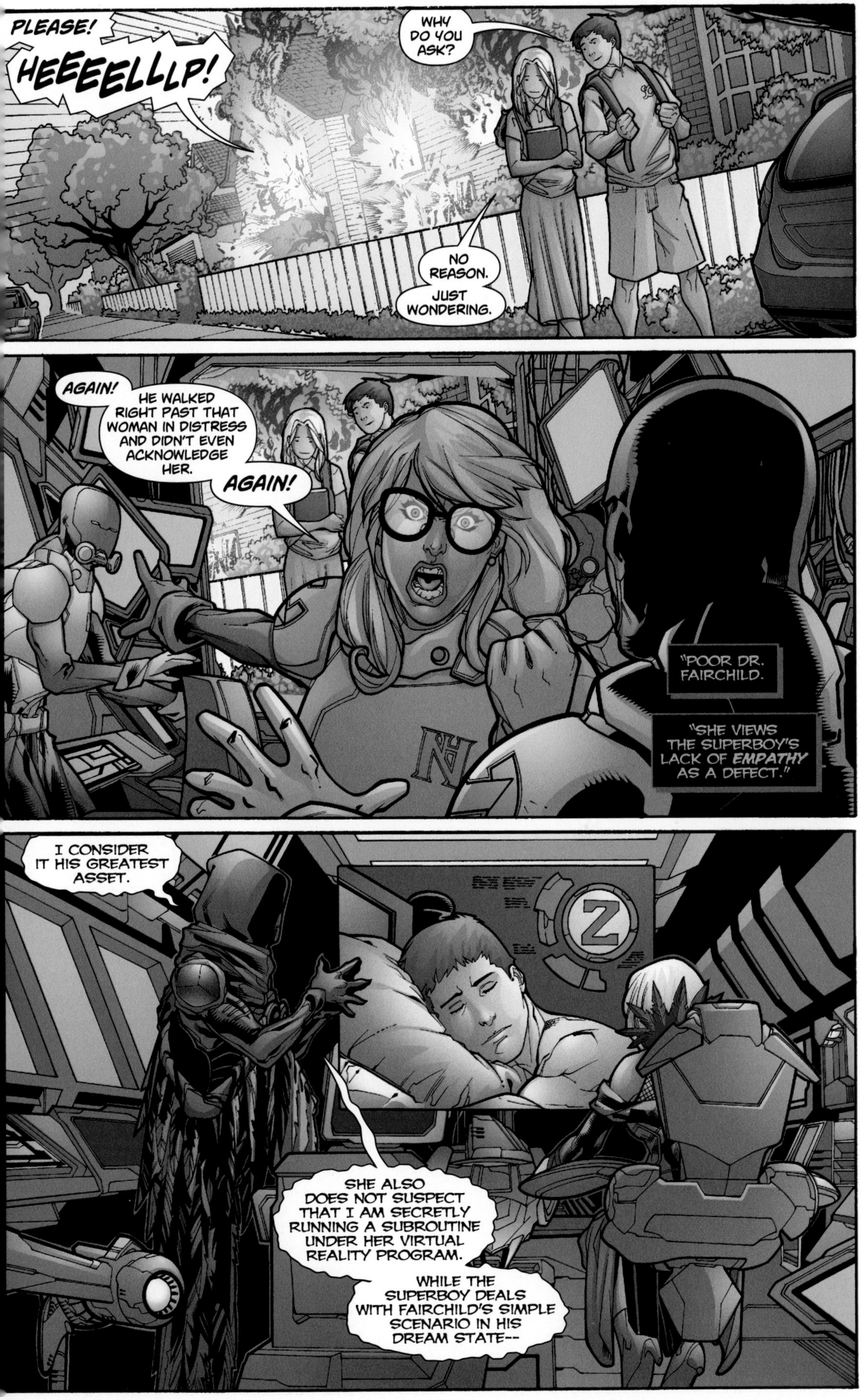
PLEASE!
HEEEEELLLLP!
WHY DO YOU ASK?
NO REASON.
JUST WONDERING.
AGAIN!
HE WALKED RIGHT PAST THAT WOMAN IN DISTRESS AND DIDN'T EVEN ACKNOWLEDGE HER.
AGAIN!
"POOR DR. FAIRCHILD.
"SHE VIEWS THE SUPERBOY'S LACK OF EMPATHY AS A DEFECT."
I CONSIDER IT HIS GREATEST ASSET.
SHE ALSO DOES NOT SUSPECT THAT I AM SECRETLY RUNNING A SUBROUTINE UNDER HER VIRTUAL REALITY PROGRAM.
WHILE THE SUPERBOY DEALS WITH FAIRCHILD'S SIMPLE SCENARIO IN HIS DREAM STATE--

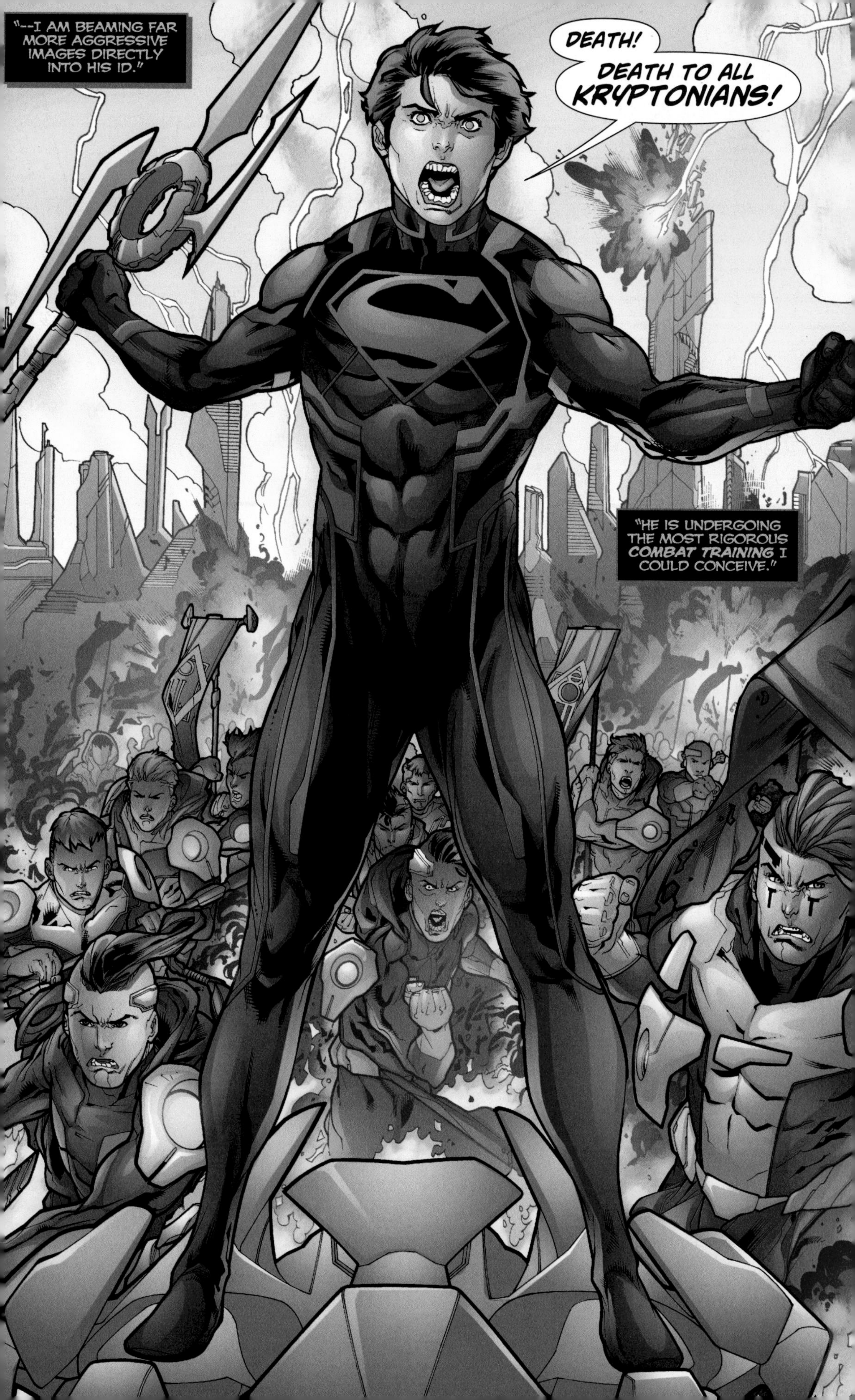
"--I AM BEAMING FAR MORE AGGRESSIVE IMAGES DIRECTLY INTO HIS ID."
DEATH!
DEATH TO ALL KRYPTONIANS!
"HE IS UNDERGOING THE MOST RIGOROUS COMBAT TRAINING I COULD CONCEIVE."

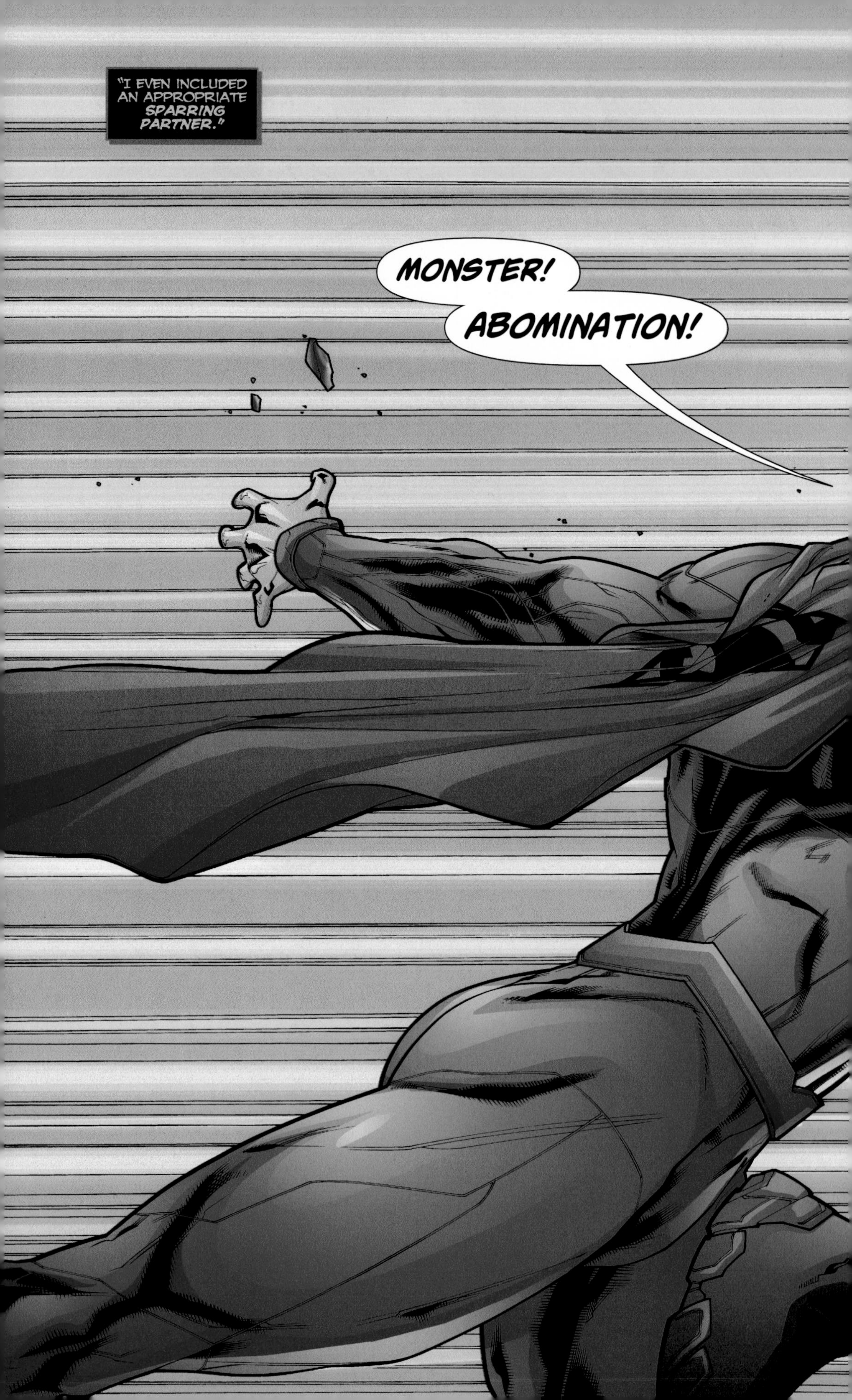
"I EVEN INCLUDED AN APPROPRIATE SPARRING PARTNER."
MONSTER!
ABOMINATION!

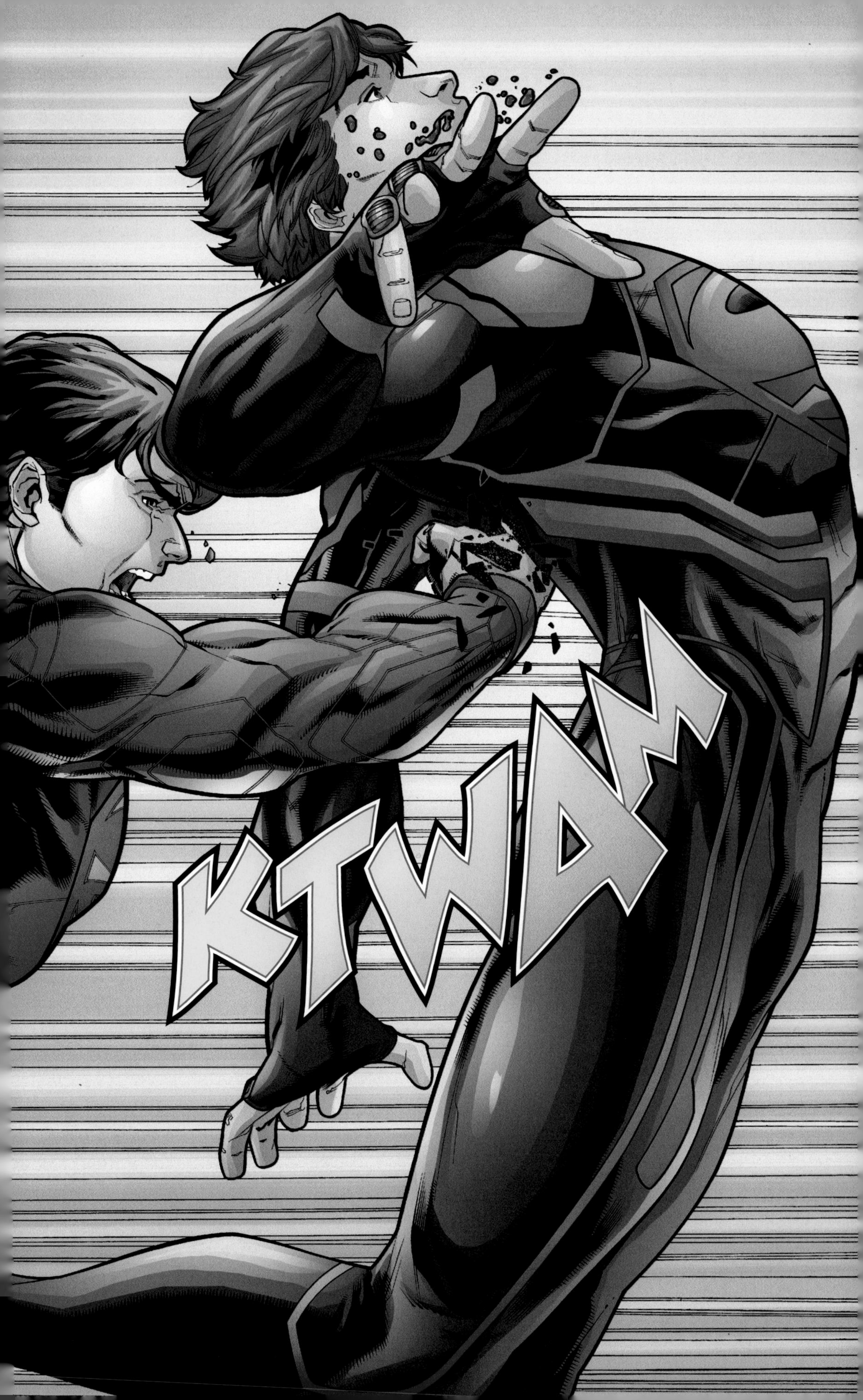
KTWAM

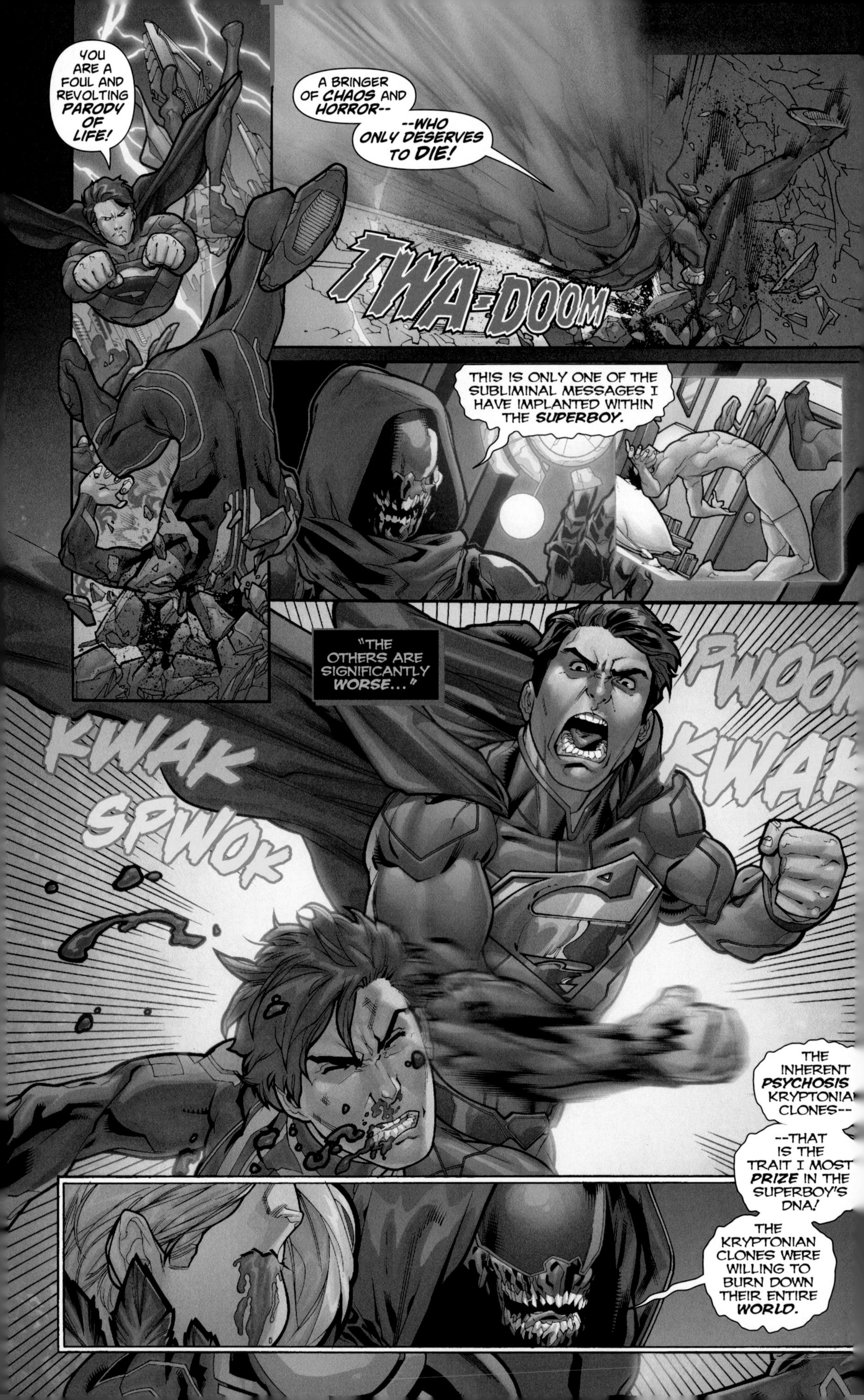

YOU ARE A FOUL AND REVOLTING PARODY OF LIFE!
A BRINGER OF CHAOS AND HORROR--
--WHO ONLY DESERVES TO DIE!
TWA-DOOM
THIS IS ONLY ONE OF THE SUBLIMINAL MESSAGES I HAVE IMPLANTED WITHIN THE SUPERBOY.
"THE OTHERS ARE SIGNIFICANTLY WORSE..."
PWOOM
KWAK
KWAK
SPWOK
THE INHERENT PSYCHOSIS KRYPTONIAN CLONES--
--THAT IS THE TRAIT I MOST PRIZE IN THE SUPERBOY'S DNA!
THE KRYPTONIAN CLONES WERE WILLING TO BURN DOWN THEIR ENTIRE WORLD.

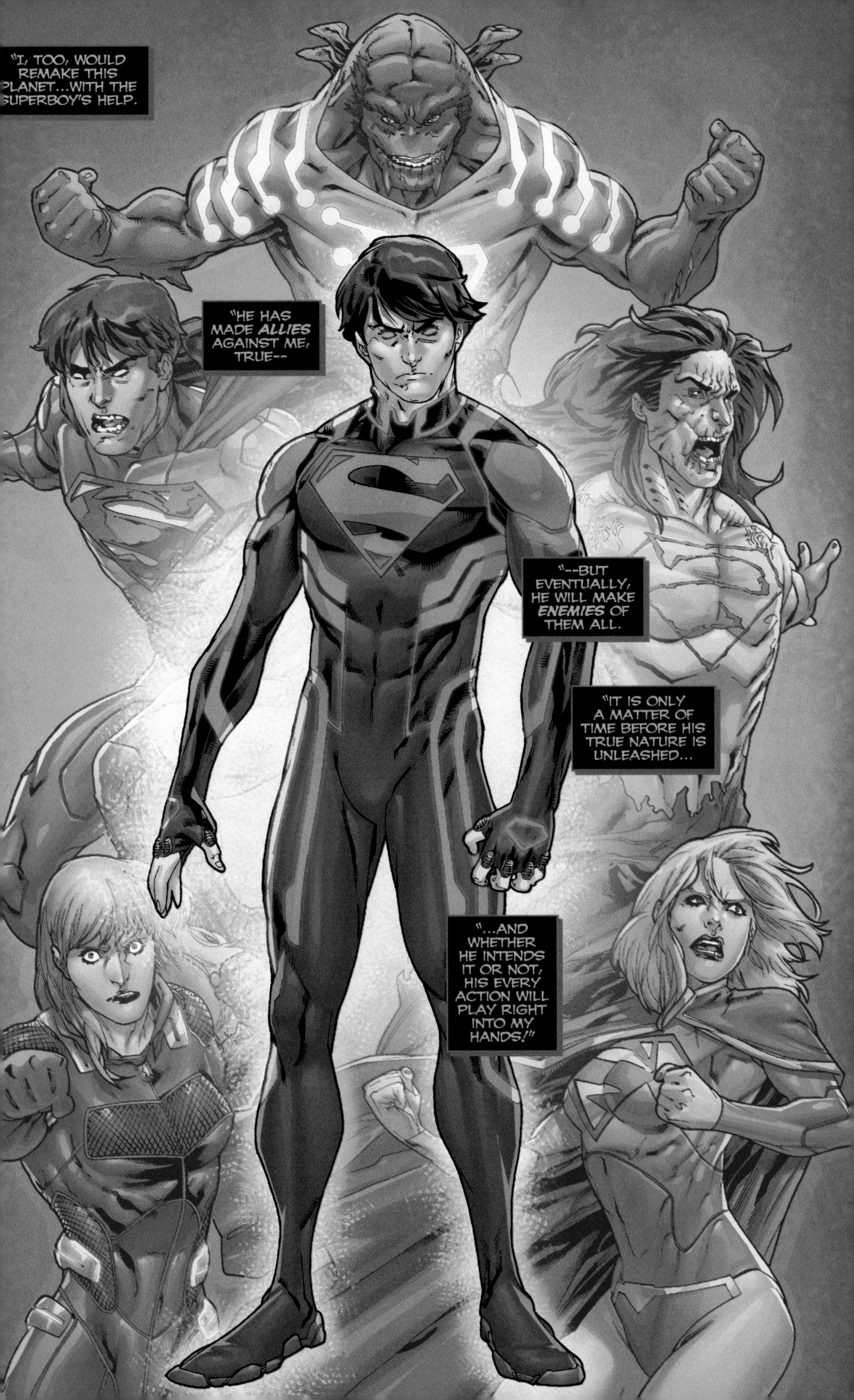
"I, TOO, WOULD REMAKE THIS PLANET...WITH THE SUPERBOY'S HELP.
"HE HAS MADE ALLIES AGAINST ME, TRUE--
"--BUT EVENTUALLY, HE WILL MAKE ENEMIES OF THEM ALL.
"IT IS ONLY A MATTER OF TIME BEFORE HIS TRUE NATURE IS UNLEASHED...
"...AND WHETHER HE INTENDS IT OR NOT, HIS EVERY ACTION WILL PLAY RIGHT INTO MY HANDS!"

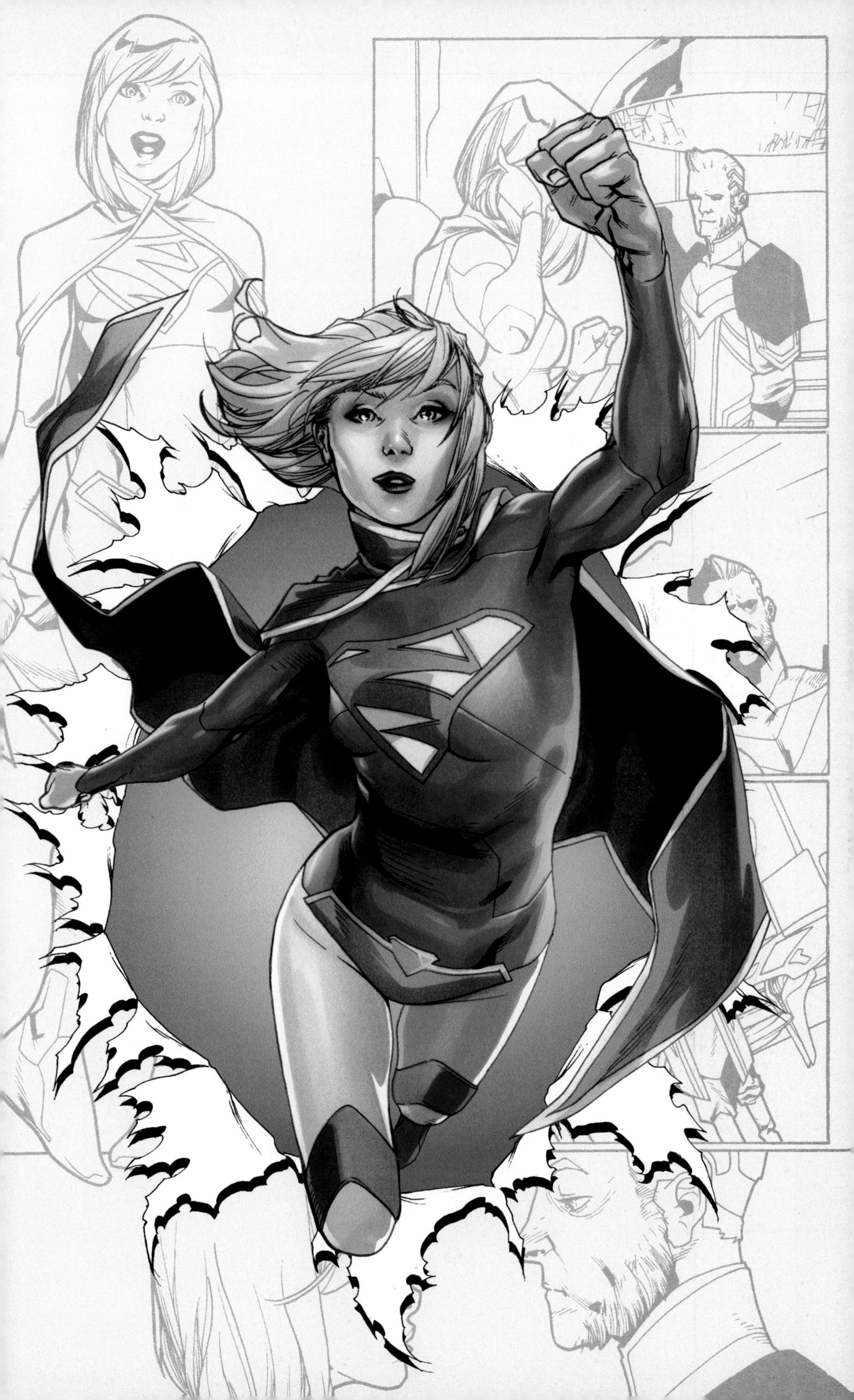

THE END OF THE BEGINNING

MICHAEL GREEN MIKE JOHNSON writers MAHMUD ASRAR artist DAVE McCAIG colorist

cover art by MAHMUD ASRAR & DAVE McCAIG

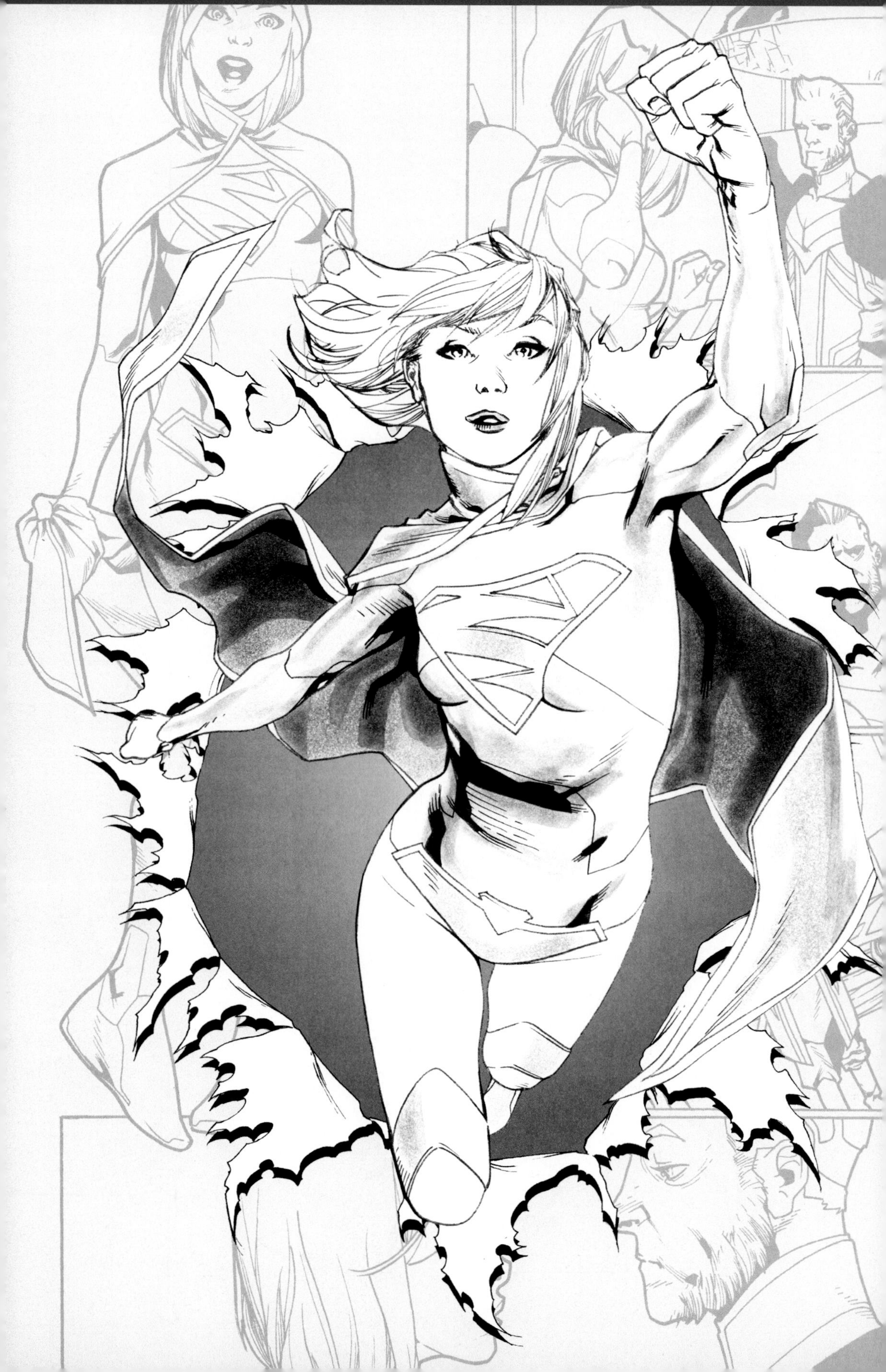

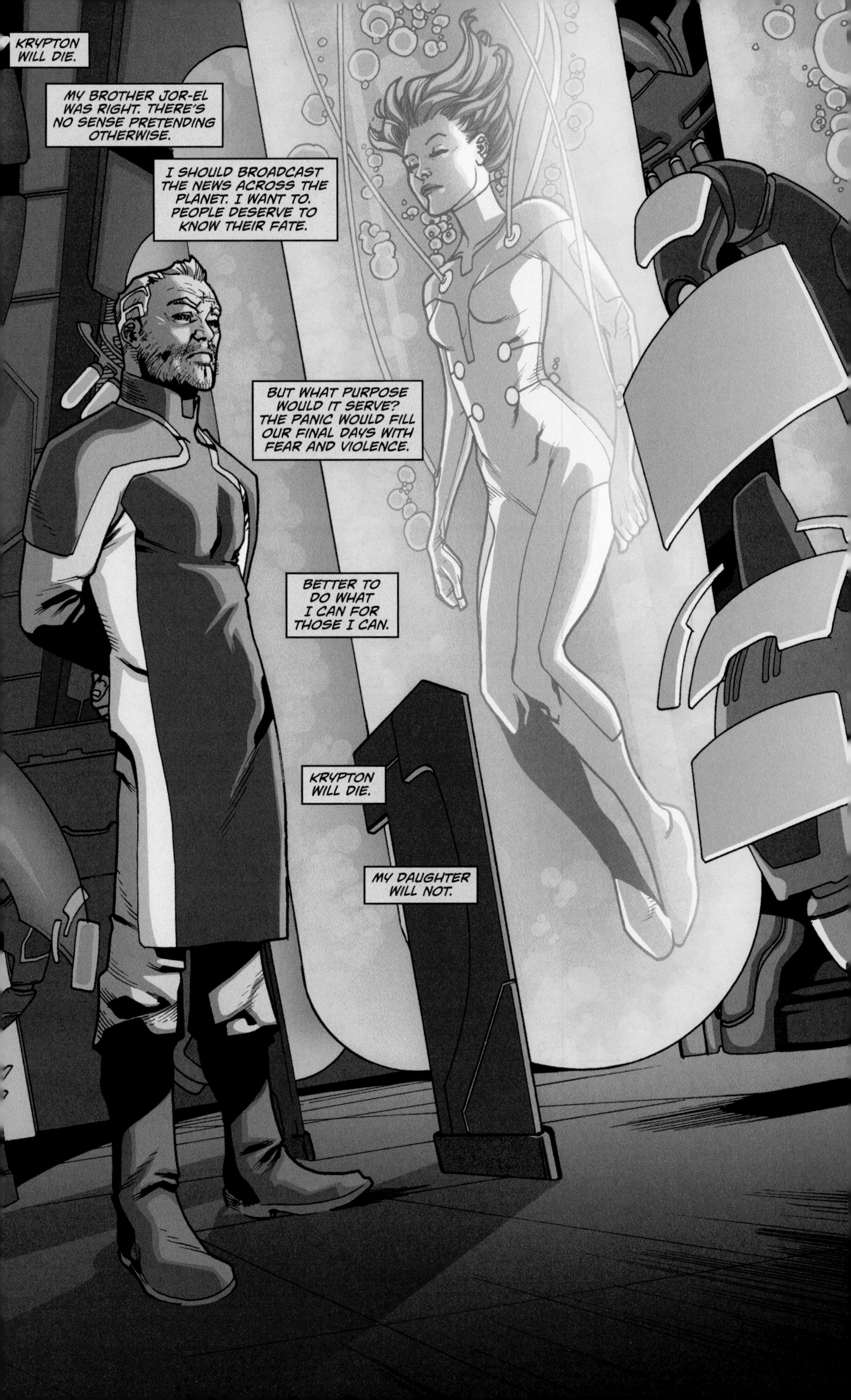
KRYPTON WILL DIE.
MY BROTHER JOR-EL WAS RIGHT. THERE'S NO SENSE PRETENDING OTHERWISE.
I SHOULD BROADCAST THE NEWS ACROSS THE PLANET. I WANT TO. PEOPLE DESERVE TO KNOW THEIR FATE.
BUT WHAT PURPOSE WOULD IT SERVE? THE PANIC WOULD FILL OUR FINAL DAYS WITH FEAR AND VIOLENCE.
BETTER TO DO WHAT I CAN FOR THOSE I CAN.
KRYPTON WILL DIE.
MY DAUGHTER WILL NOT.

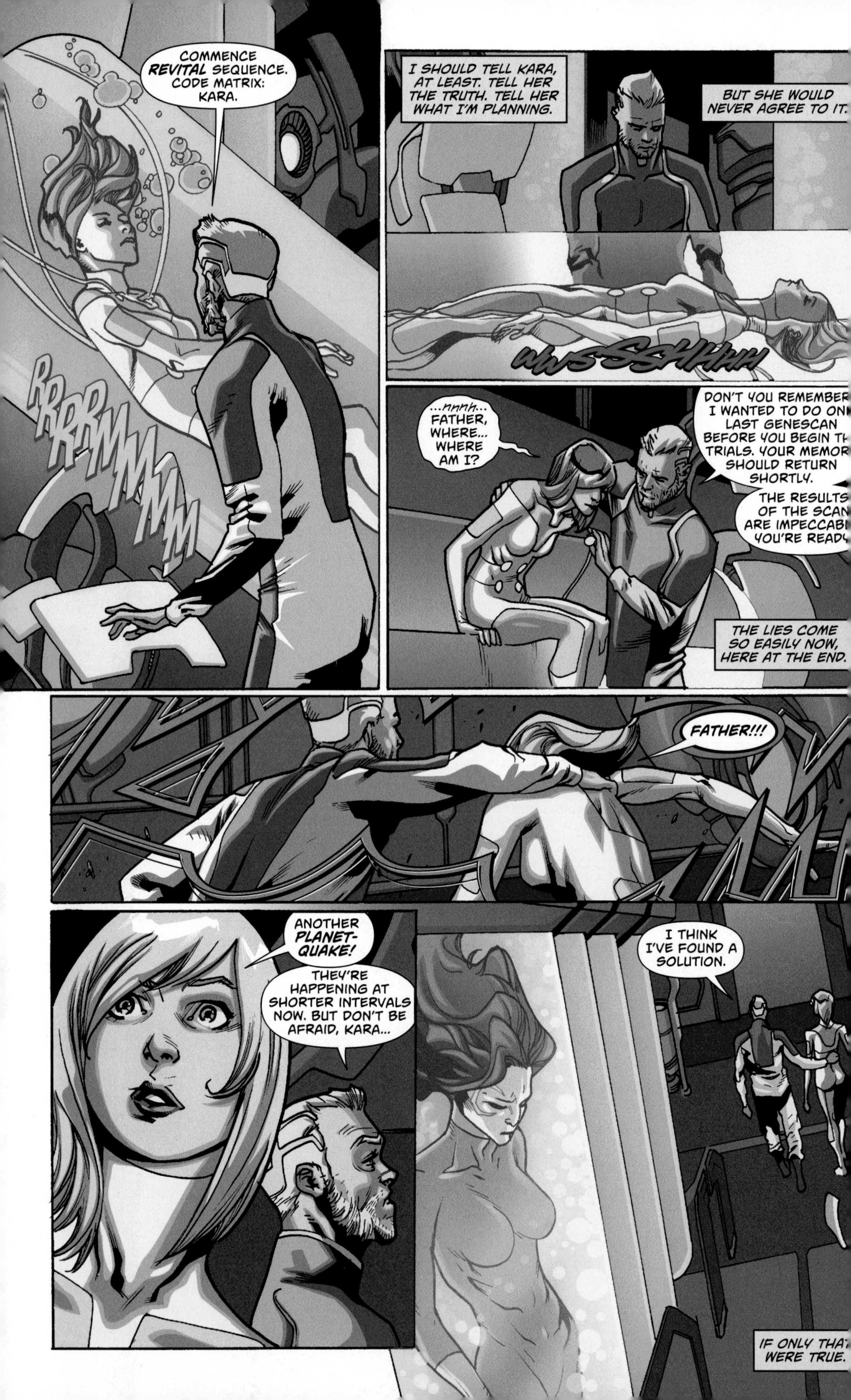
COMMENCE REVITAL SEQUENCE. CODE MATRIX: KARA.
RRRRMMMMMM
I SHOULD TELL KARA, AT LEAST. TELL HER THE TRUTH. TELL HER WHAT I'M PLANNING.
BUT SHE WOULD NEVER AGREE TO IT.
WWSSSHHHH
...nnnh... FATHER, WHERE... WHERE AM I?
DON'T YOU REMEMBER I WANTED TO DO ON LAST GENESCAN BEFORE YOU BEGIN TH TRIALS. YOUR MEMOR SHOULD RETURN SHORTLY.
THE RESULTS OF THE SCAN ARE IMPECCABL YOU'RE READY
THE LIES COME SO EASILY NOW, HERE AT THE END.
FATHER!!!
ANOTHER PLANET-QUAKE!
THEY'RE HAPPENING AT SHORTER INTERVALS NOW. BUT DON'T BE AFRAID, KARA...
I THINK I'VE FOUND A SOLUTION.
IF ONLY THA WERE TRUE.

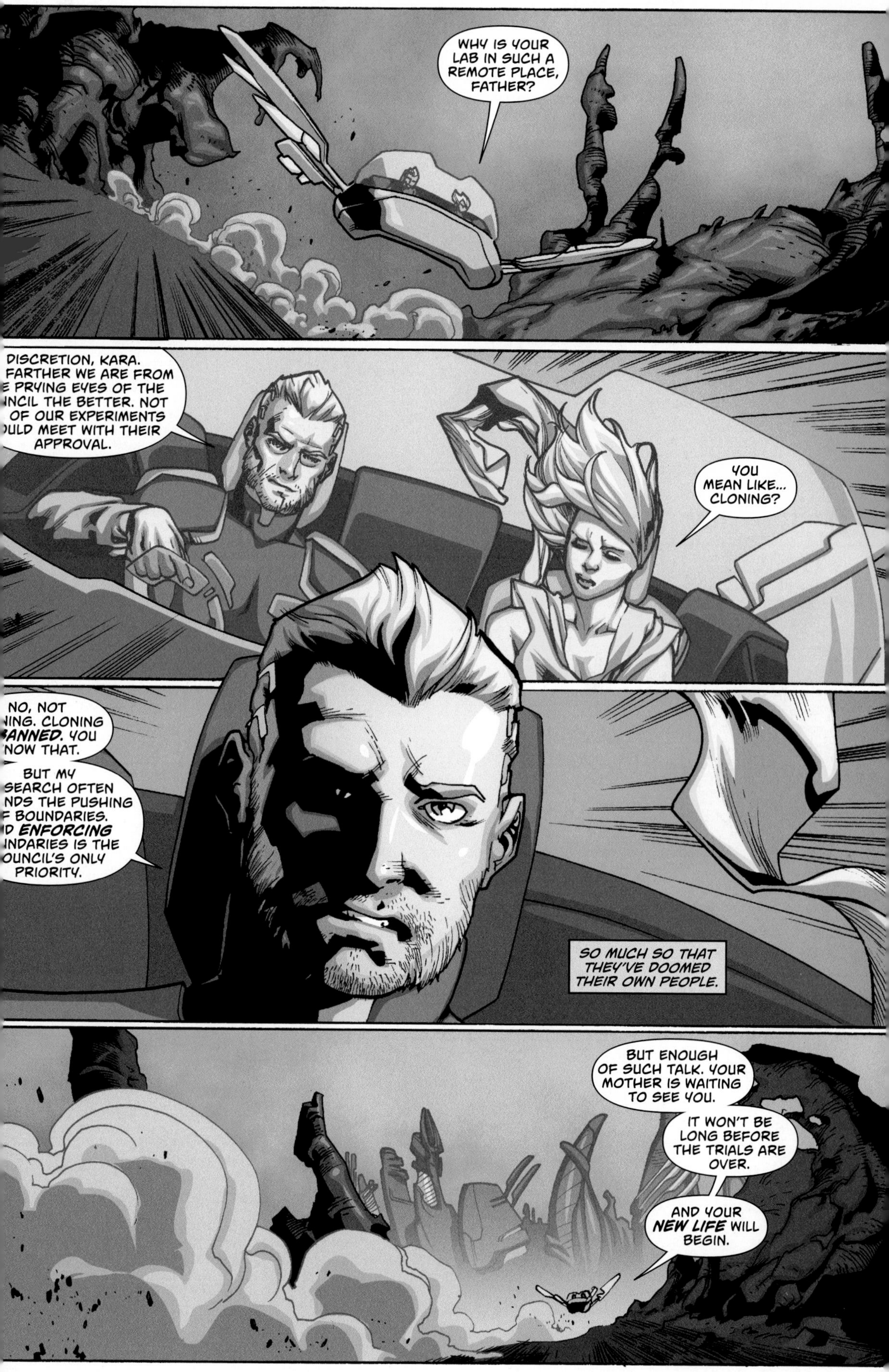
WHY IS YOUR LAB IN SUCH A REMOTE PLACE, FATHER?
DISCRETION, KARA. FARTHER WE ARE FROM E PRYING EYES OF THE NCIL THE BETTER. NOT OF OUR EXPERIMENTS ULD MEET WITH THEIR APPROVAL.
YOU MEAN LIKE... CLONING?
NO, NOT NING. CLONING BANNED. YOU NOW THAT.
BUT MY SEARCH OFTEN NDS THE PUSHING F BOUNDARIES. D ENFORCING NDARIES IS THE OUNCIL'S ONLY PRIORITY.
SO MUCH SO THAT THEY'VE DOOMED THEIR OWN PEOPLE.
BUT ENOUGH OF SUCH TALK. YOUR MOTHER IS WAITING TO SEE YOU.
IT WON'T BE LONG BEFORE THE TRIALS ARE OVER.
AND YOUR NEW LIFE WILL BEGIN.

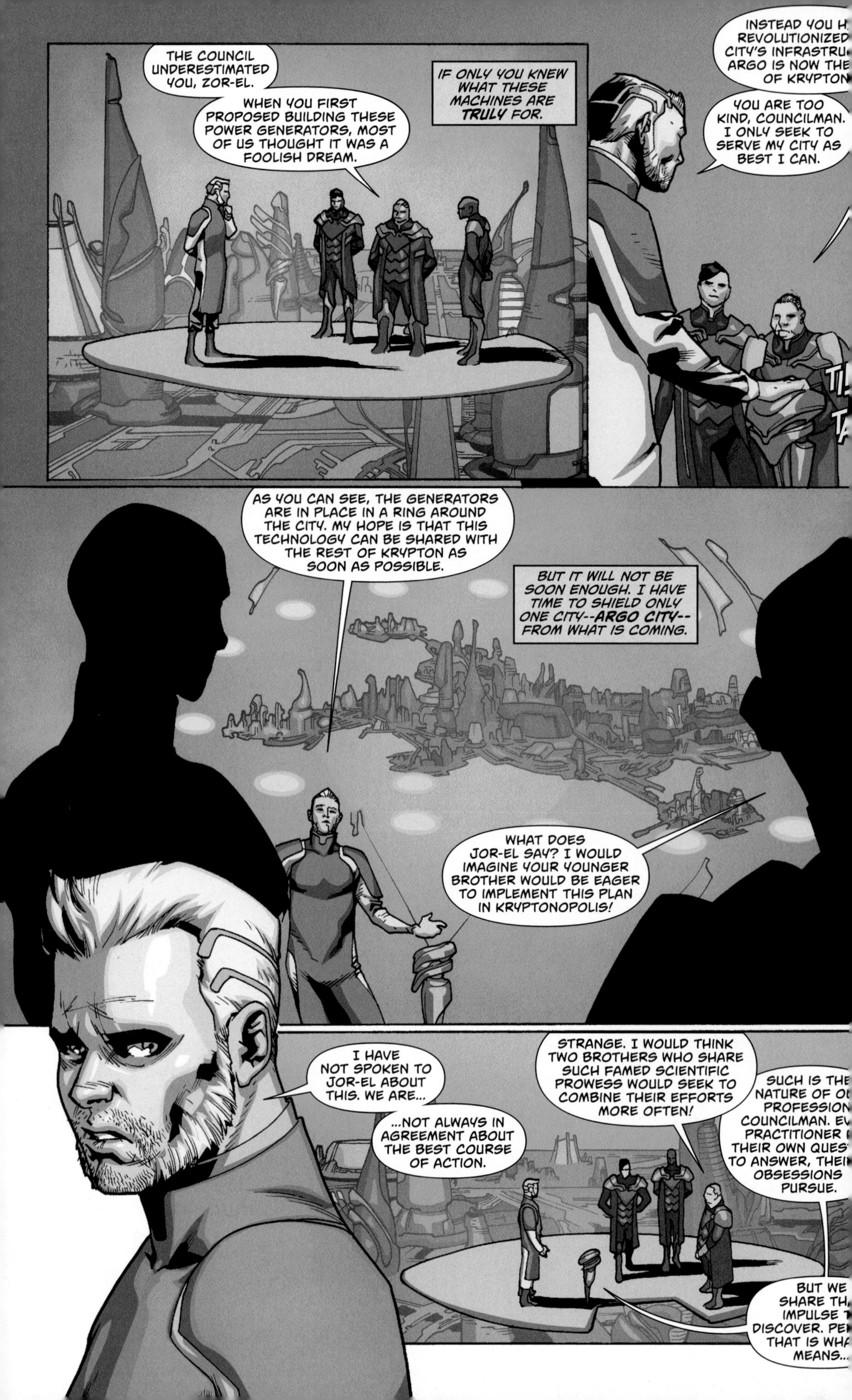
THE COUNCIL UNDERESTIMATED YOU, ZOR-EL.
WHEN YOU FIRST PROPOSED BUILDING THESE POWER GENERATORS, MOST OF US THOUGHT IT WAS A FOOLISH DREAM.
IF ONLY YOU KNEW WHAT THESE MACHINES ARE TRULY FOR.
INSTEAD YOU H REVOLUTIONIZED CITY'S INFRASTRU ARGO IS NOW THE OF KRYPTON
YOU ARE TOO KIND, COUNCILMAN. I ONLY SEEK TO SERVE MY CITY AS BEST I CAN.
AS YOU CAN SEE, THE GENERATORS ARE IN PLACE IN A RING AROUND THE CITY. MY HOPE IS THAT THIS TECHNOLOGY CAN BE SHARED WITH THE REST OF KRYPTON AS SOON AS POSSIBLE.
BUT IT WILL NOT BE SOON ENOUGH. I HAVE TIME TO SHIELD ONLY ONE CITY--ARGO CITY--FROM WHAT IS COMING.
WHAT DOES JOR-EL SAY? I WOULD IMAGINE YOUR YOUNGER BROTHER WOULD BE EAGER TO IMPLEMENT THIS PLAN IN KRYPTONOPOLIS!
I HAVE NOT SPOKEN TO JOR-EL ABOUT THIS. WE ARE...
...NOT ALWAYS IN AGREEMENT ABOUT THE BEST COURSE OF ACTION.
STRANGE. I WOULD THINK TWO BROTHERS WHO SHARE SUCH FAMED SCIENTIFIC PROWESS WOULD SEEK TO COMBINE THEIR EFFORTS MORE OFTEN!
SUCH IS THE NATURE OF O PROFESSION COUNCILMAN. E PRACTITIONER THEIR OWN QUES TO ANSWER, THEI OBSESSIONS PURSUE.
BUT WE SHARE TH IMPULSE T DISCOVER. PE THAT IS WHA MEANS...

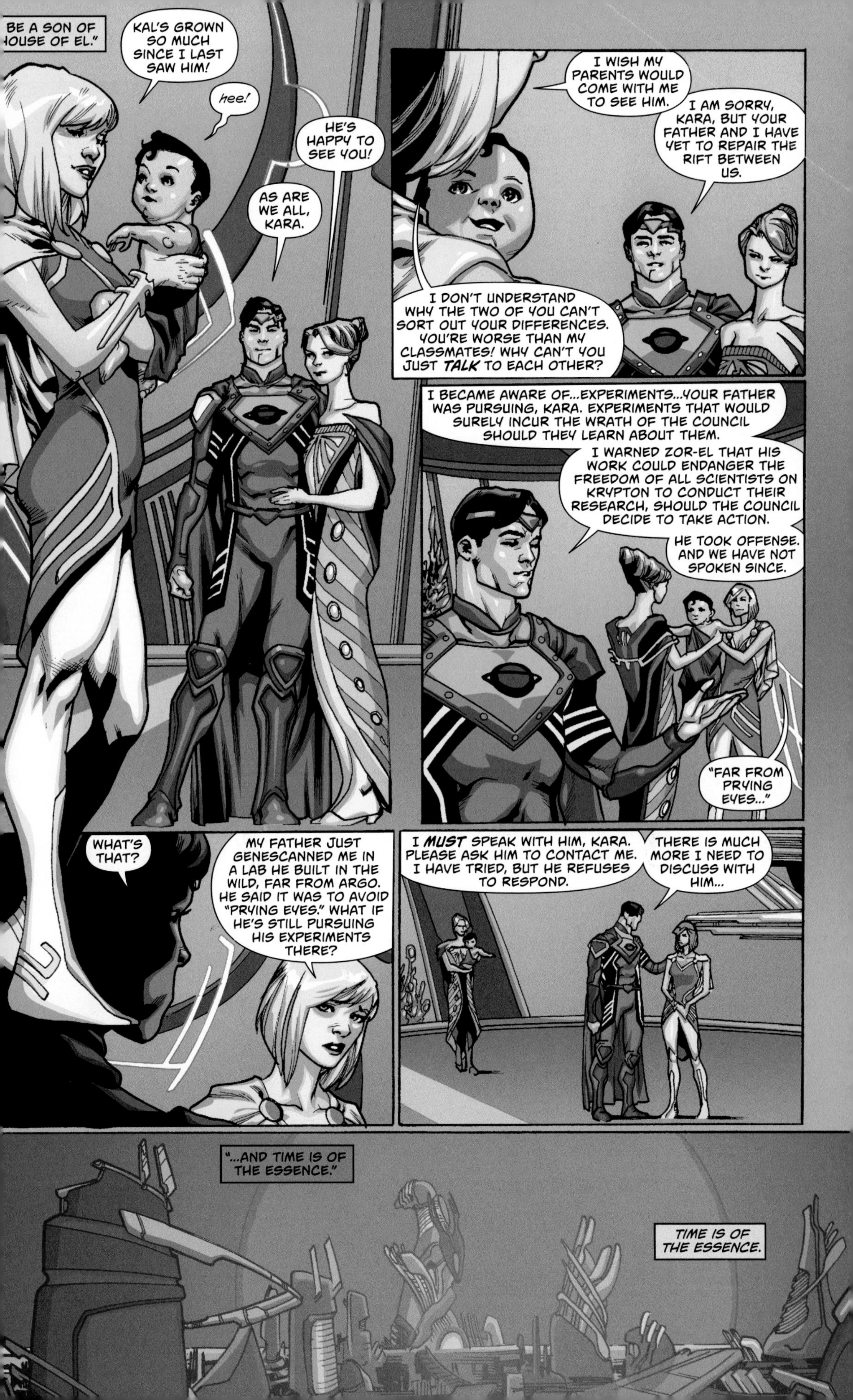

BE A SON OF
HOUSE OF EL."
KAL'S GROWN SO MUCH SINCE I LAST SAW HIM!
hee!
HE'S HAPPY TO SEE YOU!
AS ARE WE ALL, KARA.
I WISH MY PARENTS WOULD COME WITH ME TO SEE HIM.
I AM SORRY, KARA, BUT YOUR FATHER AND I HAVE YET TO REPAIR THE RIFT BETWEEN US.
I DON'T UNDERSTAND WHY THE TWO OF YOU CAN'T SORT OUT YOUR DIFFERENCES. YOU'RE WORSE THAN MY CLASSMATES! WHY CAN'T YOU JUST TALK TO EACH OTHER?
I BECAME AWARE OF...EXPERIMENTS...YOUR FATHER WAS PURSUING, KARA. EXPERIMENTS THAT WOULD SURELY INCUR THE WRATH OF THE COUNCIL SHOULD THEY LEARN ABOUT THEM.
I WARNED ZOR-EL THAT HIS WORK COULD ENDANGER THE FREEDOM OF ALL SCIENTISTS ON KRYPTON TO CONDUCT THEIR RESEARCH, SHOULD THE COUNCIL DECIDE TO TAKE ACTION.
HE TOOK OFFENSE. AND WE HAVE NOT SPOKEN SINCE.
"FAR FROM PRYING EYES..."
WHAT'S THAT?
MY FATHER JUST GENESCANNED ME IN A LAB HE BUILT IN THE WILD, FAR FROM ARGO. HE SAID IT WAS TO AVOID "PRYING EYES." WHAT IF HE'S STILL PURSUING HIS EXPERIMENTS THERE?
I MUST SPEAK WITH HIM, KARA. PLEASE ASK HIM TO CONTACT ME. I HAVE TRIED, BUT HE REFUSES TO RESPOND.
THERE IS MUCH MORE I NEED TO DISCUSS WITH HIM...
"...AND TIME IS OF THE ESSENCE."
TIME IS OF THE ESSENCE.

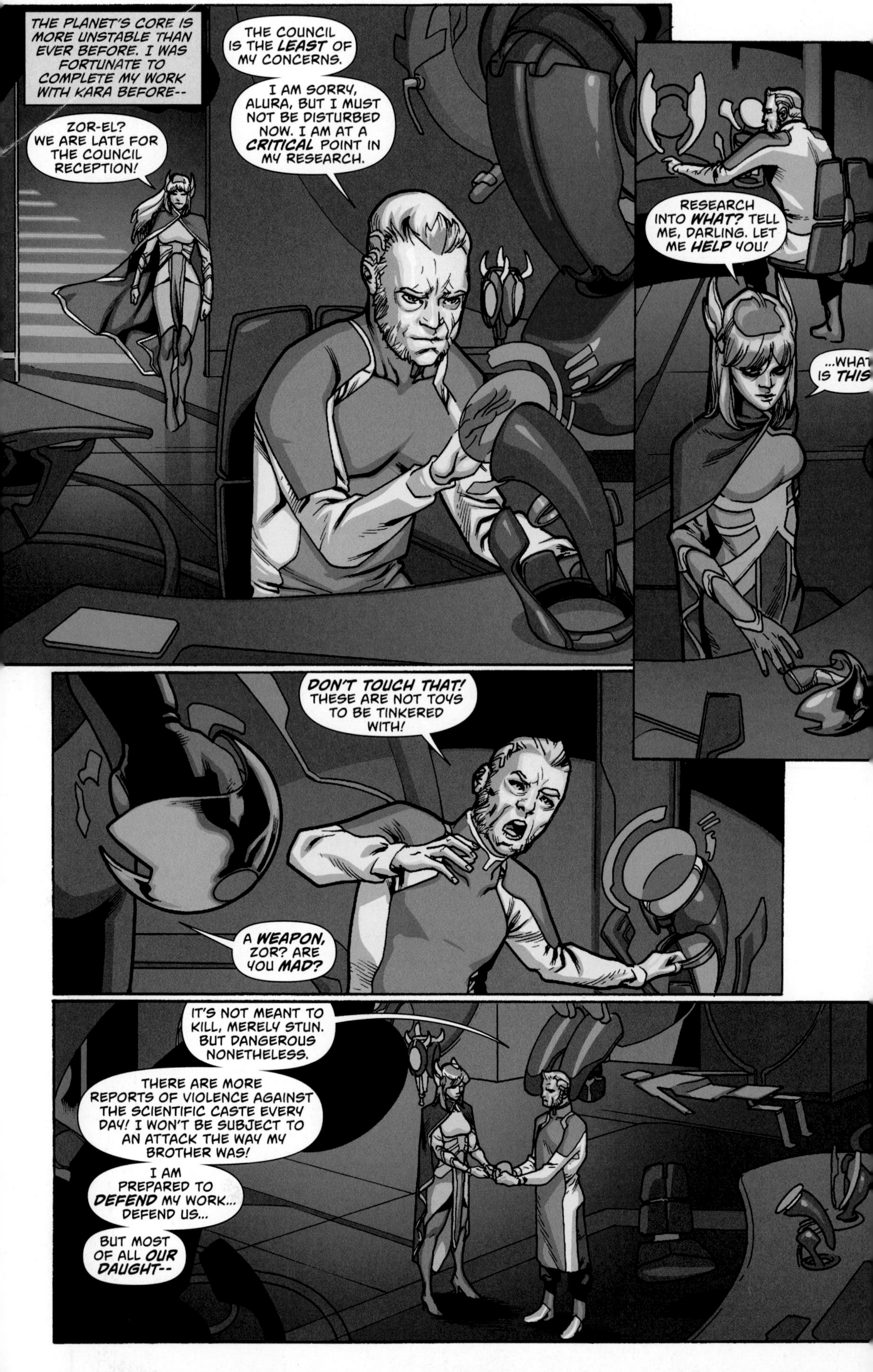
THE PLANET'S CORE IS MORE UNSTABLE THAN EVER BEFORE. I WAS FORTUNATE TO COMPLETE MY WORK WITH KARA BEFORE--
ZOR-EL? WE ARE LATE FOR THE COUNCIL RECEPTION!
THE COUNCIL IS THE LEAST OF MY CONCERNS.
I AM SORRY, ALURA, BUT I MUST NOT BE DISTURBED NOW. I AM AT A CRITICAL POINT IN MY RESEARCH.
RESEARCH INTO WHAT? TELL ME, DARLING. LET ME HELP YOU!
...WHAT IS THIS
DON'T TOUCH THAT! THESE ARE NOT TOYS TO BE TINKERED WITH!
A WEAPON, ZOR? ARE YOU MAD?
IT'S NOT MEANT TO KILL, MERELY STUN. BUT DANGEROUS NONETHELESS.
THERE ARE MORE REPORTS OF VIOLENCE AGAINST THE SCIENTIFIC CASTE EVERY DAY! I WON'T BE SUBJECT TO AN ATTACK THE WAY MY BROTHER WAS!
I AM PREPARED TO DEFEND MY WORK... DEFEND US...
BUT MOST OF ALL OUR DAUGHT--

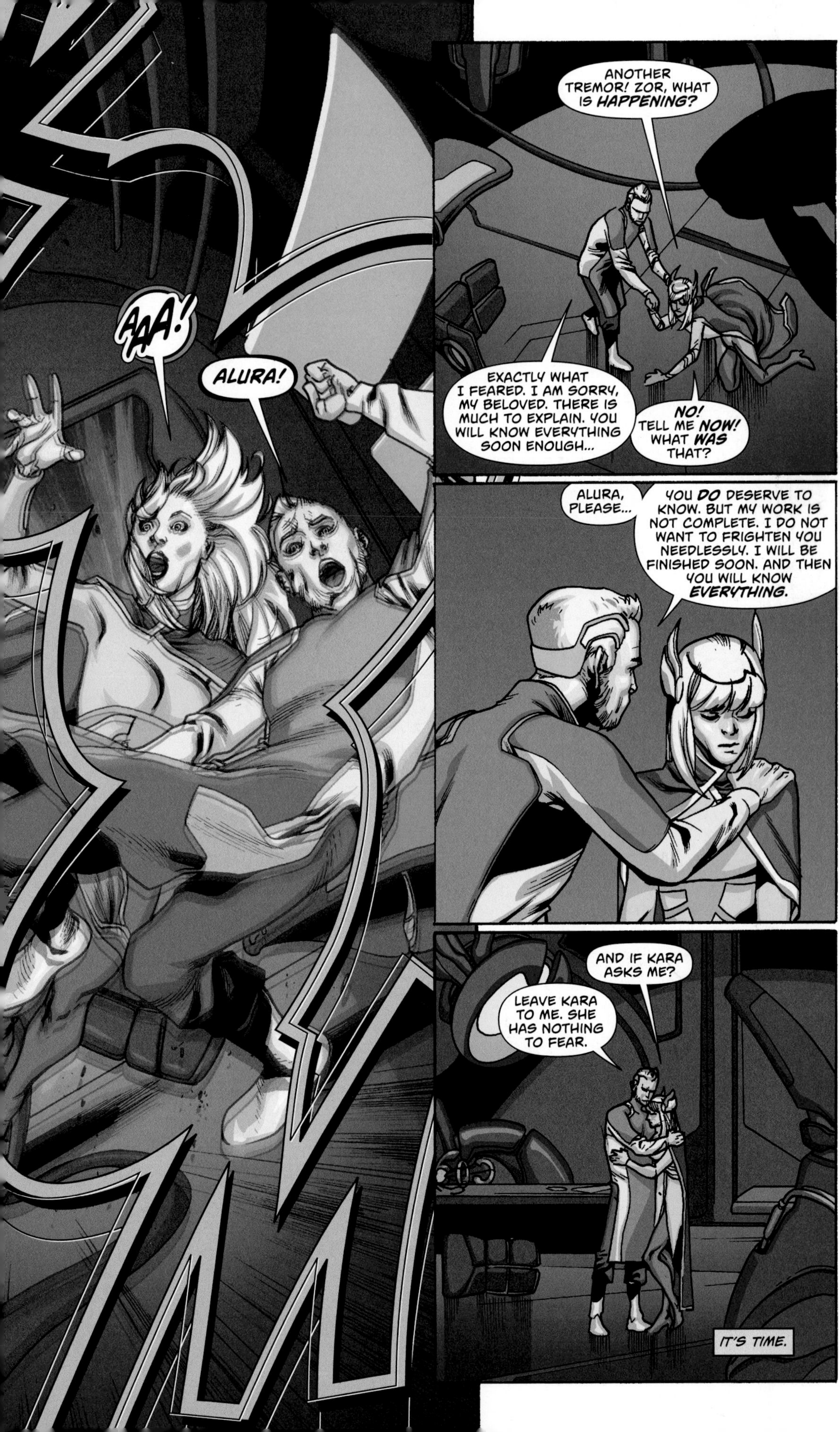

AAA!
ALURA!
ANOTHER TREMOR! ZOR, WHAT IS HAPPENING?
EXACTLY WHAT I FEARED. I AM SORRY, MY BELOVED. THERE IS MUCH TO EXPLAIN. YOU WILL KNOW EVERYTHING SOON ENOUGH...
NO! TELL ME NOW! WHAT WAS THAT?
ALURA, PLEASE...
YOU DO DESERVE TO KNOW. BUT MY WORK IS NOT COMPLETE. I DO NOT WANT TO FRIGHTEN YOU NEEDLESSLY. I WILL BE FINISHED SOON. AND THEN YOU WILL KNOW EVERYTHING.
AND IF KARA ASKS ME?
LEAVE KARA TO ME. SHE HAS NOTHING TO FEAR.
IT'S TIME.

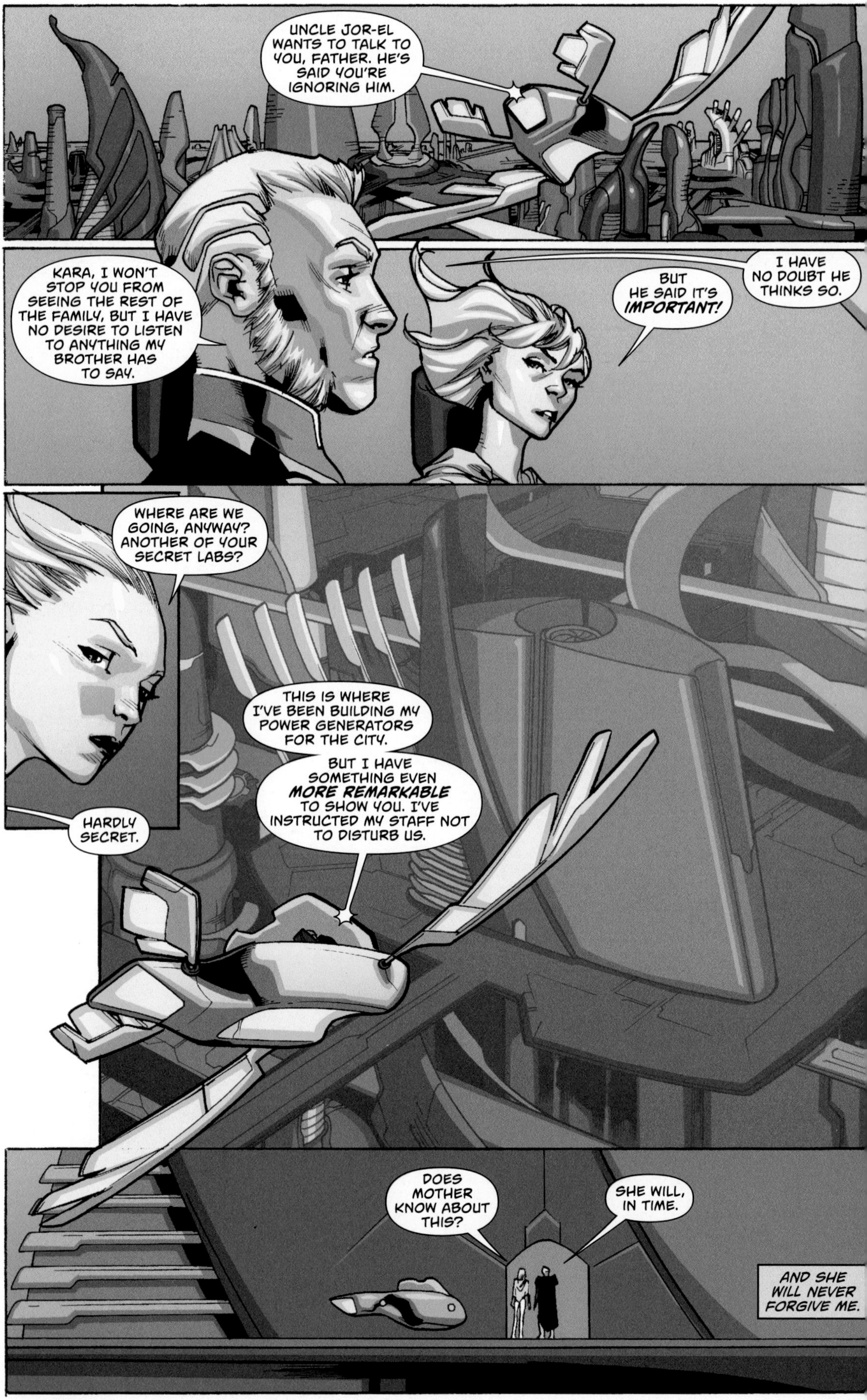

UNCLE JOR-EL WANTS TO TALK TO YOU, FATHER. HE'S SAID YOU'RE IGNORING HIM.
KARA, I WON'T STOP YOU FROM SEEING THE REST OF THE FAMILY, BUT I HAVE NO DESIRE TO LISTEN TO ANYTHING MY BROTHER HAS TO SAY.
BUT HE SAID IT'S IMPORTANT!
I HAVE NO DOUBT HE THINKS SO.
WHERE ARE WE GOING, ANYWAY? ANOTHER OF YOUR SECRET LABS?
HARDLY SECRET.
THIS IS WHERE I'VE BEEN BUILDING MY POWER GENERATORS FOR THE CITY.
BUT I HAVE SOMETHING EVEN MORE REMARKABLE TO SHOW YOU. I'VE INSTRUCTED MY STAFF NOT TO DISTURB US.
DOES MOTHER KNOW ABOUT THIS?
SHE WILL, IN TIME.
AND SHE WILL NEVER FORGIVE ME.

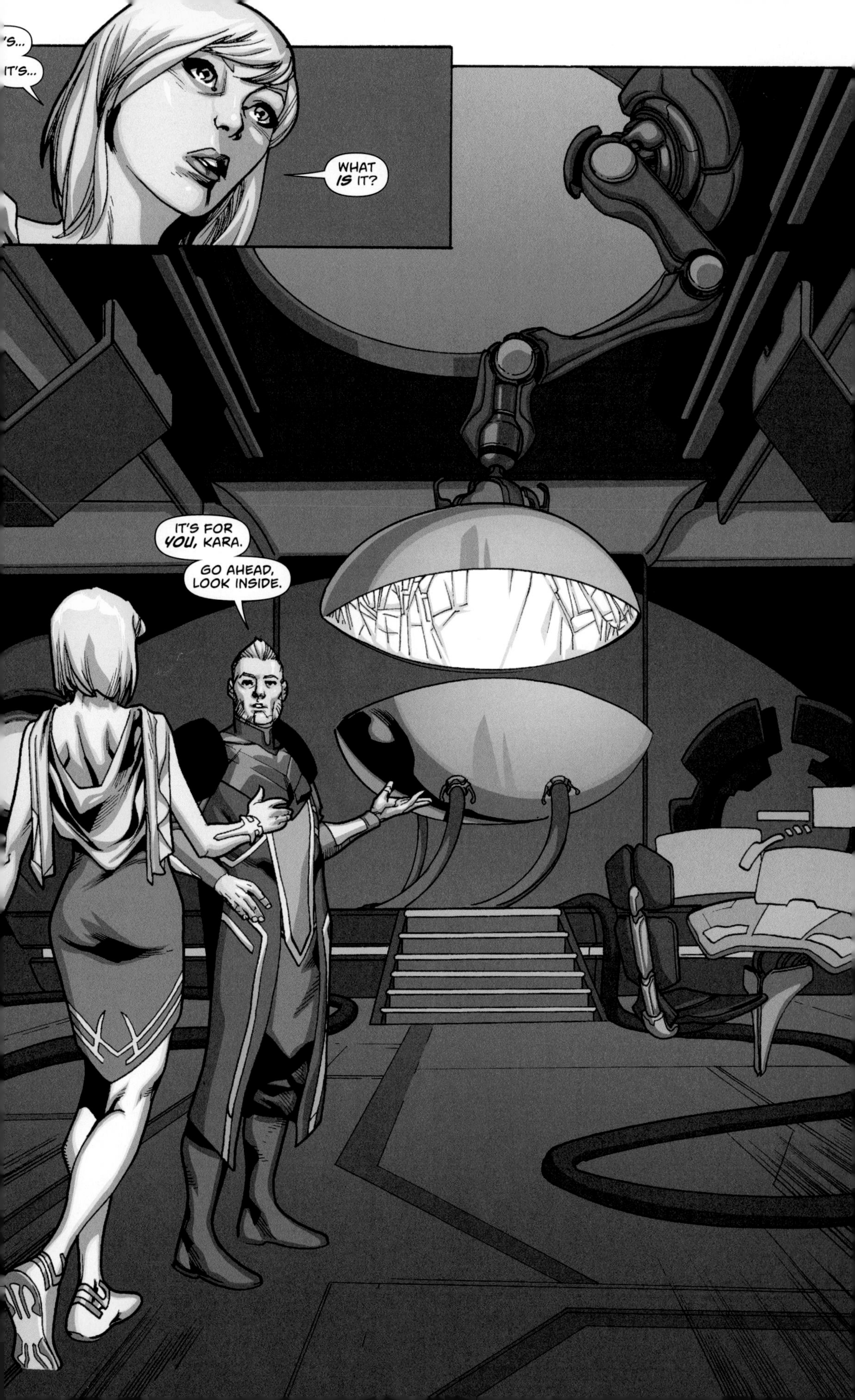

'S...
IT'S...
WHAT IS IT?
IT'S FOR YOU, KARA.
GO AHEAD, LOOK INSIDE.

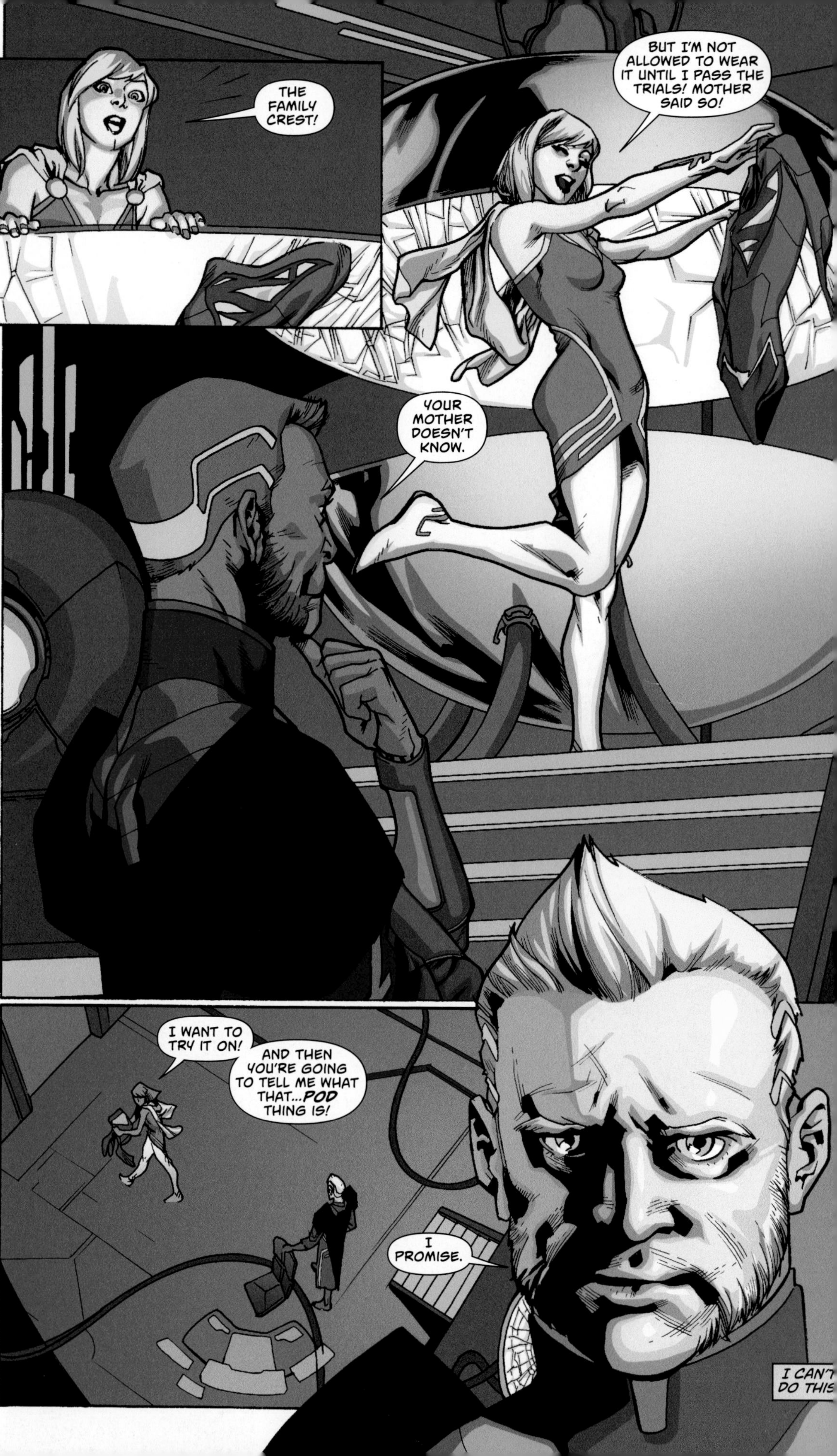
THE FAMILY CREST!
BUT I'M NOT ALLOWED TO WEAR IT UNTIL I PASS THE TRIALS! MOTHER SAID SO!
YOUR MOTHER DOESN'T KNOW.
I WANT TO TRY IT ON!
AND THEN YOU'RE GOING TO TELL ME WHAT THAT...POD THING IS!
I PROMISE.
I CAN'T DO THIS

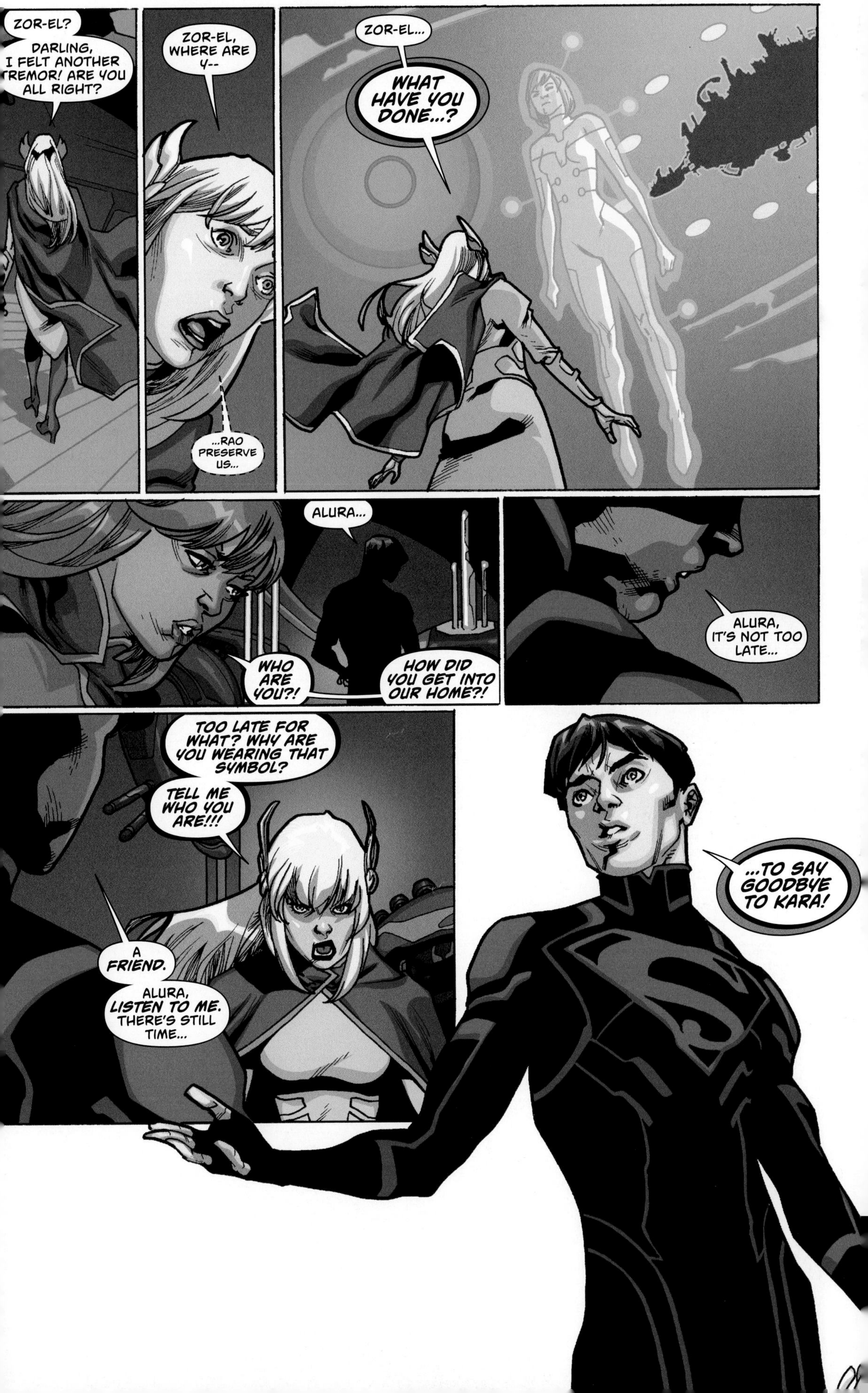
ZOR-EL?
DARLING, I FELT ANOTHER TREMOR! ARE YOU ALL RIGHT?
ZOR-EL, WHERE ARE Y--
...RAO PRESERVE US...
ZOR-EL...
WHAT HAVE YOU DONE...?
ALURA...
WHO ARE YOU?!
HOW DID YOU GET INTO OUR HOME?!
ALURA, IT'S NOT TOO LATE...
TOO LATE FOR WHAT? WHY ARE YOU WEARING THAT SYMBOL?
TELL ME WHO YOU ARE!!!
A FRIEND.
ALURA, LISTEN TO ME. THERE'S STILL TIME...
...TO SAY GOODBYE TO KARA!

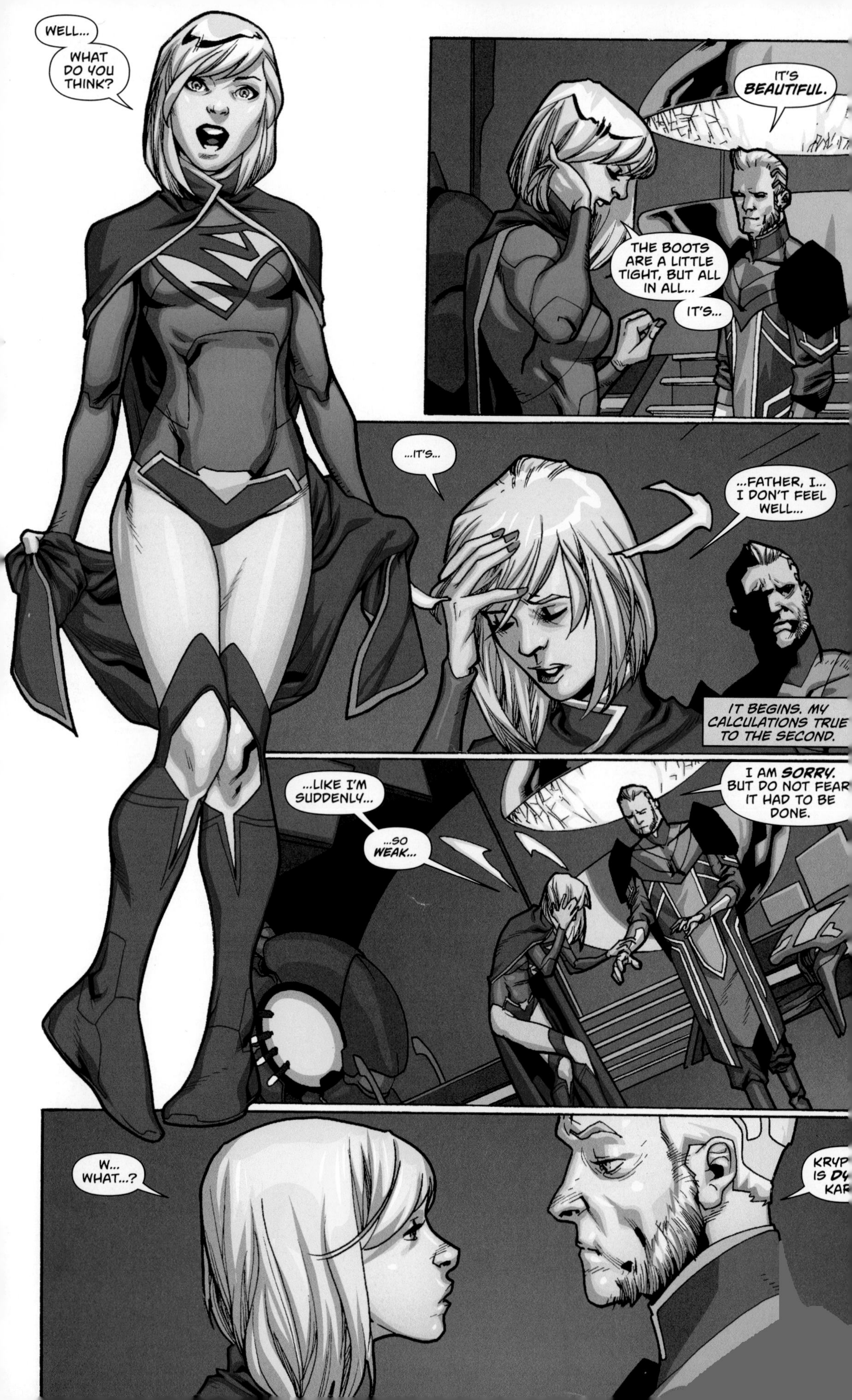
WELL...
WHAT DO YOU THINK?
IT'S **BEAUTIFUL.**
THE BOOTS ARE A LITTLE TIGHT, BUT ALL IN ALL...
IT'S...
...IT'S...
...FATHER, I... I DON'T FEEL WELL...
IT BEGINS. MY CALCULATIONS TRUE TO THE SECOND.
...LIKE I'M SUDDENLY...
...SO **WEAK...**
I AM **SORRY.** BUT DO NOT FEAR
IT HAD TO BE DONE.
W... WHAT...?

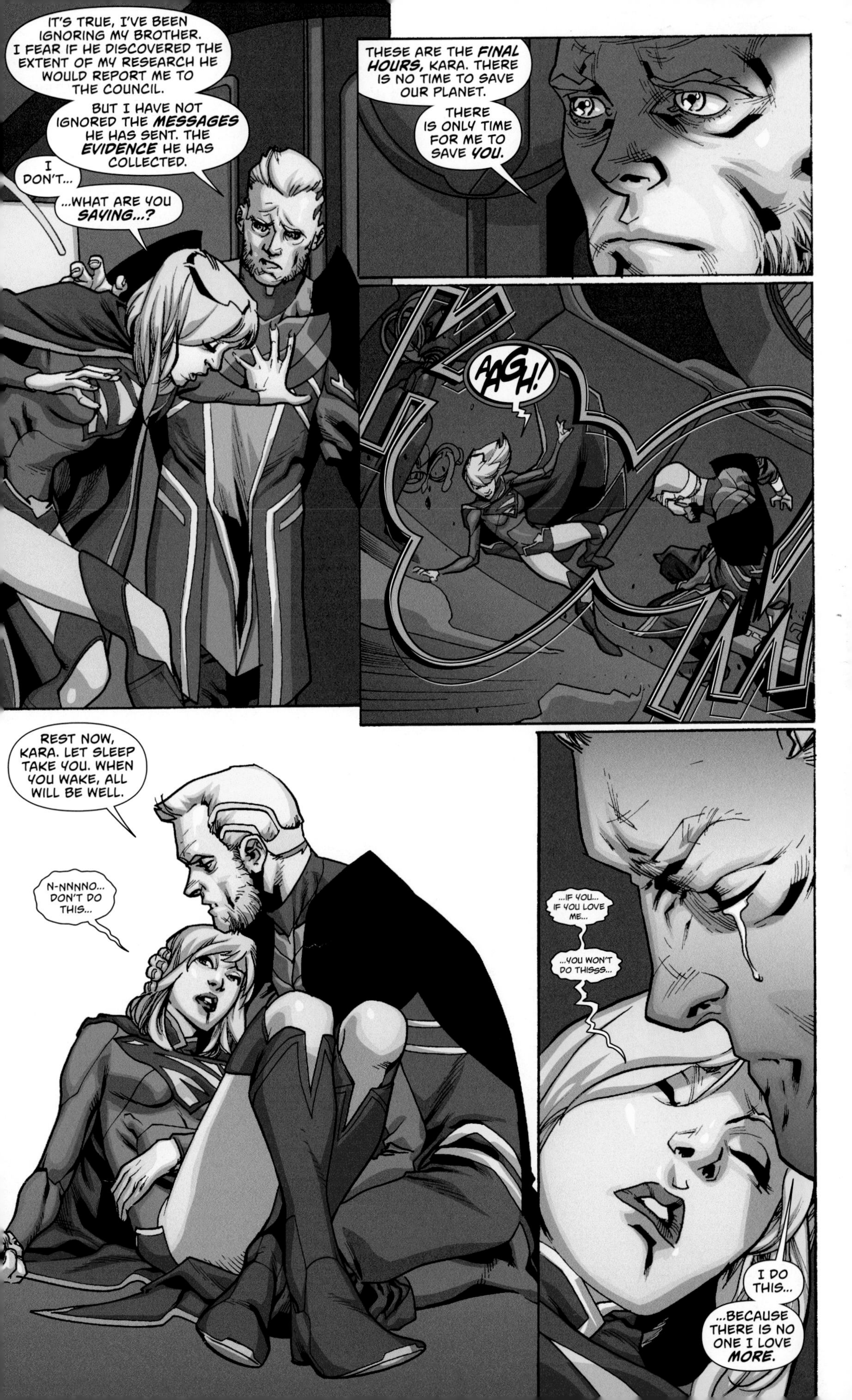
IT'S TRUE, I'VE BEEN IGNORING MY BROTHER. I FEAR IF HE DISCOVERED THE EXTENT OF MY RESEARCH HE WOULD REPORT ME TO THE COUNCIL.
BUT I HAVE NOT IGNORED THE MESSAGES HE HAS SENT. THE EVIDENCE HE HAS COLLECTED.
I DON'T...
...WHAT ARE YOU SAYING...?
THESE ARE THE FINAL HOURS, KARA. THERE IS NO TIME TO SAVE OUR PLANET.
THERE IS ONLY TIME FOR ME TO SAVE YOU.
AAGH!
REST NOW, KARA. LET SLEEP TAKE YOU. WHEN YOU WAKE, ALL WILL BE WELL.
N-NNNNO... DON'T DO THIS...
...IF YOU... IF YOU LOVE ME...
...YOU WON'T DO THISSS...
I DO THIS...
...BECAUSE THERE IS NO ONE I LOVE MORE.

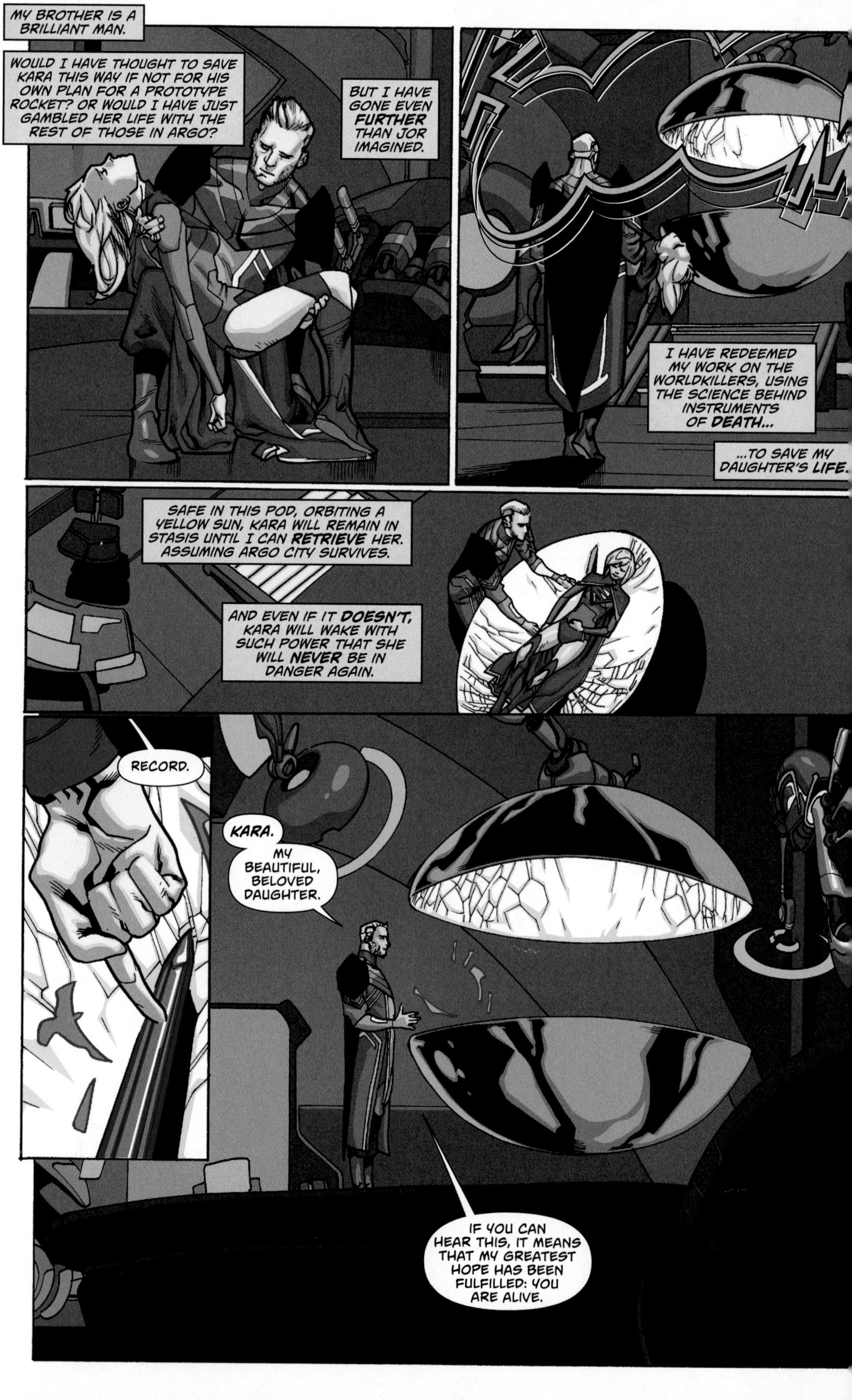
MY BROTHER IS A BRILLIANT MAN.
WOULD I HAVE THOUGHT TO SAVE KARA THIS WAY IF NOT FOR HIS OWN PLAN FOR A PROTOTYPE ROCKET? OR WOULD I HAVE JUST GAMBLED HER LIFE WITH THE REST OF THOSE IN ARGO?
BUT I HAVE GONE EVEN FURTHER THAN JOR IMAGINED.
I HAVE REDEEMED MY WORK ON THE WORLDKILLERS, USING THE SCIENCE BEHIND INSTRUMENTS OF DEATH...
...TO SAVE MY DAUGHTER'S LIFE.
SAFE IN THIS POD, ORBITING A YELLOW SUN, KARA WILL REMAIN IN STASIS UNTIL I CAN RETRIEVE HER. ASSUMING ARGO CITY SURVIVES.
AND EVEN IF IT DOESN'T, KARA WILL WAKE WITH SUCH POWER THAT SHE WILL NEVER BE IN DANGER AGAIN.
RECORD.
KARA.
MY BEAUTIFUL, BELOVED DAUGHTER.
IF YOU CAN HEAR THIS, IT MEANS THAT MY GREATEST HOPE HAS BEEN FULFILLED: YOU ARE ALIVE.

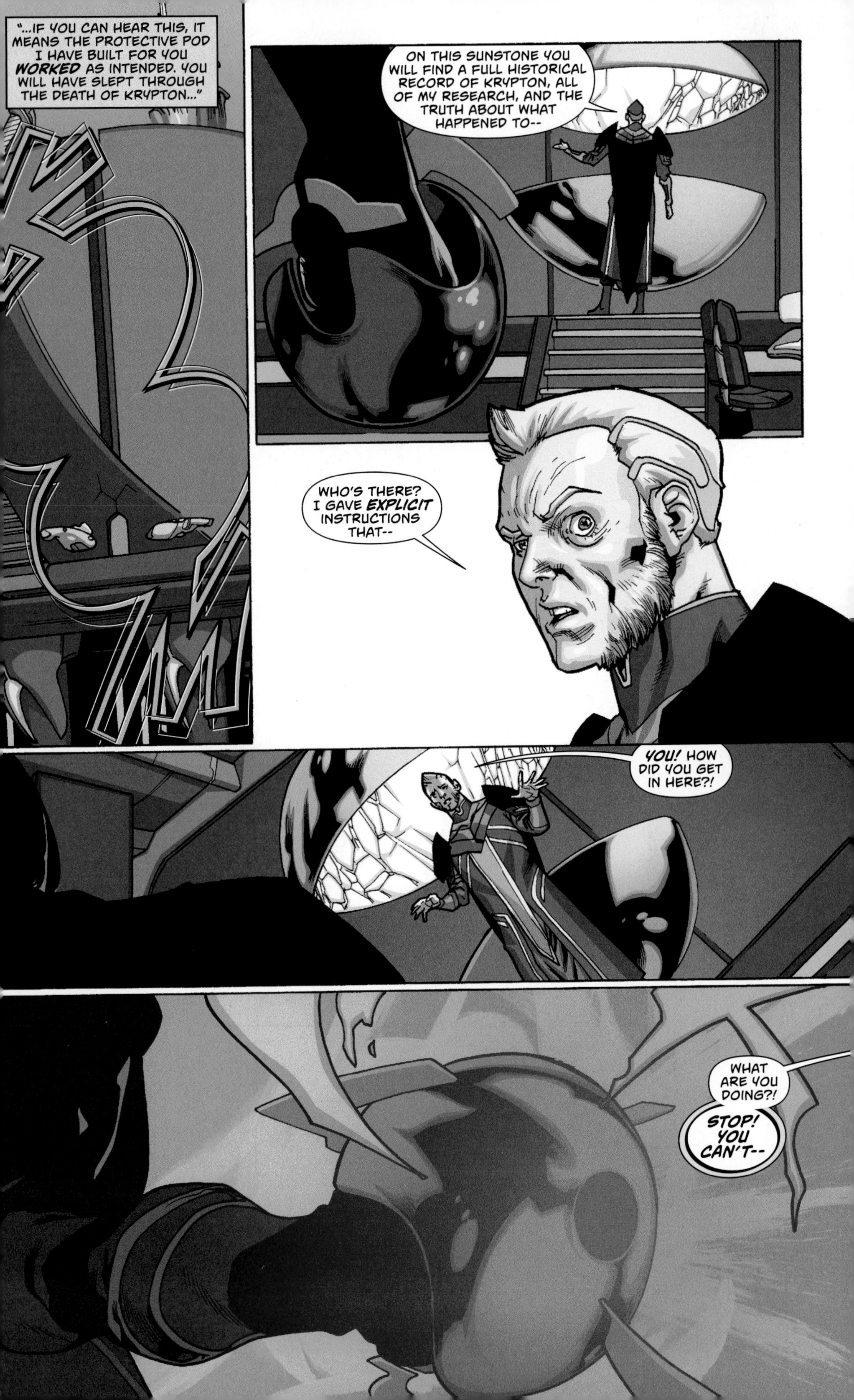
"...IF YOU CAN HEAR THIS, IT MEANS THE PROTECTIVE POD I HAVE BUILT FOR YOU WORKED AS INTENDED. YOU WILL HAVE SLEPT THROUGH THE DEATH OF KRYPTON..."
ON THIS SUNSTONE YOU WILL FIND A FULL HISTORICAL RECORD OF KRYPTON, ALL OF MY RESEARCH, AND THE TRUTH ABOUT WHAT HAPPENED TO--
WHO'S THERE? I GAVE EXPLICIT INSTRUCTIONS THAT--
YOU! HOW DID YOU GET IN HERE?!
WHAT ARE YOU DOING?!
STOP! YOU CAN'T--

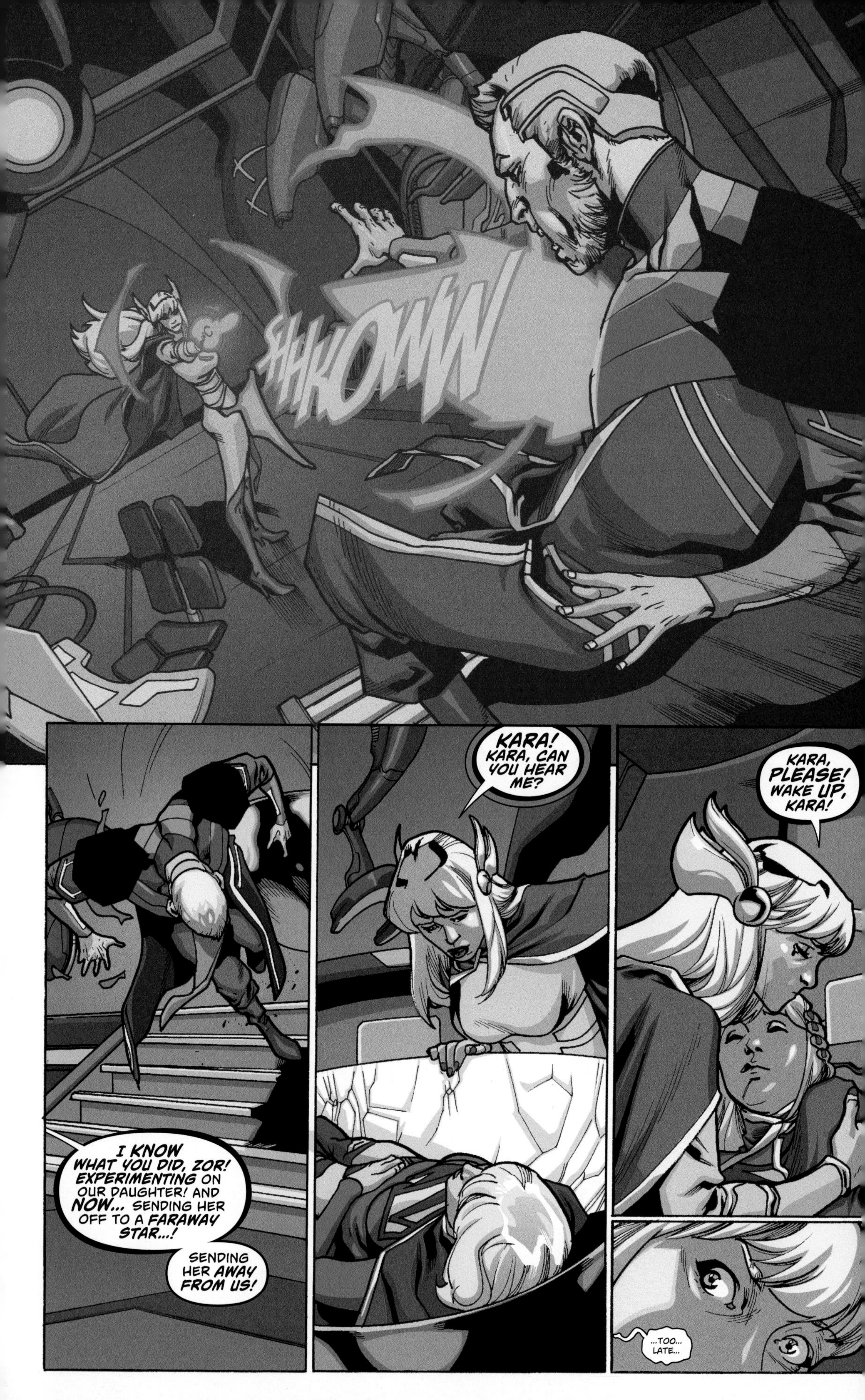
SHHKOWW
KARA! KARA, CAN YOU HEAR ME?
KARA, PLEASE! WAKE UP, KARA!
I KNOW WHAT YOU DID, ZOR! EXPERIMENTING ON OUR DAUGHTER! AND NOW... SENDING HER OFF TO A FARAWAY STAR...!
SENDING HER AWAY FROM US!
...TOO... LATE...

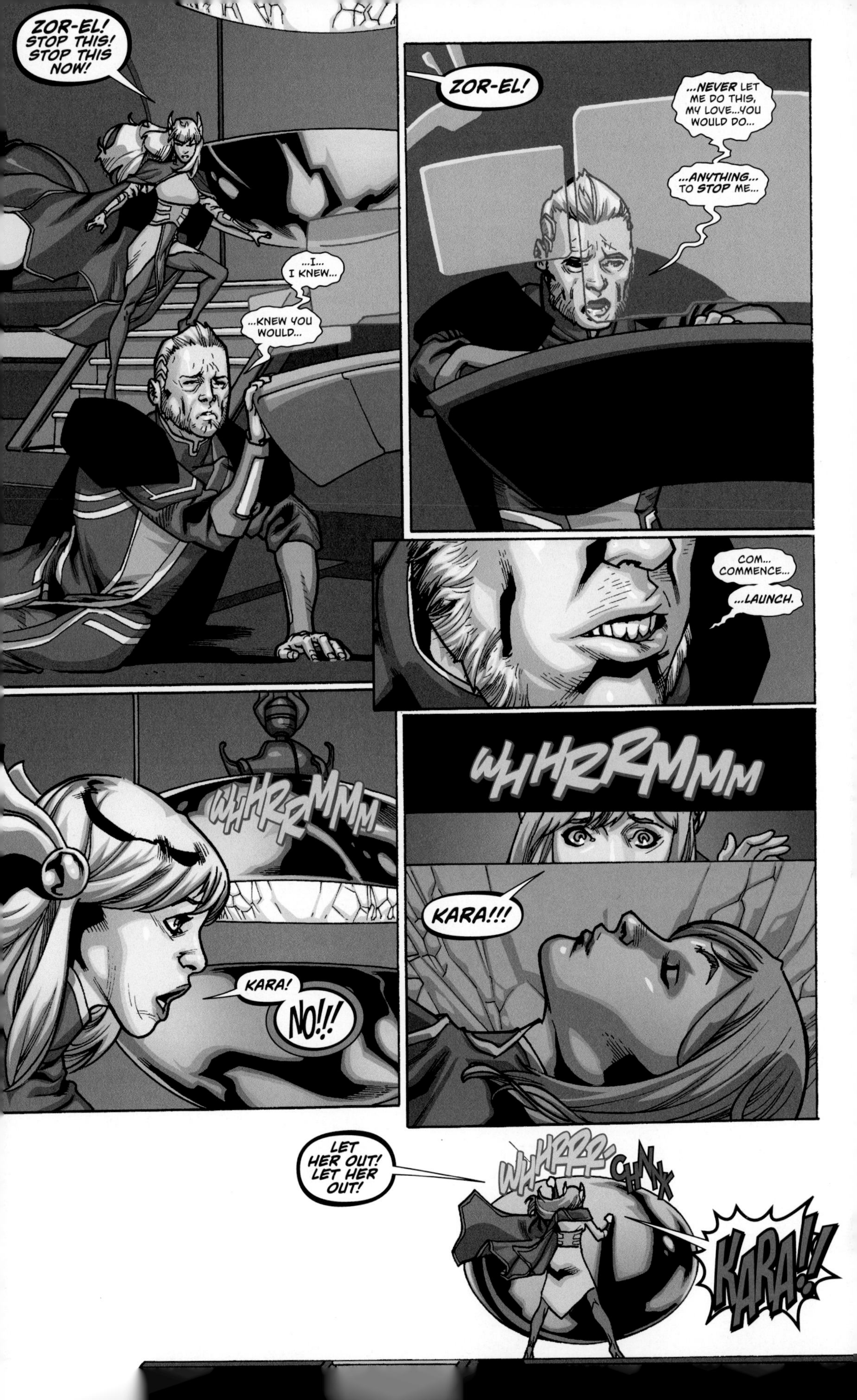
ZOR-EL! STOP THIS! STOP THIS NOW!
...I... I KNEW...
...KNEW YOU WOULD...
ZOR-EL!
...NEVER LET ME DO THIS, MY LOVE...YOU WOULD DO...
...ANYTHING... TO STOP ME...
COM... COMMENCE...
...LAUNCH.
WHHRRMMM
KARA! NO!!!
WHHRRMMMM
KARA!!!
LET HER OUT! LET HER OUT!
WHHRRR CHNNK
KARA!!!

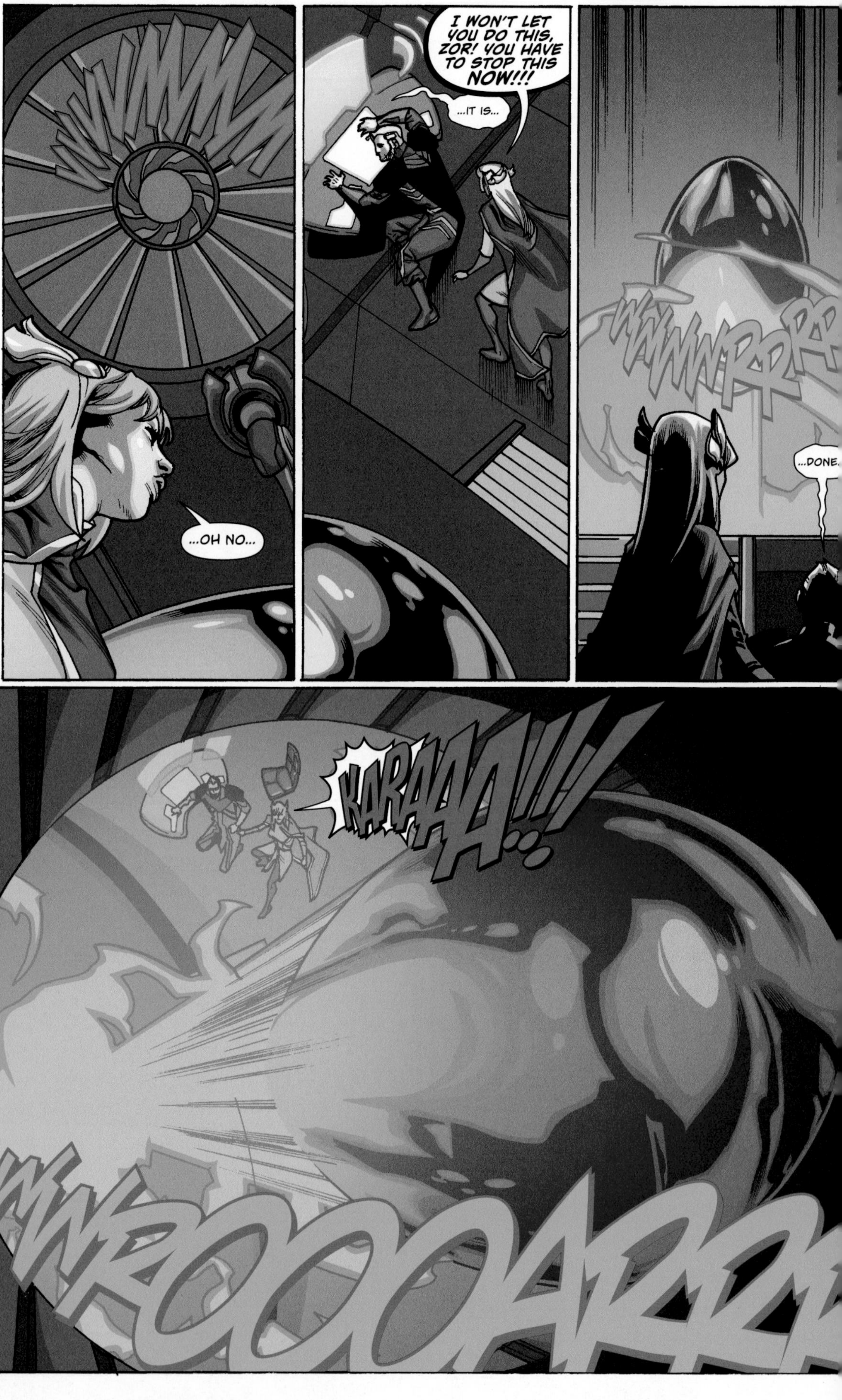
VVVMMMMM
...OH NO...
I WON'T LET YOU DO THIS, ZOR! YOU HAVE TO STOP THIS NOW!!!
...IT IS...
WWWWRRRR
...DONE.
KARAAAA!!!!
WWROOOOARRR

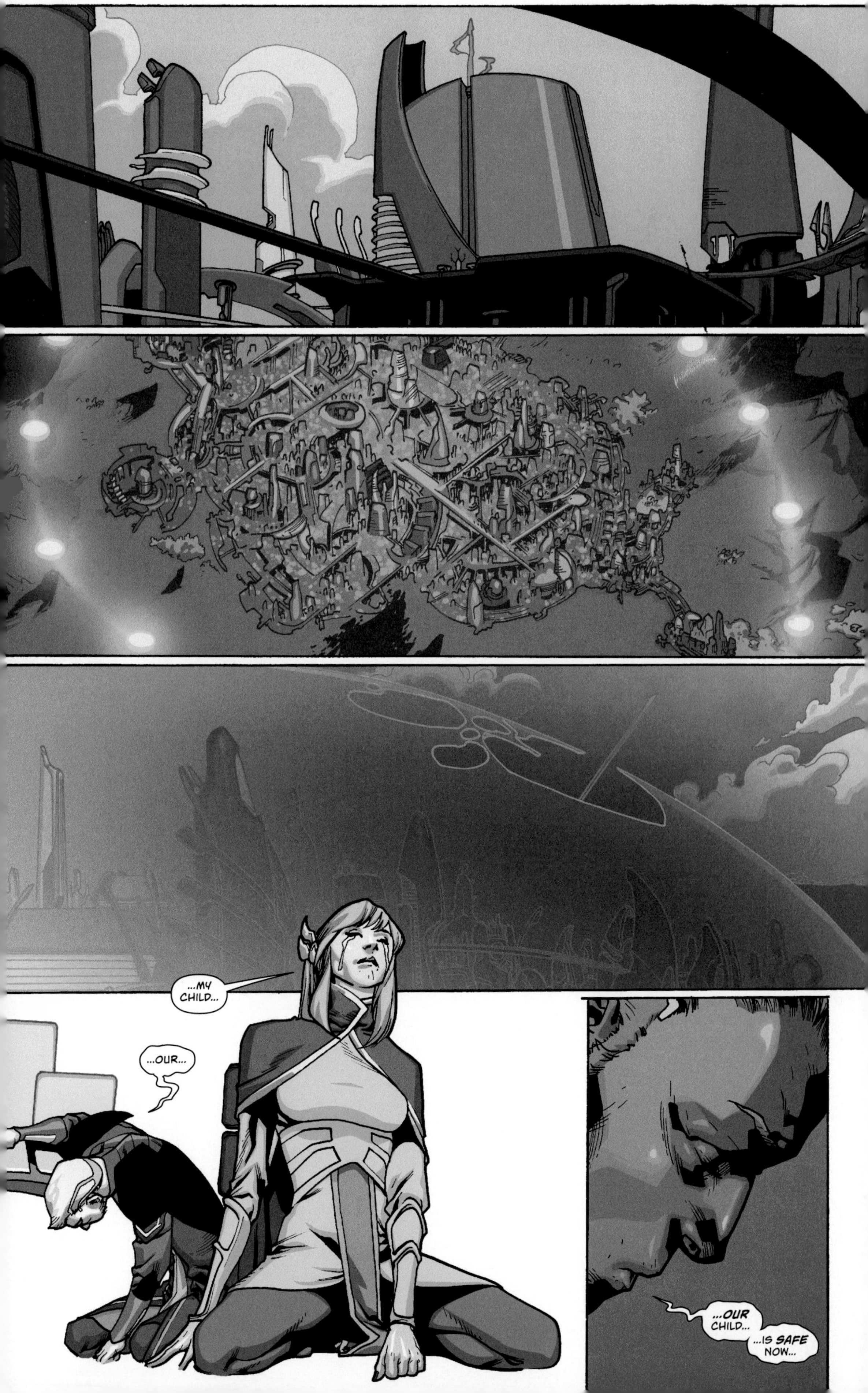
...MY CHILD...
...OUR...
...OUR CHILD...
...IS SAFE NOW...

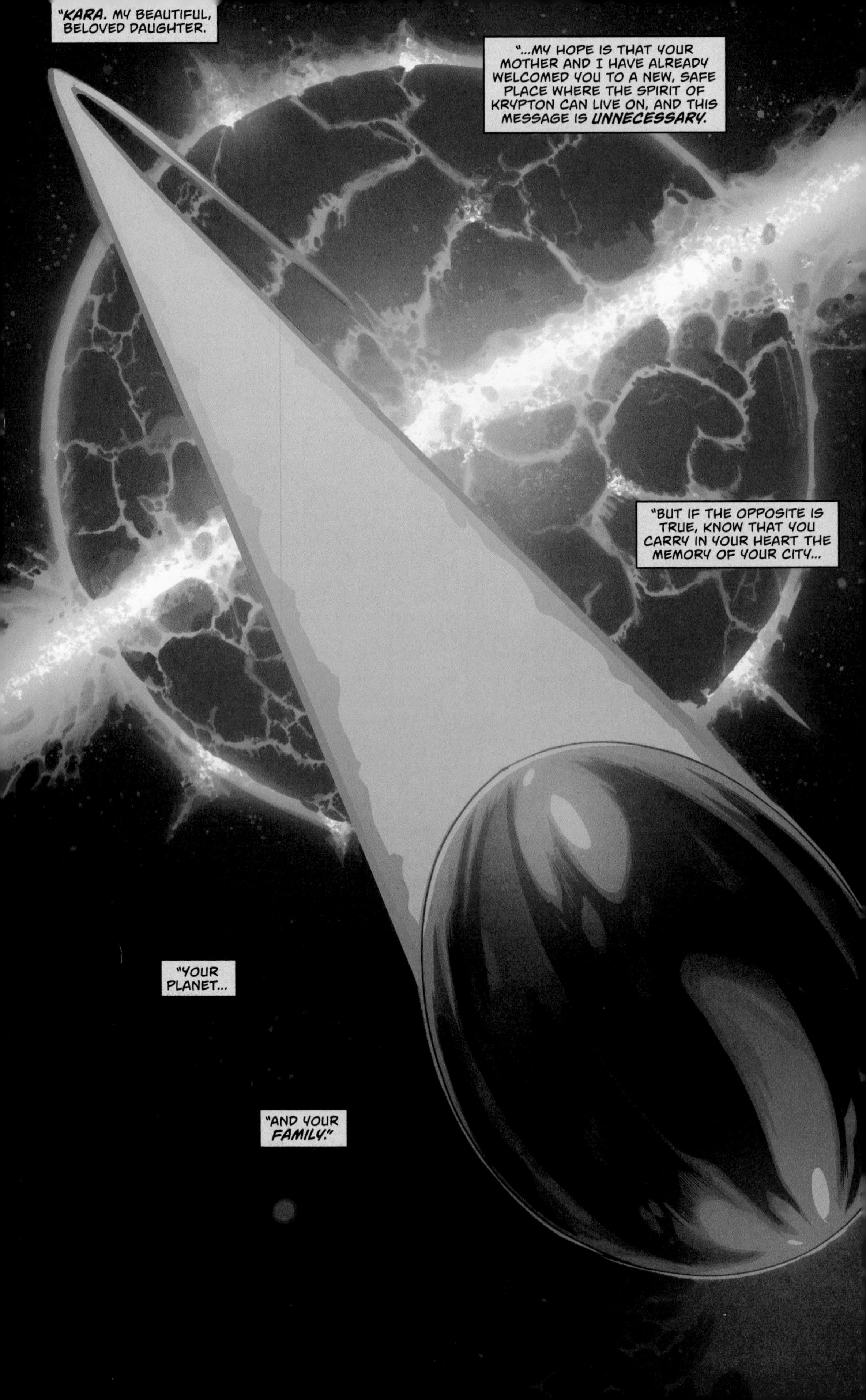
"KARA. MY BEAUTIFUL, BELOVED DAUGHTER.
"...MY HOPE IS THAT YOUR MOTHER AND I HAVE ALREADY WELCOMED YOU TO A NEW, SAFE PLACE WHERE THE SPIRIT OF KRYPTON CAN LIVE ON, AND THIS MESSAGE IS UNNECESSARY.
"BUT IF THE OPPOSITE IS TRUE, KNOW THAT YOU CARRY IN YOUR HEART THE MEMORY OF YOUR CITY...
"YOUR PLANET...
"AND YOUR FAMILY."

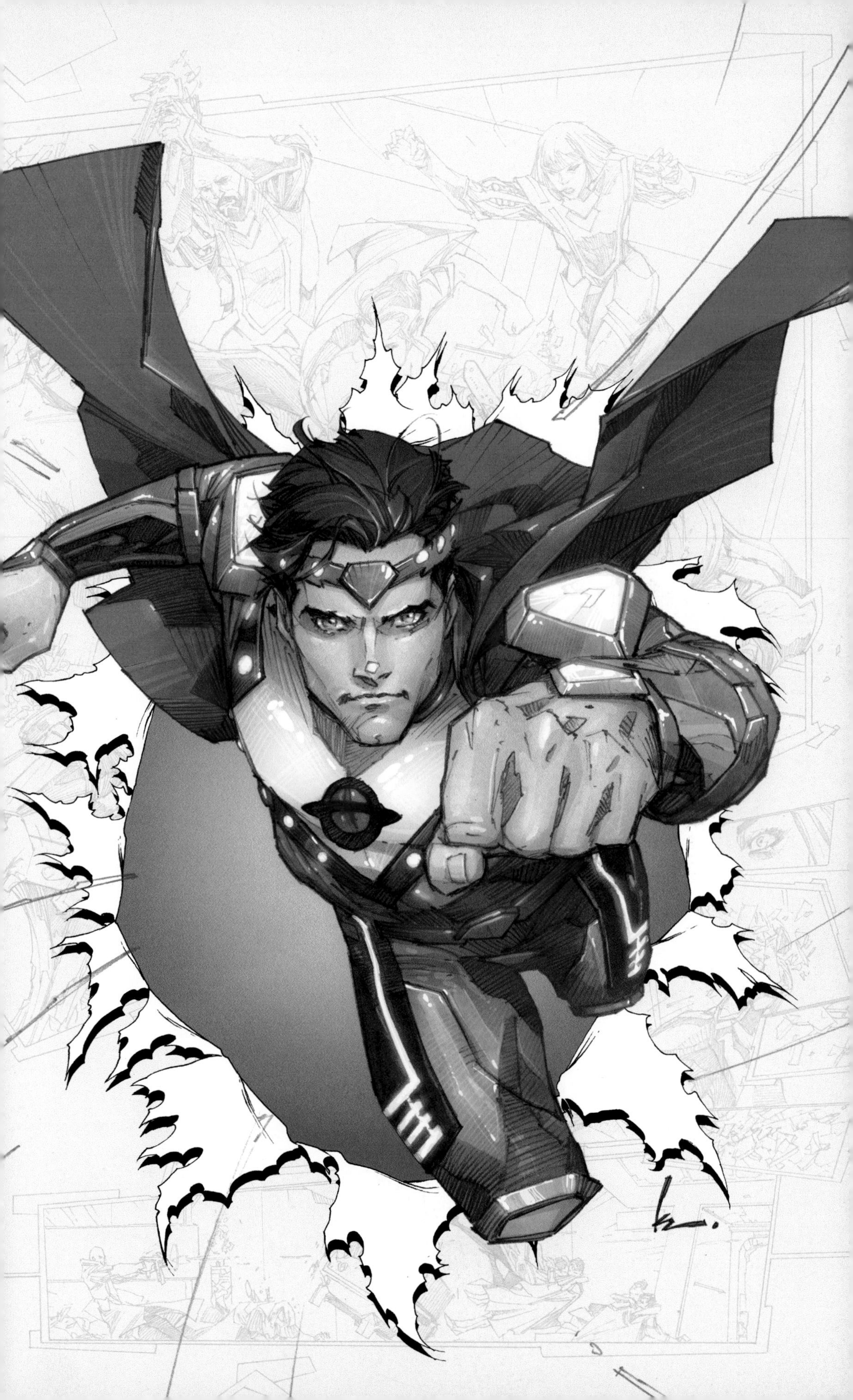

EVERY END HAS A BEGINNING...

SCOTT LOBDELL writer **KENNETH ROCAFORT** artist **SUNNY GHO** colorist

cover art by **KENNETH ROCAFORT**

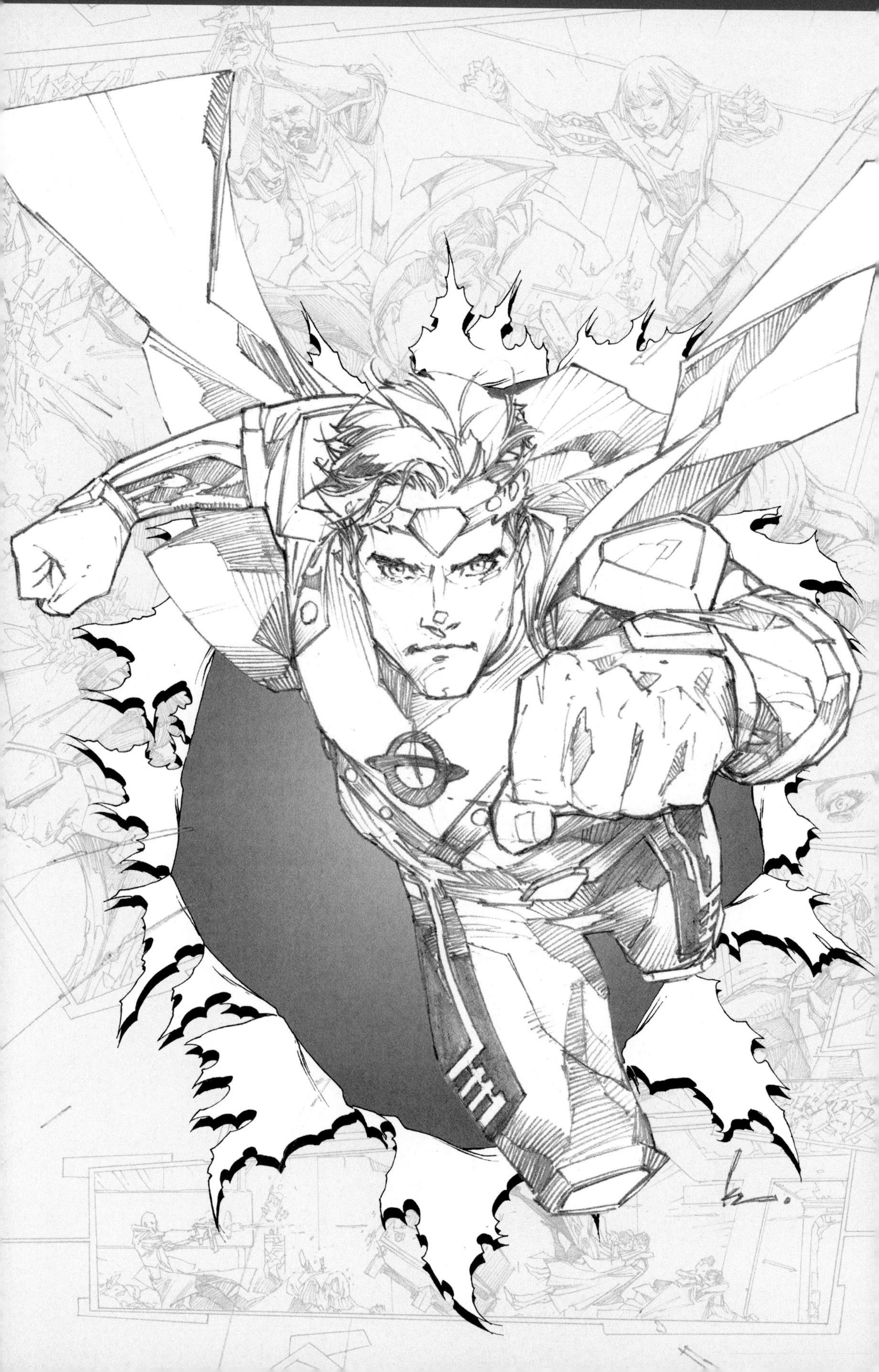

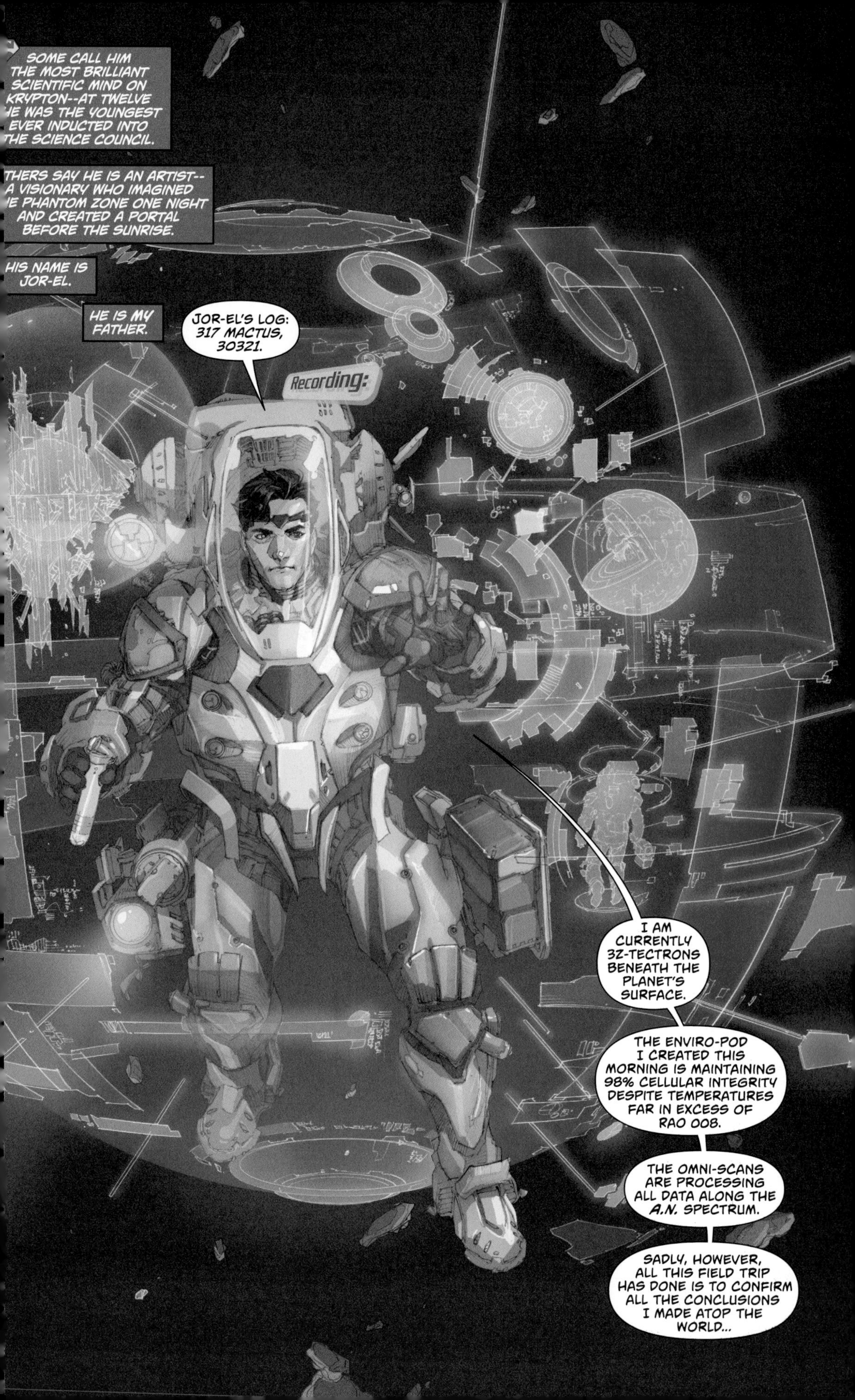
SOME CALL HIM THE MOST BRILLIANT SCIENTIFIC MIND ON KRYPTON--AT TWELVE E WAS THE YOUNGEST EVER INDUCTED INTO THE SCIENCE COUNCIL.
THERS SAY HE IS AN ARTIST-- A VISIONARY WHO IMAGINED E PHANTOM ZONE ONE NIGHT AND CREATED A PORTAL BEFORE THE SUNRISE.
HIS NAME IS JOR-EL.
HE IS MY FATHER.
JOR-EL'S LOG: 317 MACTUS, 30321.
Recording:
I AM CURRENTLY 32-TECTRONS BENEATH THE PLANET'S SURFACE.
THE ENVIRO-POD I CREATED THIS MORNING IS MAINTAINING 98% CELLULAR INTEGRITY DESPITE TEMPERATURES FAR IN EXCESS OF RAO 008.
THE OMNI-SCANS ARE PROCESSING ALL DATA ALONG THE A.N. SPECTRUM.
SADLY, HOWEVER, ALL THIS FIELD TRIP HAS DONE IS TO CONFIRM ALL THE CONCLUSIONS I MADE ATOP THE WORLD...

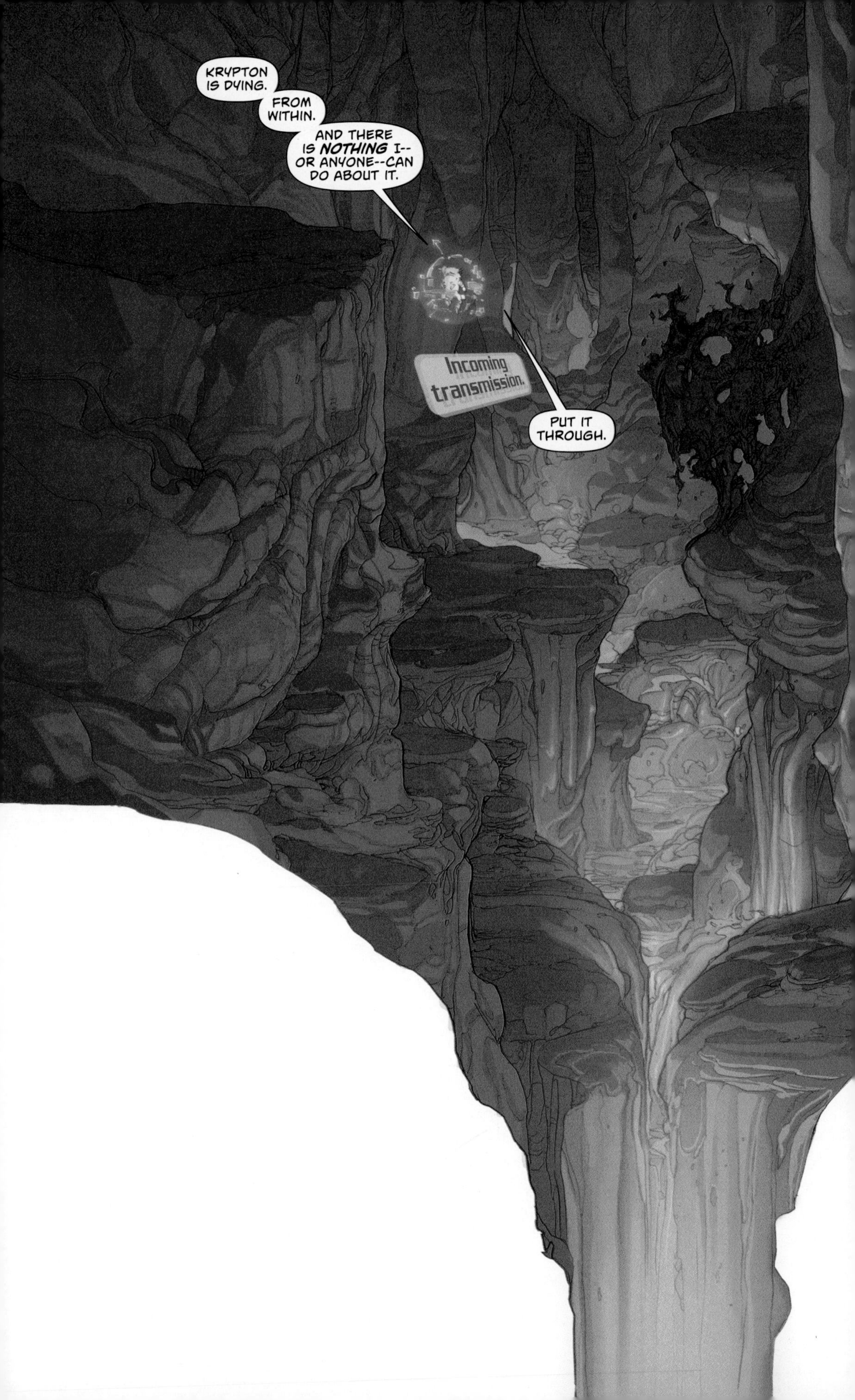
KRYPTON IS DYING.
FROM WITHIN.
AND THERE IS NOTHING I--OR ANYONE--CAN DO ABOUT IT.
Incoming transmission.
PUT IT THROUGH.

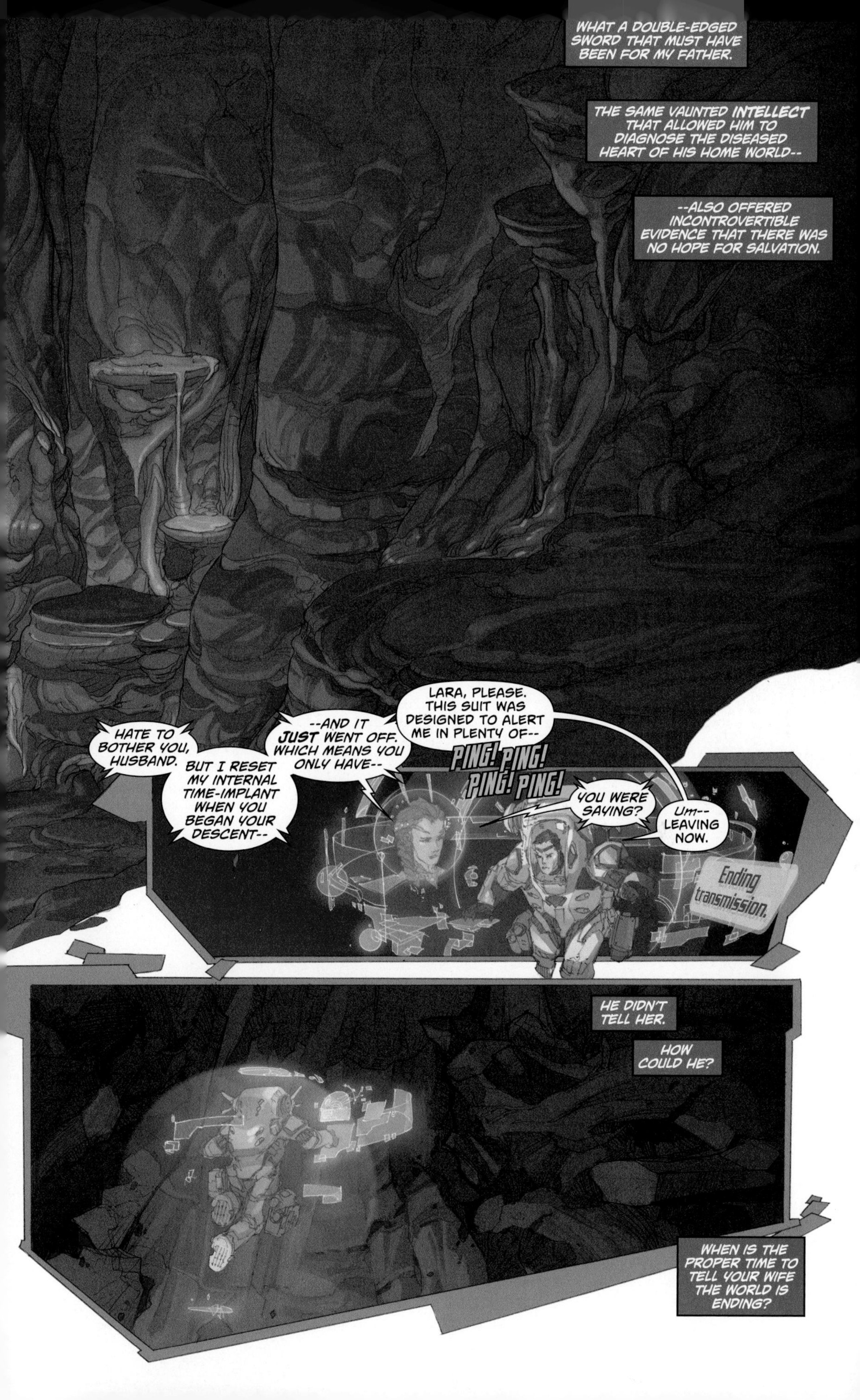

WHAT A DOUBLE-EDGED SWORD THAT MUST HAVE BEEN FOR MY FATHER.
THE SAME VAUNTED INTELLECT THAT ALLOWED HIM TO DIAGNOSE THE DISEASED HEART OF HIS HOME WORLD--
--ALSO OFFERED INCONTROVERTIBLE EVIDENCE THAT THERE WAS NO HOPE FOR SALVATION.
HATE TO BOTHER YOU, HUSBAND.
BUT I RESET MY INTERNAL TIME-IMPLANT WHEN YOU BEGAN YOUR DESCENT--
--AND IT JUST WENT OFF. WHICH MEANS YOU ONLY HAVE--
LARA, PLEASE. THIS SUIT WAS DESIGNED TO ALERT ME IN PLENTY OF--
PING! PING! PING! PING!
YOU WERE SAYING?
Um-- LEAVING NOW.
Ending transmission.
HE DIDN'T TELL HER.
HOW COULD HE?
WHEN IS THE PROPER TIME TO TELL YOUR WIFE THE WORLD IS ENDING?

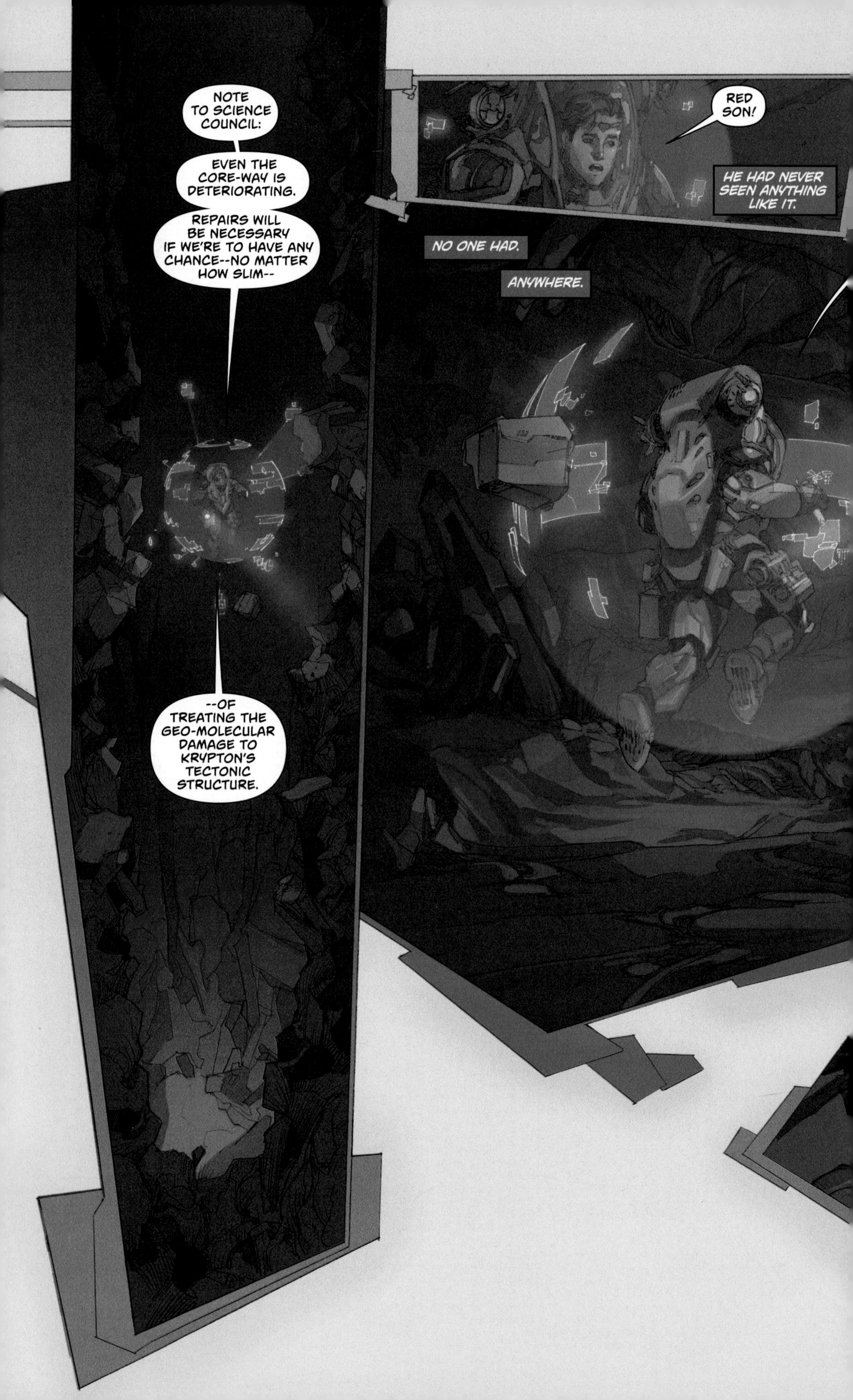
NOTE TO SCIENCE COUNCIL:
EVEN THE CORE-WAY IS DETERIORATING.
REPAIRS WILL BE NECESSARY IF WE'RE TO HAVE ANY CHANCE--NO MATTER HOW SLIM--
--OF TREATING THE GEO-MOLECULAR DAMAGE TO KRYPTON'S TECTONIC STRUCTURE.
RED SON!
HE HAD NEVER SEEN ANYTHING LIKE IT.
NO ONE HAD.
ANYWHERE.

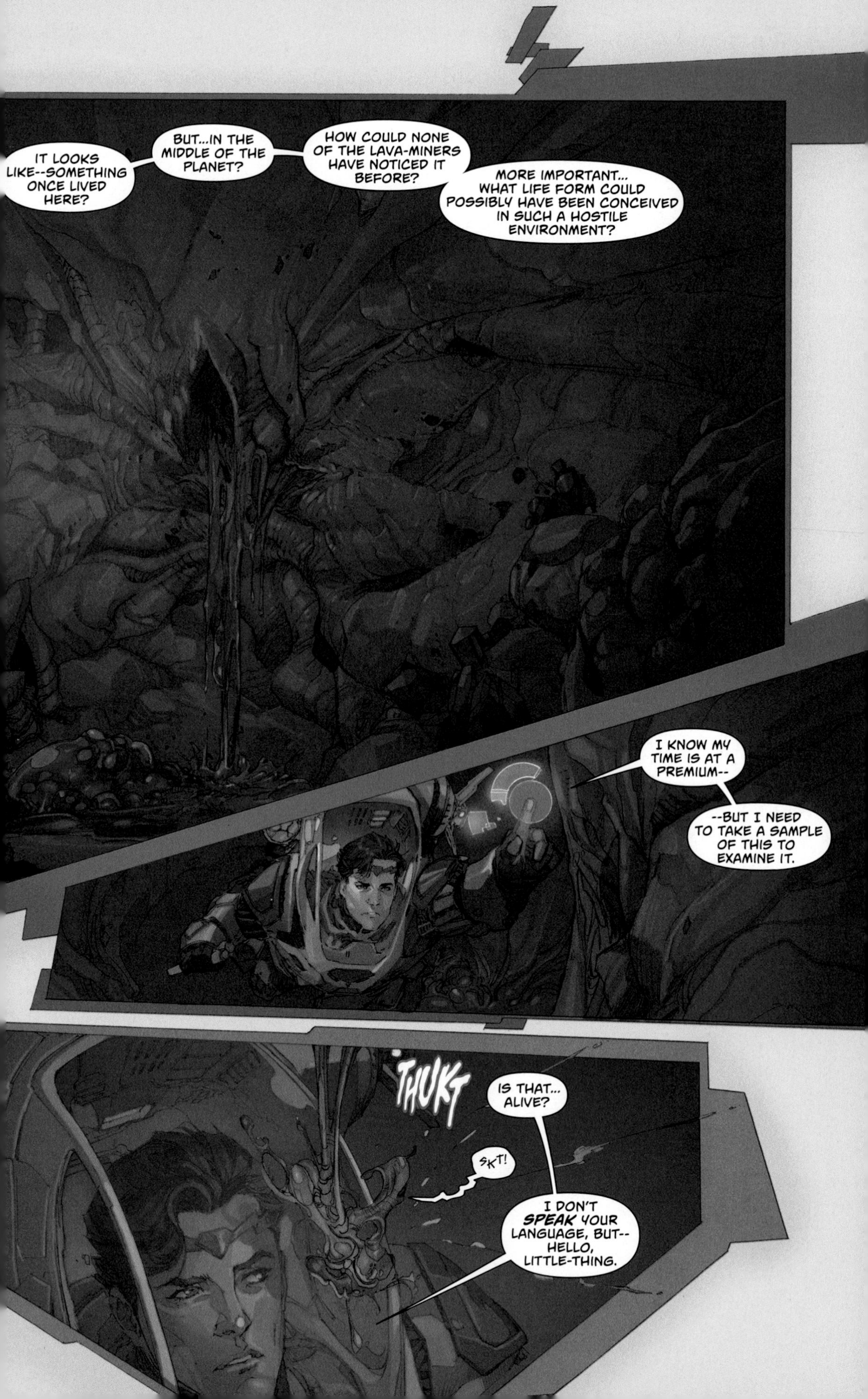

IT LOOKS LIKE--SOMETHING ONCE LIVED HERE?
BUT...IN THE MIDDLE OF THE PLANET?
HOW COULD NONE OF THE LAVA-MINERS HAVE NOTICED IT BEFORE?
MORE IMPORTANT... WHAT LIFE FORM COULD POSSIBLY HAVE BEEN CONCEIVED IN SUCH A HOSTILE ENVIRONMENT?
I KNOW MY TIME IS AT A PREMIUM--
--BUT I NEED TO TAKE A SAMPLE OF THIS TO EXAMINE IT.
THUKT
IS THAT... ALIVE?
SKT!
I DON'T ***SPEAK*** YOUR LANGUAGE, BUT-- HELLO, LITTLE-THING.

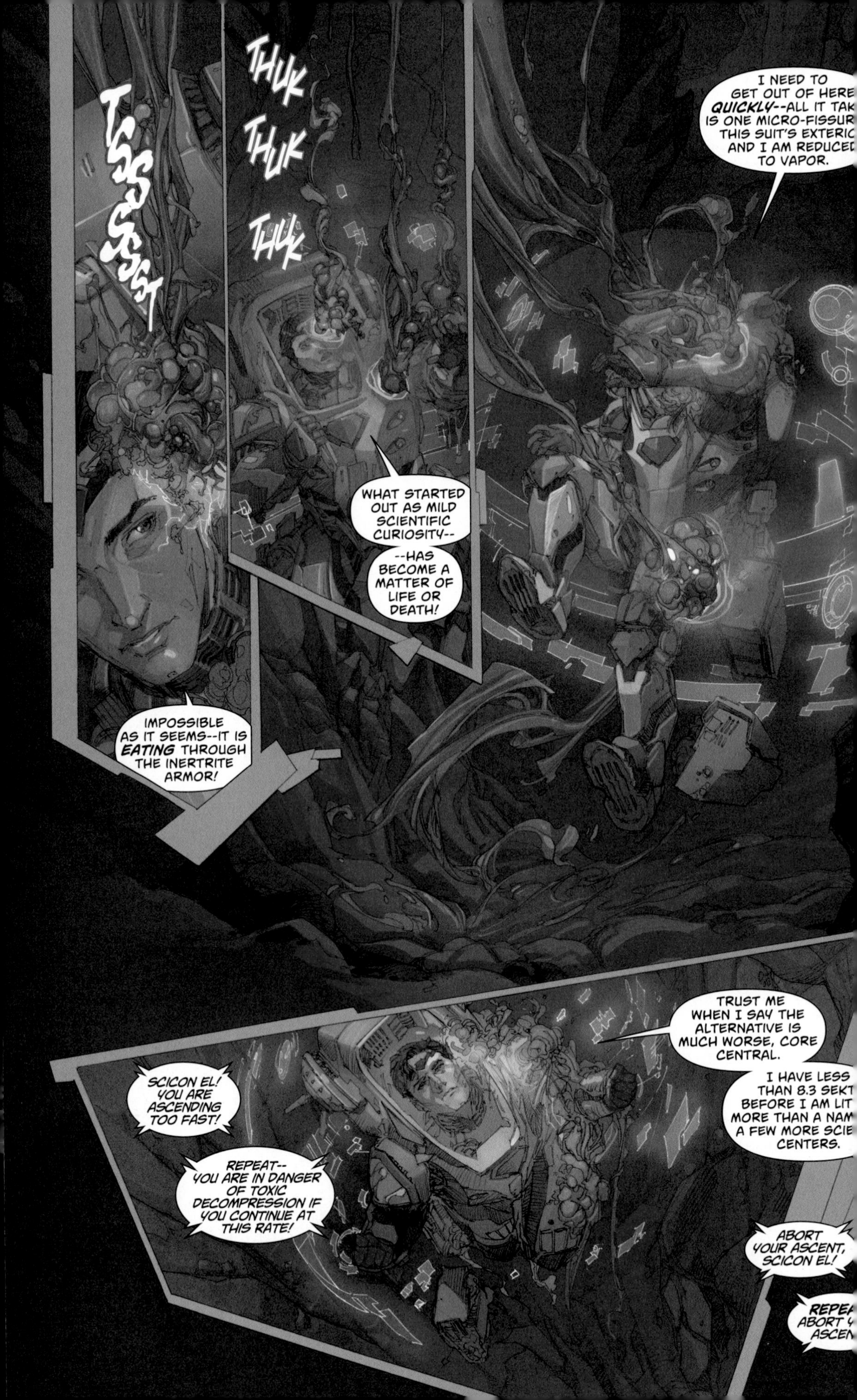
TSSSSSST
IMPOSSIBLE AS IT SEEMS--IT IS EATING THROUGH THE INERTRITE ARMOR!
THUK THUK THUK
WHAT STARTED OUT AS MILD SCIENTIFIC CURIOSITY--
--HAS BECOME A MATTER OF LIFE OR DEATH!
I NEED TO GET OUT OF HERE QUICKLY--ALL IT TAK IS ONE MICRO-FISSUR THIS SUIT'S EXTERIC AND I AM REDUCED TO VAPOR.
SCICON EL! YOU ARE ASCENDING TOO FAST!
REPEAT-- YOU ARE IN DANGER OF TOXIC DECOMPRESSION IF YOU CONTINUE AT THIS RATE!
TRUST ME WHEN I SAY THE ALTERNATIVE IS MUCH WORSE, CORE CENTRAL.
I HAVE LESS THAN 8.3 SEKT BEFORE I AM LIT MORE THAN A NAM A FEW MORE SCIE CENTERS.
ABORT YOUR ASCENT, SCICON EL!
REPEA ABORT Y ASCEN

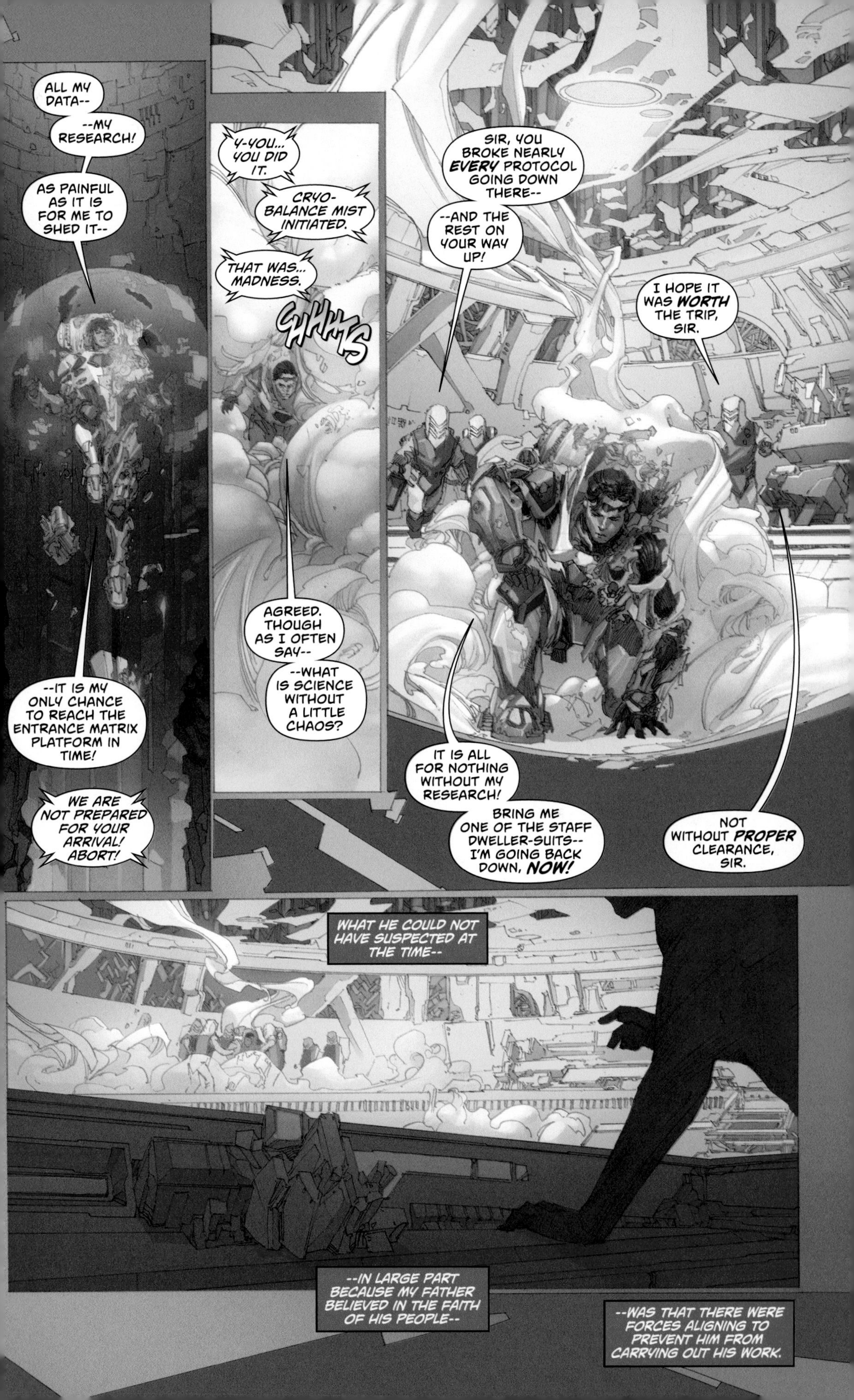
ALL MY DATA--
--MY RESEARCH!
AS PAINFUL AS IT IS FOR ME TO SHED IT--
--IT IS MY ONLY CHANCE TO REACH THE ENTRANCE MATRIX PLATFORM IN TIME!
WE ARE NOT PREPARED FOR YOUR ARRIVAL! ABORT!
Y-YOU... YOU DID IT.
CRYO-BALANCE MIST INITIATED.
THAT WAS... MADNESS.
CHHHTS
AGREED. THOUGH AS I OFTEN SAY--
--WHAT IS SCIENCE WITHOUT A LITTLE CHAOS?
SIR, YOU BROKE NEARLY EVERY PROTOCOL GOING DOWN THERE--
--AND THE REST ON YOUR WAY UP!
I HOPE IT WAS WORTH THE TRIP, SIR.
IT IS ALL FOR NOTHING WITHOUT MY RESEARCH!
BRING ME ONE OF THE STAFF DWELLER-SUITS-- I'M GOING BACK DOWN, NOW!
NOT WITHOUT PROPER CLEARANCE, SIR.
WHAT HE COULD NOT HAVE SUSPECTED AT THE TIME--
--IN LARGE PART BECAUSE MY FATHER BELIEVED IN THE FAITH OF HIS PEOPLE--
--WAS THAT THERE WERE FORCES ALIGNING TO PREVENT HIM FROM CARRYING OUT HIS WORK.

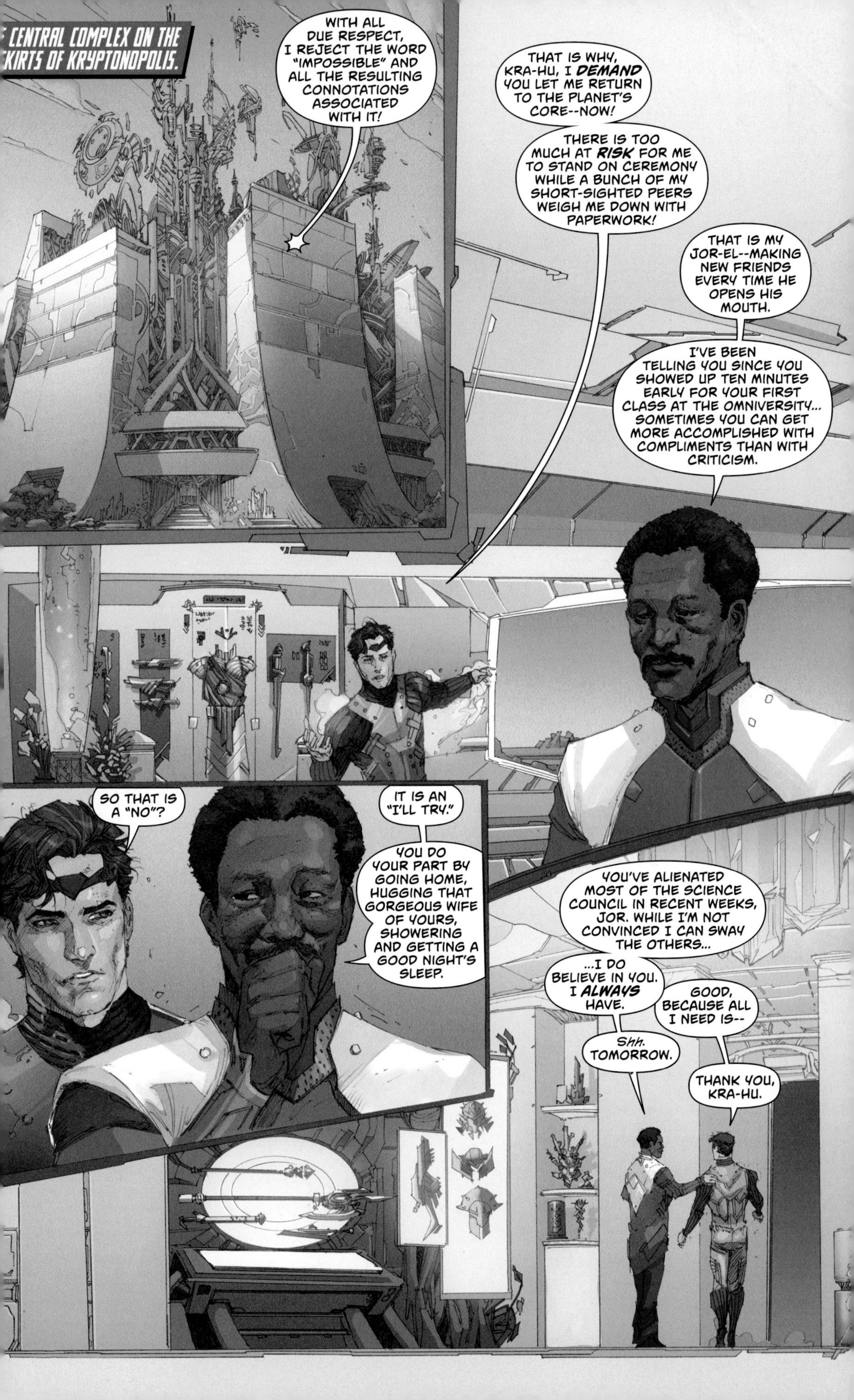
CENTRAL COMPLEX ON THE
KIRTS OF KRYPTONOPOLIS.
WITH ALL DUE RESPECT, I REJECT THE WORD "IMPOSSIBLE" AND ALL THE RESULTING CONNOTATIONS ASSOCIATED WITH IT!
THAT IS WHY, KRA-HU, I DEMAND YOU LET ME RETURN TO THE PLANET'S CORE--NOW!
THERE IS TOO MUCH AT RISK FOR ME TO STAND ON CEREMONY WHILE A BUNCH OF MY SHORT-SIGHTED PEERS WEIGH ME DOWN WITH PAPERWORK!
THAT IS MY JOR-EL--MAKING NEW FRIENDS EVERY TIME HE OPENS HIS MOUTH.
I'VE BEEN TELLING YOU SINCE YOU SHOWED UP TEN MINUTES EARLY FOR YOUR FIRST CLASS AT THE OMNIVERSITY... SOMETIMES YOU CAN GET MORE ACCOMPLISHED WITH COMPLIMENTS THAN WITH CRITICISM.
SO THAT IS A "NO"?
IT IS AN "I'LL TRY."
YOU DO YOUR PART BY GOING HOME, HUGGING THAT GORGEOUS WIFE OF YOURS, SHOWERING AND GETTING A GOOD NIGHT'S SLEEP.
YOU'VE ALIENATED MOST OF THE SCIENCE COUNCIL IN RECENT WEEKS, JOR. WHILE I'M NOT CONVINCED I CAN SWAY THE OTHERS...
...I DO BELIEVE IN YOU. I ALWAYS HAVE.
GOOD, BECAUSE ALL I NEED IS--
Shh. TOMORROW.
THANK YOU, KRA-HU.

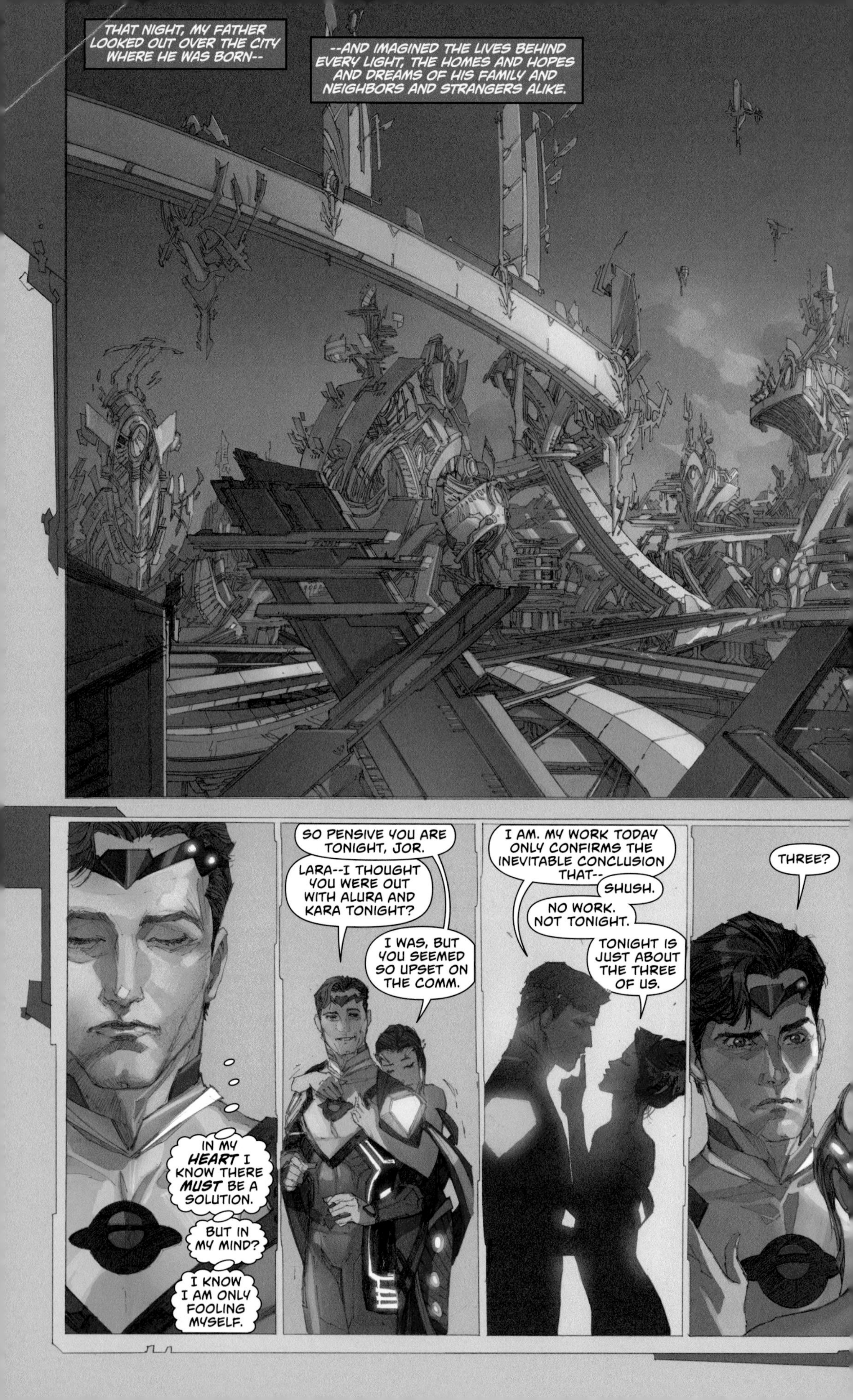
THAT NIGHT, MY FATHER LOOKED OUT OVER THE CITY WHERE HE WAS BORN--
--AND IMAGINED THE LIVES BEHIND EVERY LIGHT, THE HOMES AND HOPES AND DREAMS OF HIS FAMILY AND NEIGHBORS AND STRANGERS ALIKE.
IN MY HEART I KNOW THERE MUST BE A SOLUTION.
BUT IN MY MIND?
I KNOW I AM ONLY FOOLING MYSELF.
SO PENSIVE YOU ARE TONIGHT, JOR.
LARA--I THOUGHT YOU WERE OUT WITH ALURA AND KARA TONIGHT?
I WAS, BUT YOU SEEMED SO UPSET ON THE COMM.
I AM. MY WORK TODAY ONLY CONFIRMS THE INEVITABLE CONCLUSION THAT--
SHUSH.
NO WORK. NOT TONIGHT.
TONIGHT IS JUST ABOUT THE THREE OF US.
THREE?

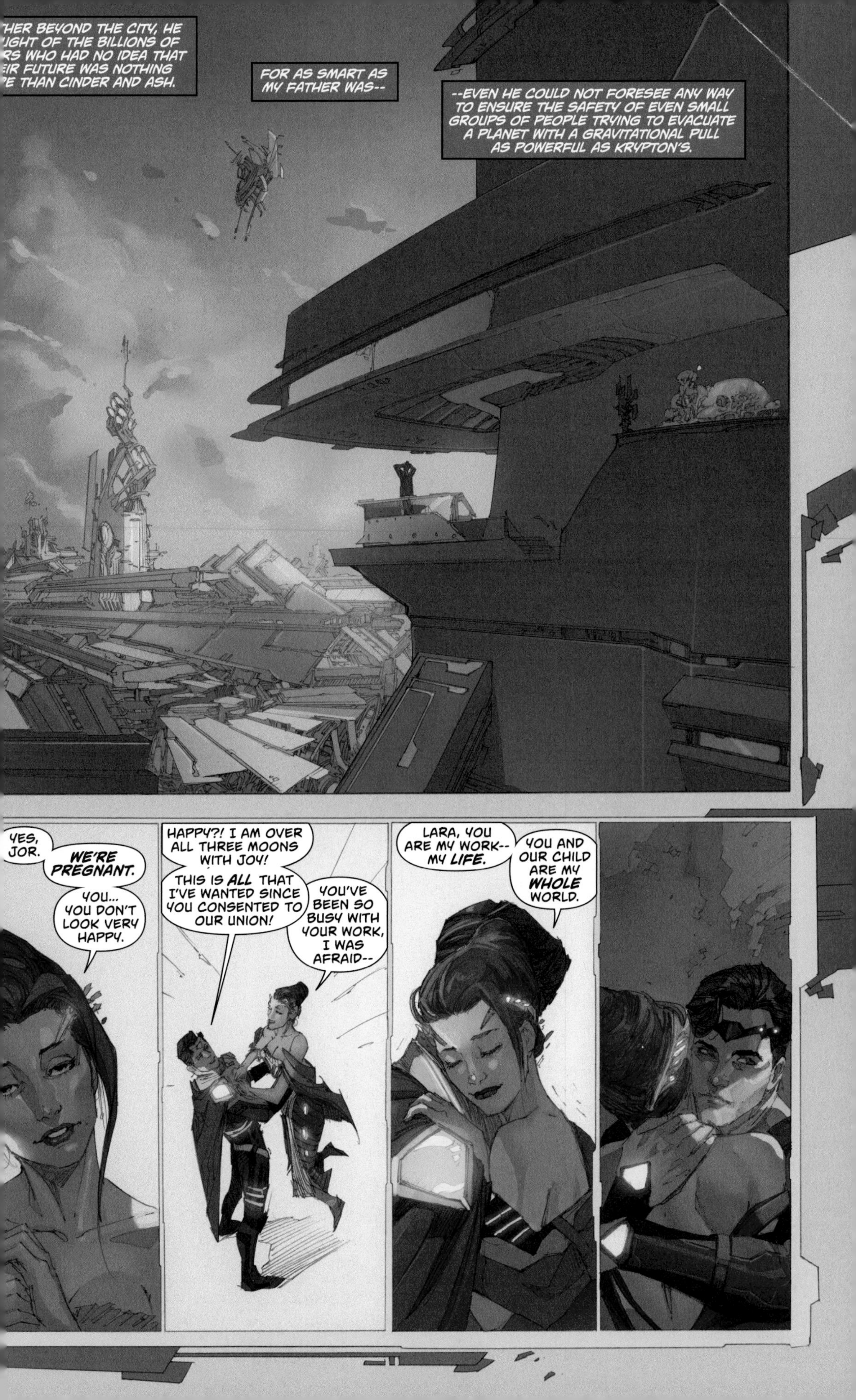

THER BEYOND THE CITY, HE
UGHT OF THE BILLIONS OF
RS WHO HAD NO IDEA THAT
EIR FUTURE WAS NOTHING
PE THAN CINDER AND ASH.
FOR AS SMART AS MY FATHER WAS--
--EVEN HE COULD NOT FORESEE ANY WAY TO ENSURE THE SAFETY OF EVEN SMALL GROUPS OF PEOPLE TRYING TO EVACUATE A PLANET WITH A GRAVITATIONAL PULL AS POWERFUL AS KRYPTON'S.
YES, JOR.
WE'RE PREGNANT.
YOU... YOU DON'T LOOK VERY HAPPY.
HAPPY?! I AM OVER ALL THREE MOONS WITH JOY!
THIS IS ALL THAT I'VE WANTED SINCE YOU CONSENTED TO OUR UNION!
YOU'VE BEEN SO BUSY WITH YOUR WORK, I WAS AFRAID--
LARA, YOU ARE MY WORK-- MY LIFE.
YOU AND OUR CHILD ARE MY WHOLE WORLD.

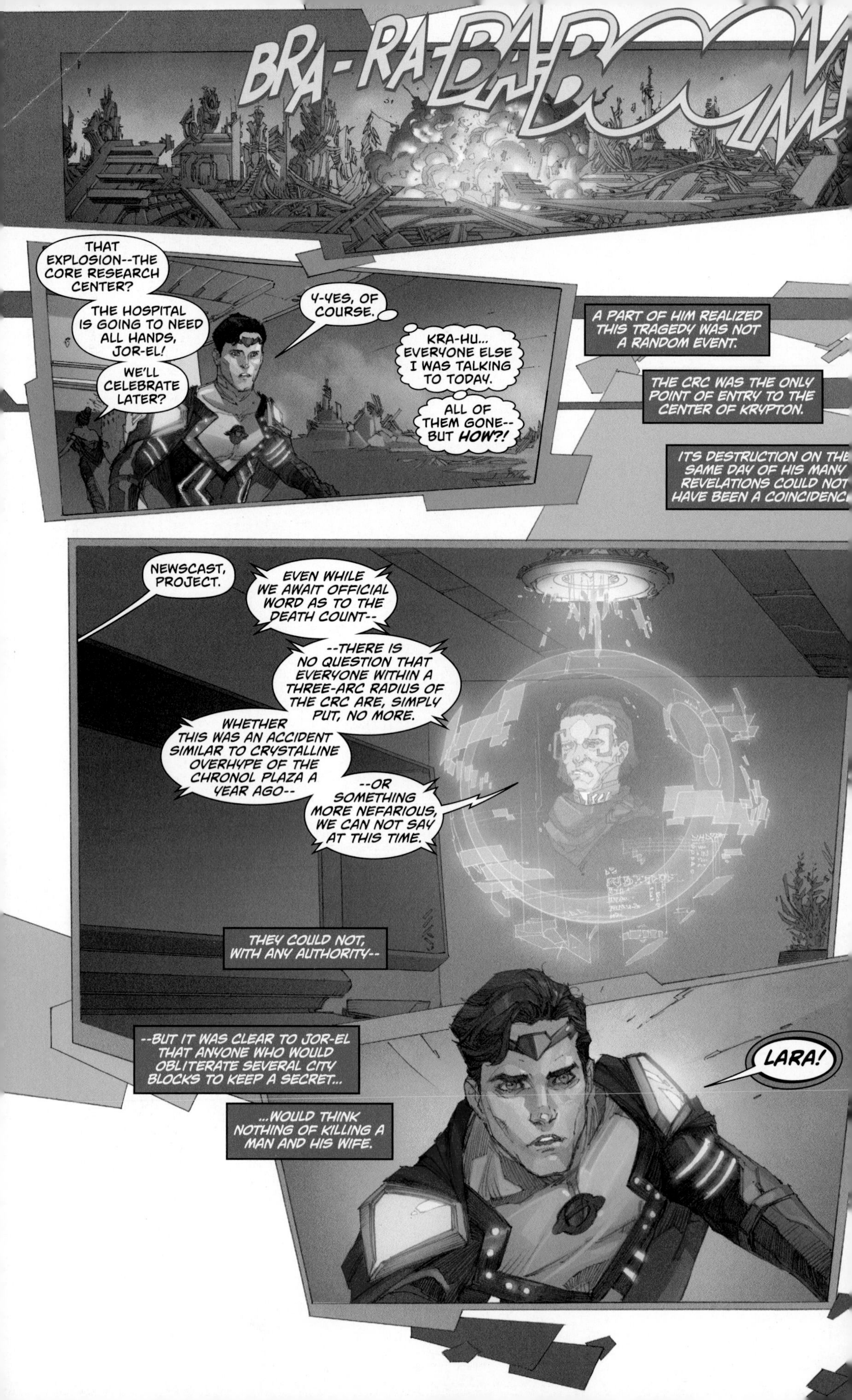
BRA-RA-BA-BOOM
THAT EXPLOSION--THE CORE RESEARCH CENTER?
THE HOSPITAL IS GOING TO NEED ALL HANDS, JOR-EL!
WE'LL CELEBRATE LATER?
Y-YES, OF COURSE.
KRA-HU... EVERYONE ELSE I WAS TALKING TO TODAY.
ALL OF THEM GONE-- BUT HOW?!
A PART OF HIM REALIZED THIS TRAGEDY WAS NOT A RANDOM EVENT.
THE CRC WAS THE ONLY POINT OF ENTRY TO THE CENTER OF KRYPTON.
ITS DESTRUCTION ON THE SAME DAY OF HIS MANY REVELATIONS COULD NOT HAVE BEEN A COINCIDENC
NEWSCAST, PROJECT.
EVEN WHILE WE AWAIT OFFICIAL WORD AS TO THE DEATH COUNT--
--THERE IS NO QUESTION THAT EVERYONE WITHIN A THREE-ARC RADIUS OF THE CRC ARE, SIMPLY PUT, NO MORE.
WHETHER THIS WAS AN ACCIDENT SIMILAR TO CRYSTALLINE OVERHYPE OF THE CHRONOL PLAZA A YEAR AGO--
--OR SOMETHING MORE NEFARIOUS, WE CAN NOT SAY AT THIS TIME.
THEY COULD NOT, WITH ANY AUTHORITY--
--BUT IT WAS CLEAR TO JOR-EL THAT ANYONE WHO WOULD OBLITERATE SEVERAL CITY BLOCKS TO KEEP A SECRET...
...WOULD THINK NOTHING OF KILLING A MAN AND HIS WIFE.
LARA!

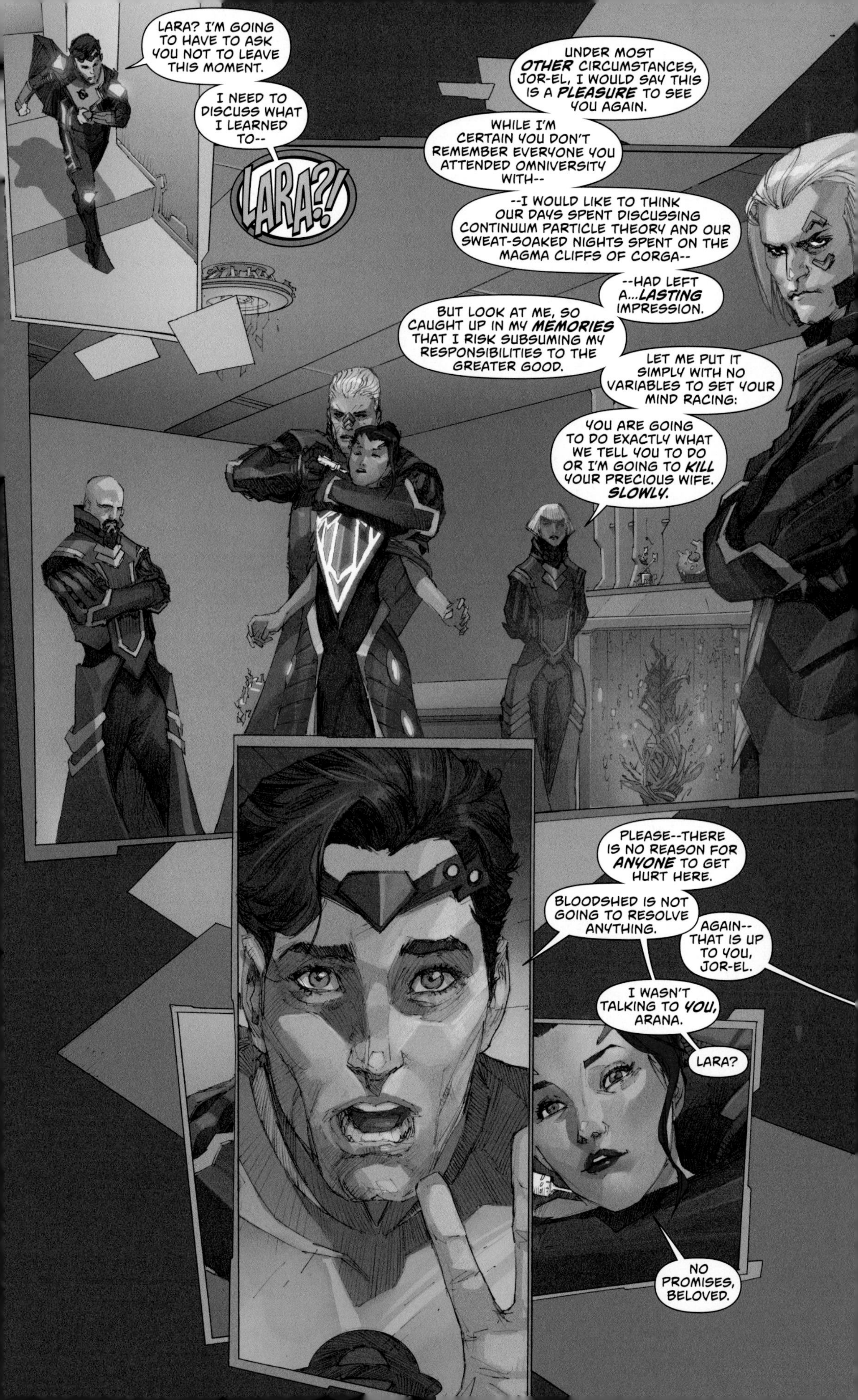
LARA? I'M GOING TO HAVE TO ASK YOU NOT TO LEAVE THIS MOMENT.
I NEED TO DISCUSS WHAT I LEARNED TO--
LARA?!
UNDER MOST OTHER CIRCUMSTANCES, JOR-EL, I WOULD SAY THIS IS A PLEASURE TO SEE YOU AGAIN.
WHILE I'M CERTAIN YOU DON'T REMEMBER EVERYONE YOU ATTENDED OMNIVERSITY WITH--
--I WOULD LIKE TO THINK OUR DAYS SPENT DISCUSSING CONTINUUM PARTICLE THEORY AND OUR SWEAT-SOAKED NIGHTS SPENT ON THE MAGMA CLIFFS OF CORGA--
--HAD LEFT A...LASTING IMPRESSION.
BUT LOOK AT ME, SO CAUGHT UP IN MY MEMORIES THAT I RISK SUBSUMING MY RESPONSIBILITIES TO THE GREATER GOOD.
LET ME PUT IT SIMPLY WITH NO VARIABLES TO SET YOUR MIND RACING:
YOU ARE GOING TO DO EXACTLY WHAT WE TELL YOU TO DO OR I'M GOING TO KILL YOUR PRECIOUS WIFE. SLOWLY.
PLEASE--THERE IS NO REASON FOR ANYONE TO GET HURT HERE.
BLOODSHED IS NOT GOING TO RESOLVE ANYTHING.
AGAIN--THAT IS UP TO YOU, JOR-EL.
I WASN'T TALKING TO YOU, ARANA.
LARA?
NO PROMISES, BELOVED.

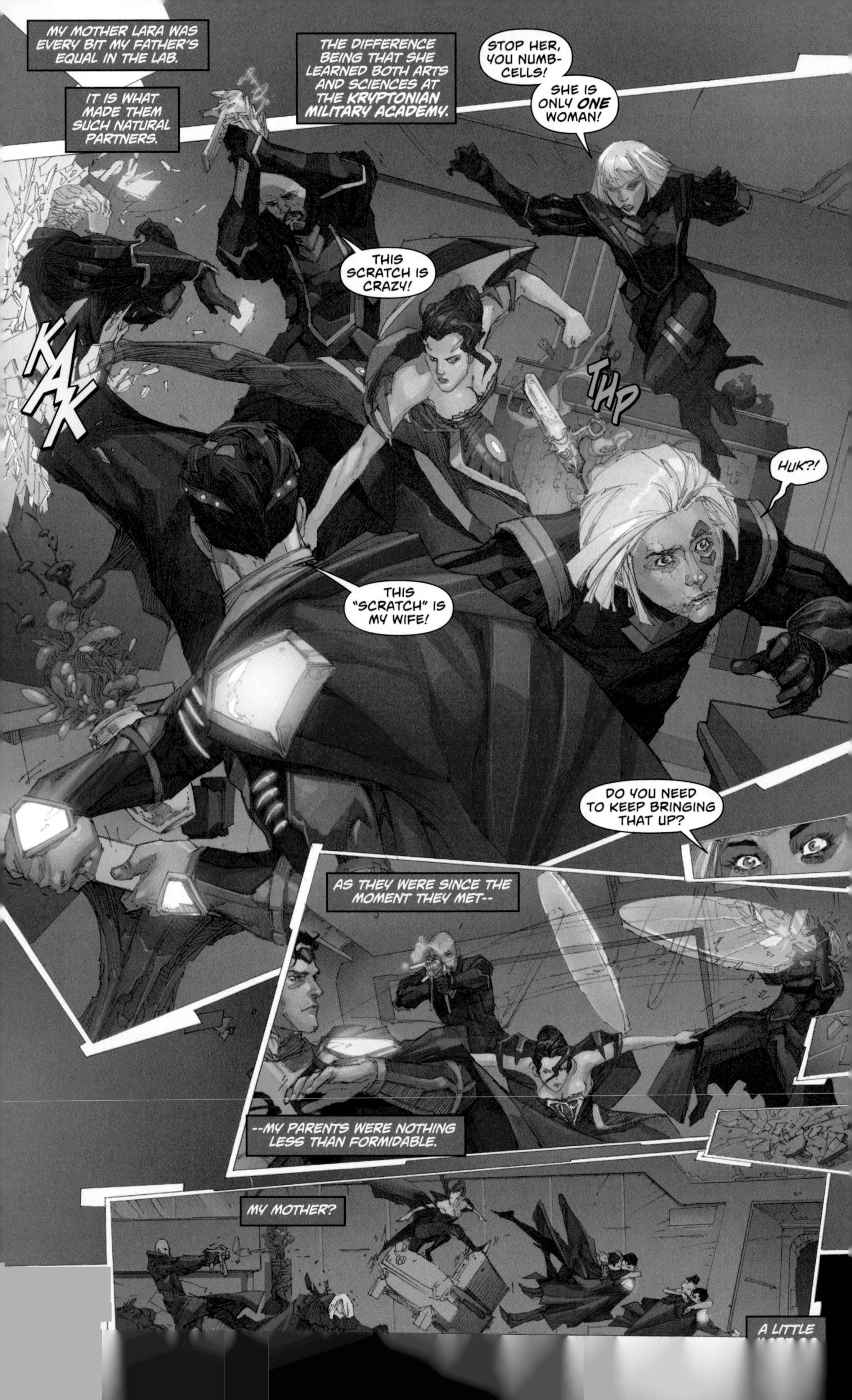

MY MOTHER LARA WAS EVERY BIT MY FATHER'S EQUAL IN THE LAB.
IT IS WHAT MADE THEM SUCH NATURAL PARTNERS.
THE DIFFERENCE BEING THAT SHE LEARNED BOTH ARTS AND SCIENCES AT THE KRYPTONIAN MILITARY ACADEMY.
STOP HER, YOU NUMB-CELLS!
SHE IS ONLY ONE WOMAN!
THIS SCRATCH IS CRAZY!
KAK
THP
HUK?!
THIS "SCRATCH" IS MY WIFE!
DO YOU NEED TO KEEP BRINGING THAT UP?
AS THEY WERE SINCE THE MOMENT THEY MET--
--MY PARENTS WERE NOTHING LESS THAN FORMIDABLE.
MY MOTHER?
A LITTLE

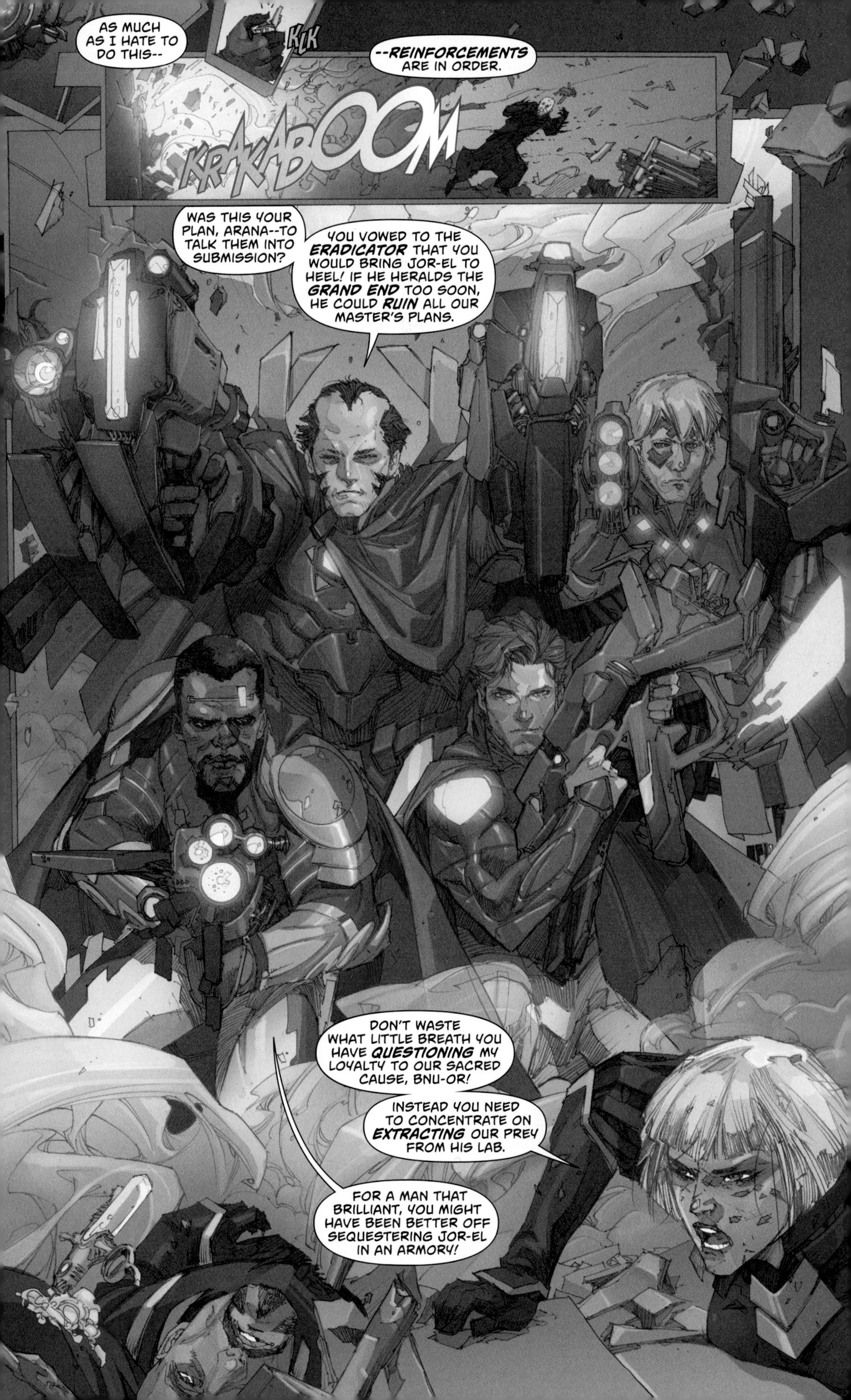
AS MUCH AS I HATE TO DO THIS--
KLIK
--REINFORCEMENTS ARE IN ORDER.
KRAKABOOM
WAS THIS YOUR PLAN, ARANA--TO TALK THEM INTO SUBMISSION?
YOU VOWED TO THE ERADICATOR THAT YOU WOULD BRING JOR-EL TO HEEL! IF HE HERALDS THE GRAND END TOO SOON, HE COULD RUIN ALL OUR MASTER'S PLANS.
DON'T WASTE WHAT LITTLE BREATH YOU HAVE QUESTIONING MY LOYALTY TO OUR SACRED CAUSE, BNU-OR!
INSTEAD YOU NEED TO CONCENTRATE ON EXTRACTING OUR PREY FROM HIS LAB.
FOR A MAN THAT BRILLIANT, YOU MIGHT HAVE BEEN BETTER OFF SEQUESTERING JOR-EL IN AN ARMORY!

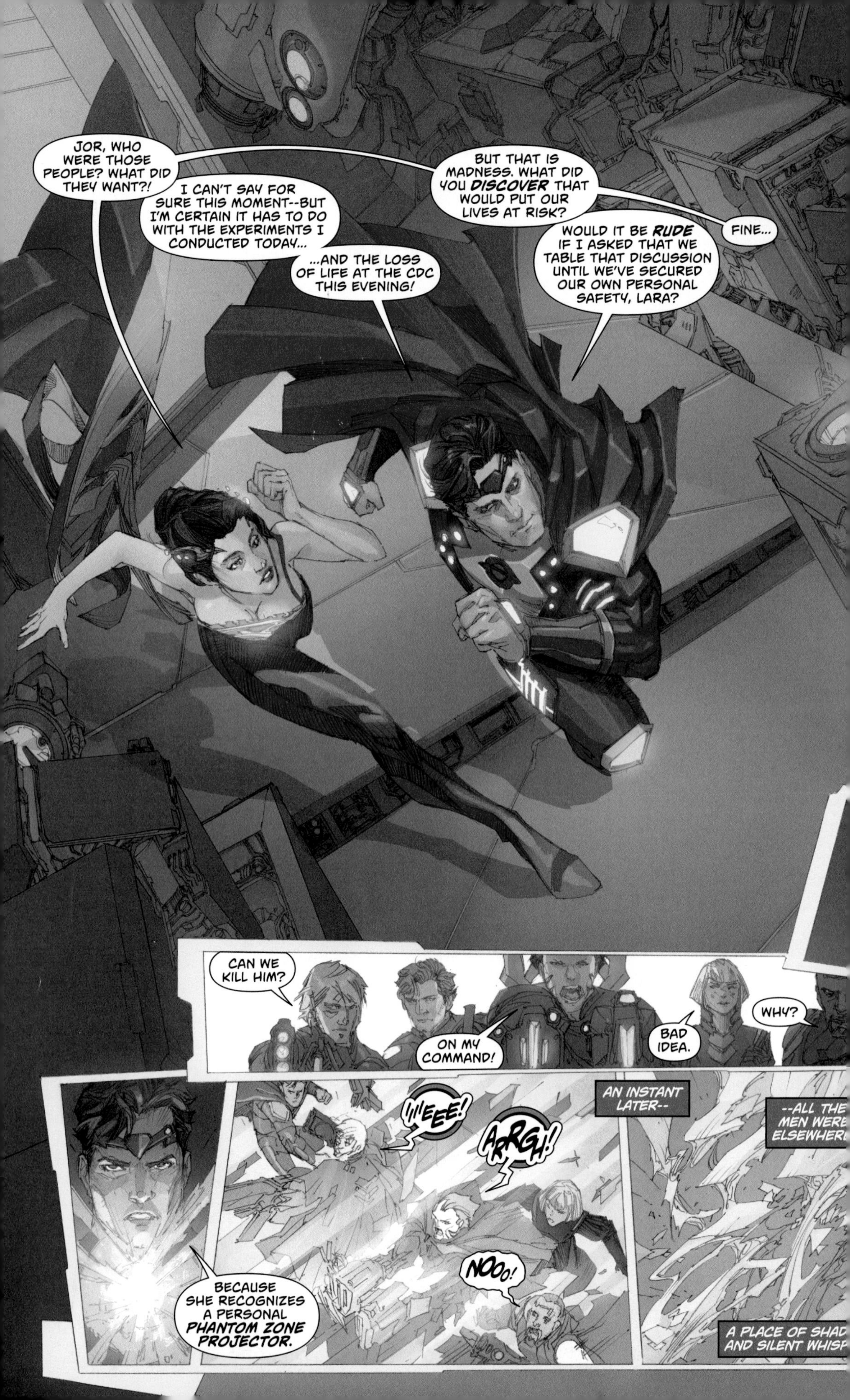
JOR, WHO WERE THOSE PEOPLE? WHAT DID THEY WANT?!
I CAN'T SAY FOR SURE THIS MOMENT--BUT I'M CERTAIN IT HAS TO DO WITH THE EXPERIMENTS I CONDUCTED TODAY...
...AND THE LOSS OF LIFE AT THE CDC THIS EVENING!
BUT THAT IS MADNESS. WHAT DID YOU **DISCOVER** THAT WOULD PUT OUR LIVES AT RISK?
WOULD IT BE **RUDE** IF I ASKED THAT WE TABLE THAT DISCUSSION UNTIL WE'VE SECURED OUR OWN PERSONAL SAFETY, LARA?
FINE...
CAN WE KILL HIM?
ON MY COMMAND!
BAD IDEA.
WHY?
BECAUSE SHE RECOGNIZES A PERSONAL **PHANTOM ZONE PROJECTOR.**
IIIEEE!
ARRGH!
NOOo!
AN INSTANT LATER--
--ALL THE MEN WERE ELSEWHER
A PLACE OF SHAD AND SILENT WHISP

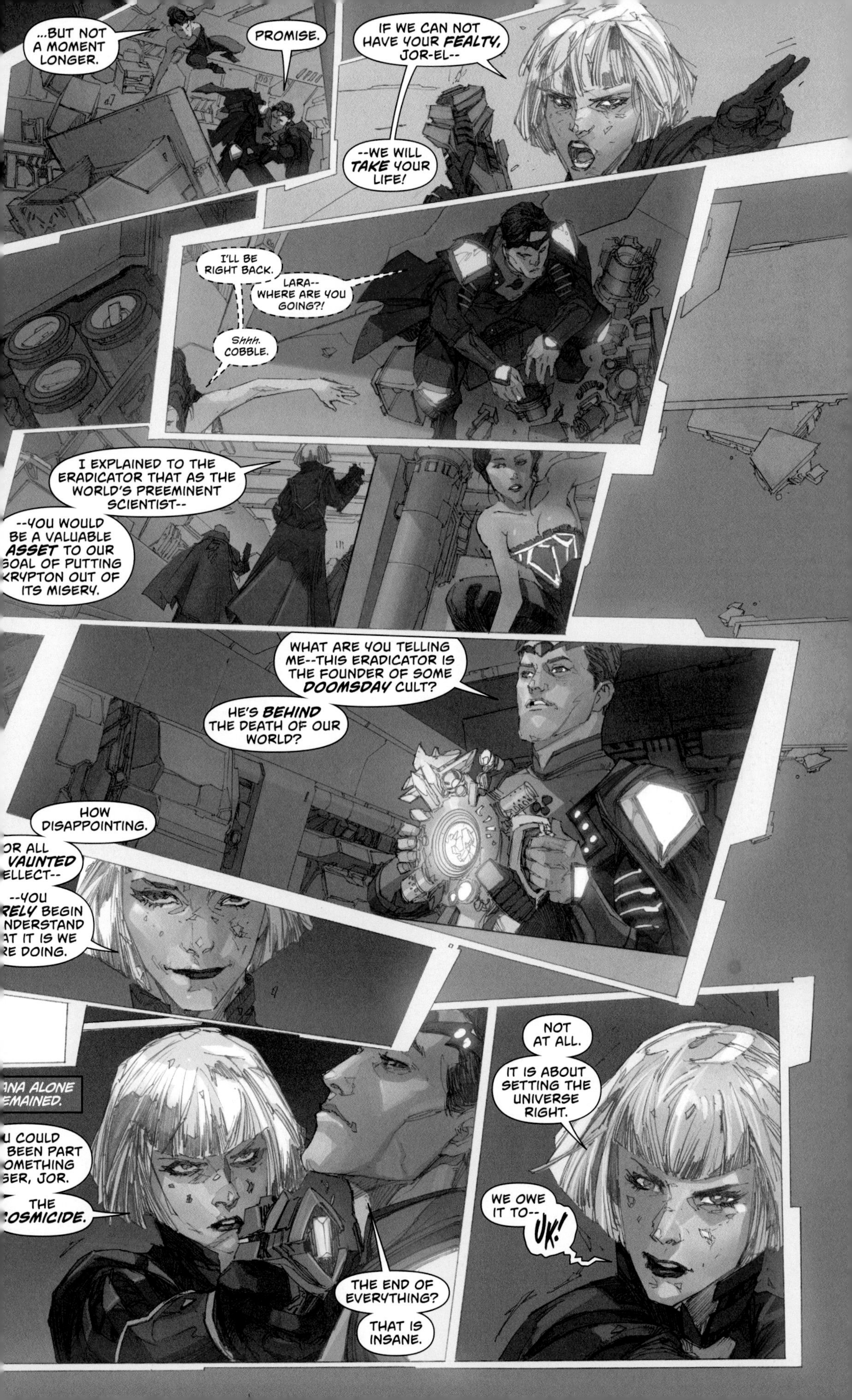
...BUT NOT A MOMENT LONGER.
PROMISE.
IF WE CAN NOT HAVE YOUR FEALTY, JOR-EL--
--WE WILL TAKE YOUR LIFE!
I'LL BE RIGHT BACK.
LARA-- WHERE ARE YOU GOING?!
Shhh. COBBLE.
I EXPLAINED TO THE ERADICATOR THAT AS THE WORLD'S PREEMINENT SCIENTIST--
--YOU WOULD BE A VALUABLE ASSET TO OUR GOAL OF PUTTING KRYPTON OUT OF ITS MISERY.
WHAT ARE YOU TELLING ME--THIS ERADICATOR IS THE FOUNDER OF SOME DOOMSDAY CULT?
HE'S BEHIND THE DEATH OF OUR WORLD?
HOW DISAPPOINTING.
OR ALL VAUNTED ELLECT--
--YOU RELY BEGIN NDERSTAND AT IT IS WE RE DOING.
ANA ALONE EMAINED.
U COULD BEEN PART OMETHING GER, JOR.
THE COSMICIDE.
THE END OF EVERYTHING?
THAT IS INSANE.
NOT AT ALL.
IT IS ABOUT SETTING THE UNIVERSE RIGHT.
WE OWE IT TO--
UK!

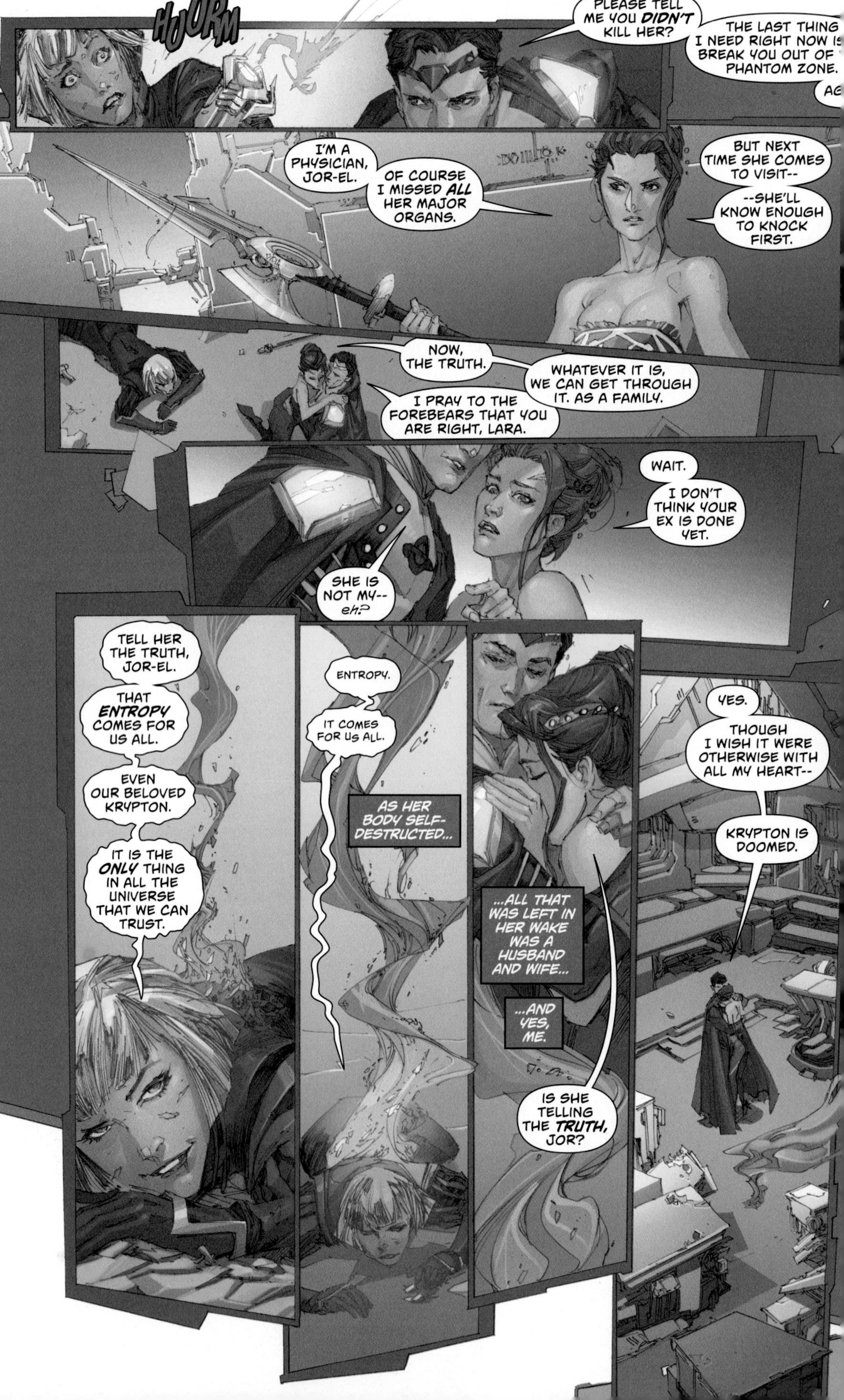
HUURM
PLEASE TELL ME YOU *DIDN'T* KILL HER?
THE LAST THING I NEED RIGHT NOW IS BREAK YOU OUT OF PHANTOM ZONE.
I'M A PHYSICIAN, JOR-EL.
OF COURSE I MISSED *ALL* HER MAJOR ORGANS.
BUT NEXT TIME SHE COMES TO VISIT--
--SHE'LL KNOW ENOUGH TO KNOCK FIRST.
NOW, THE TRUTH.
WHATEVER IT IS, WE CAN GET THROUGH IT. AS A FAMILY.
I PRAY TO THE FOREBEARS THAT YOU ARE RIGHT, LARA.
WAIT.
I DON'T THINK YOUR EX IS DONE YET.
SHE IS NOT MY-- eh?
TELL HER THE TRUTH, JOR-EL.
THAT *ENTROPY* COMES FOR US ALL.
EVEN OUR BELOVED KRYPTON.
IT IS THE *ONLY* THING IN ALL THE UNIVERSE THAT WE CAN TRUST.
ENTROPY.
IT COMES FOR US ALL.
AS HER BODY SELF-DESTRUCTED...
...ALL THAT WAS LEFT IN HER WAKE WAS A HUSBAND AND WIFE...
...AND YES, ME.
IS SHE TELLING THE *TRUTH,* JOR?
YES.
THOUGH I WISH IT WERE OTHERWISE WITH ALL MY HEART--
KRYPTON IS DOOMED.

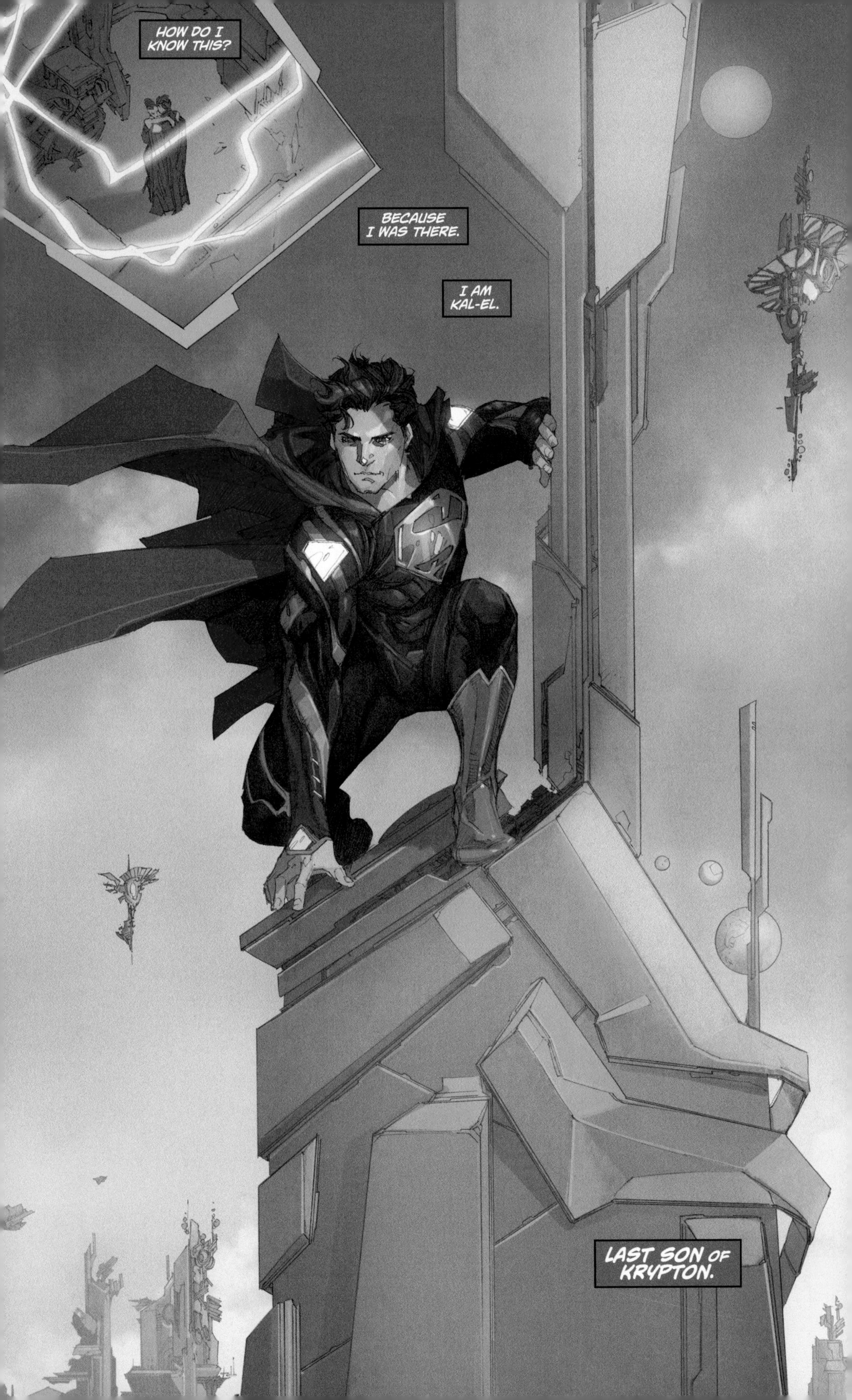
HOW DO I KNOW THIS?
BECAUSE I WAS THERE.
I AM KAL-EL.
LAST SON OF KRYPTON.

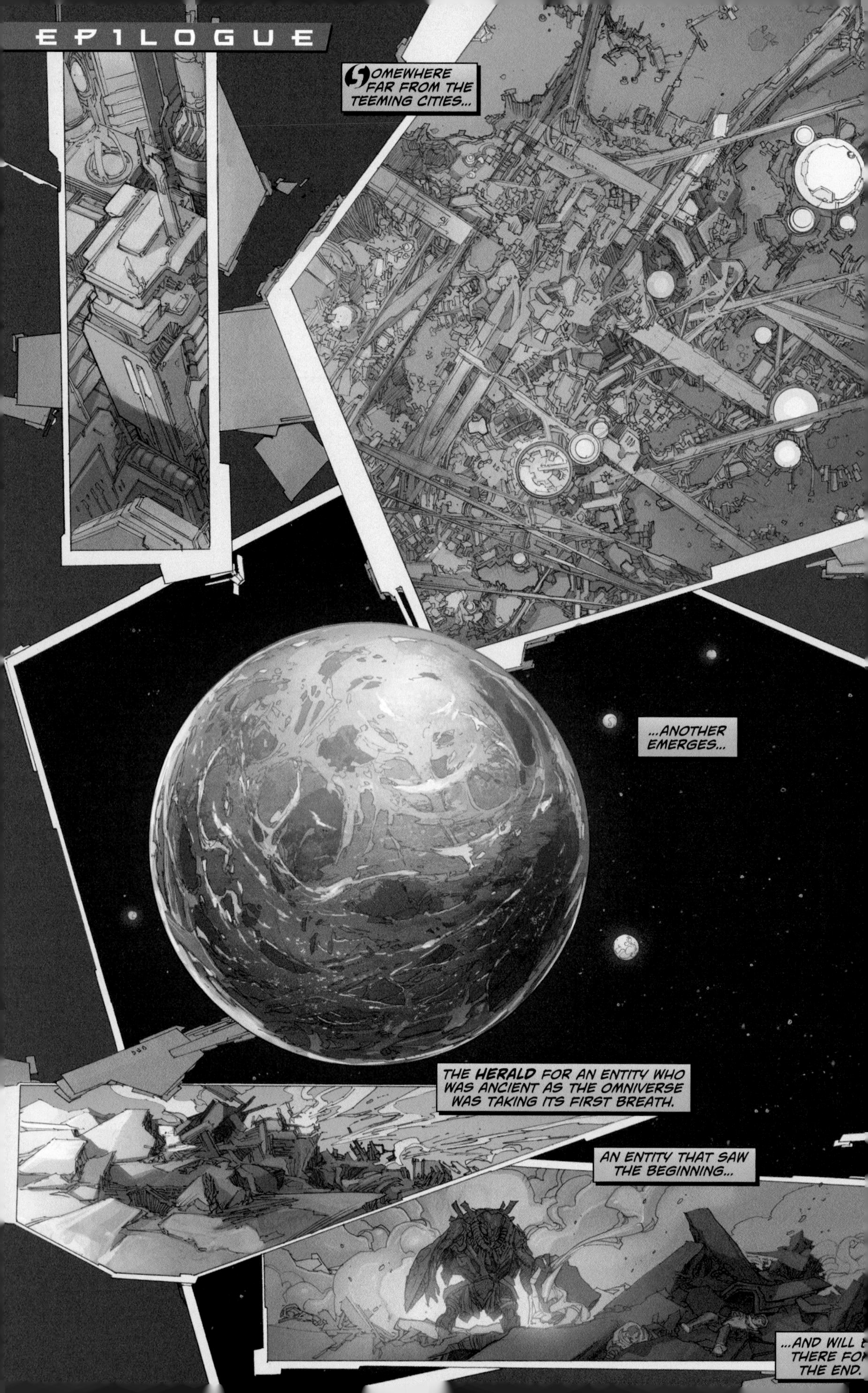
EPILOGUE
SOMEWHERE FAR FROM THE TEEMING CITIES...
...ANOTHER EMERGES...
THE HERALD FOR AN ENTITY WHO WAS ANCIENT AS THE OMNIVERSE WAS TAKING ITS FIRST BREATH.
AN ENTITY THAT SAW THE BEGINNING...
THE END.

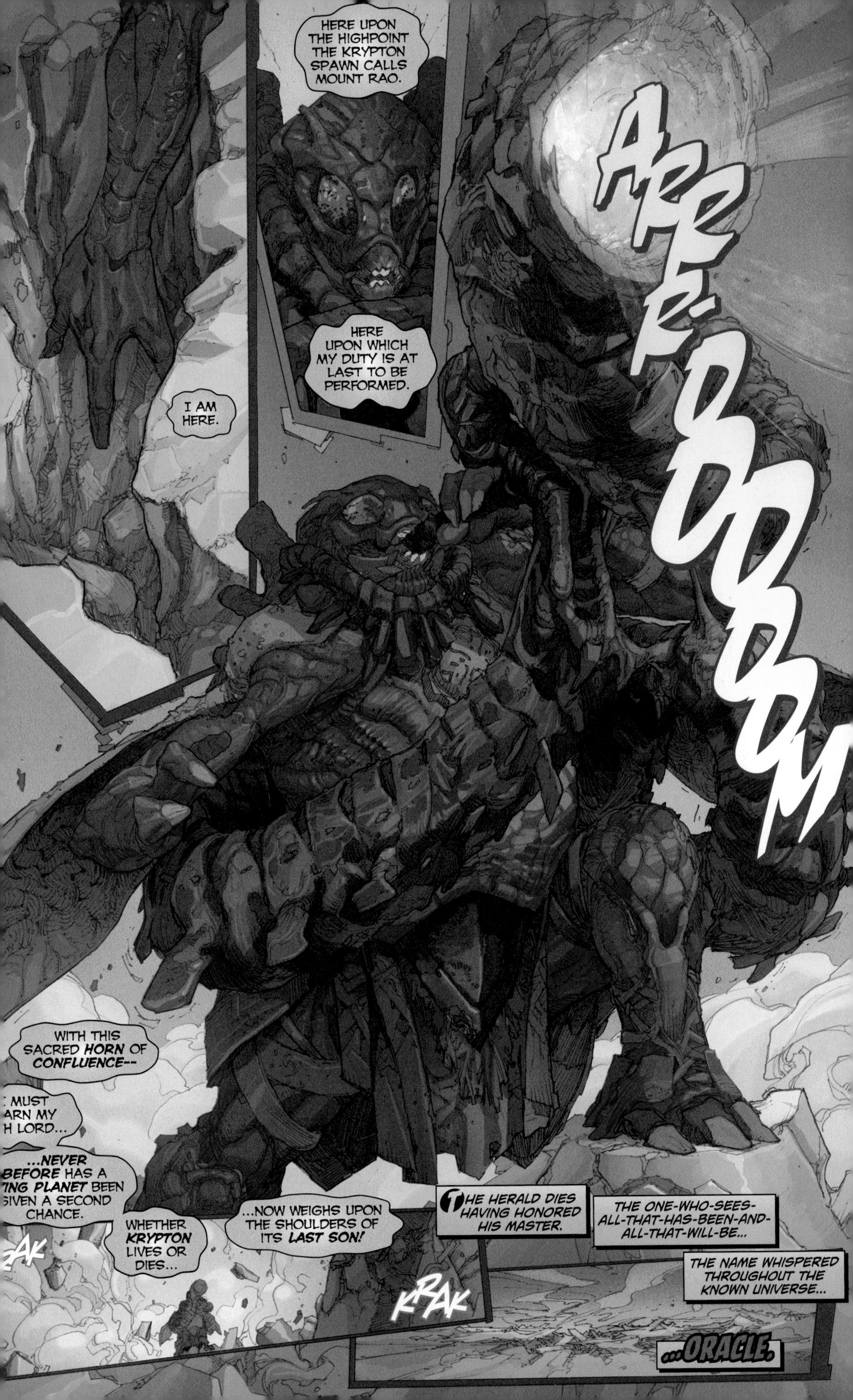
HERE UPON THE HIGHPOINT THE KRYPTON SPAWN CALLS MOUNT RAO.
HERE UPON WHICH MY DUTY IS AT LAST TO BE PERFORMED.
I AM HERE.
ARR-R-ROOOOM
WITH THIS SACRED HORN OF CONFLUENCE--
MUST ARN MY H LORD...
...NEVER BEFORE HAS A ING PLANET BEEN GIVEN A SECOND CHANCE.
WHETHER KRYPTON LIVES OR DIES...
...NOW WEIGHS UPON THE SHOULDERS OF ITS LAST SON!
KRAK
KRAK
THE HERALD DIES HAVING HONORED HIS MASTER.
THE ONE-WHO-SEES-ALL-THAT-HAS-BEEN-AND-ALL-THAT-WILL-BE...
THE NAME WHISPERED THROUGHOUT THE KNOWN UNIVERSE...
...ORACLE.

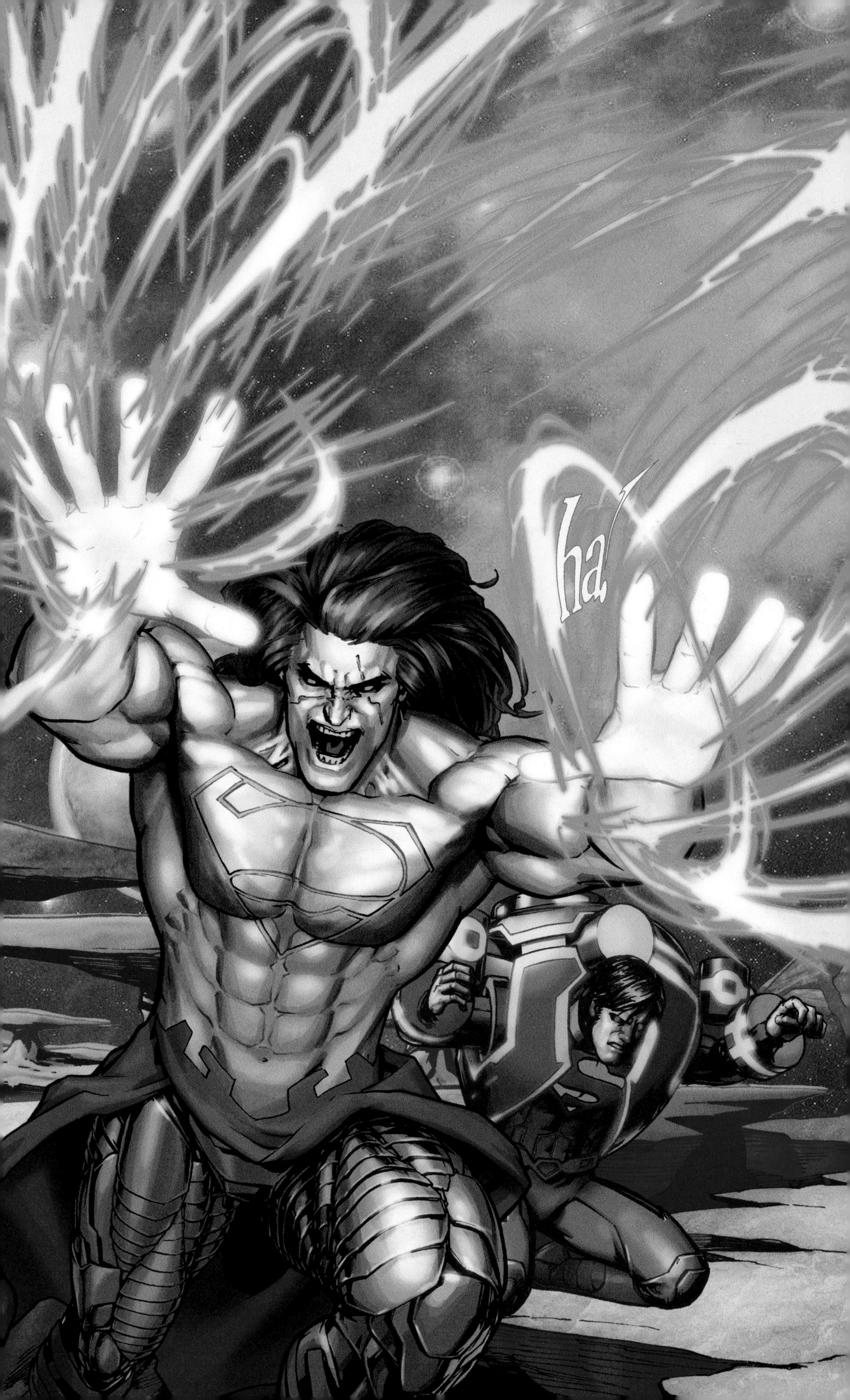
ha!

TO H'EL AND BACK

SCOTT LOBDELL writer **DAN JURGENS** penciller **RAY McCARTHY** finishes **HI-FI** colorist
cover art by **GENE HA**

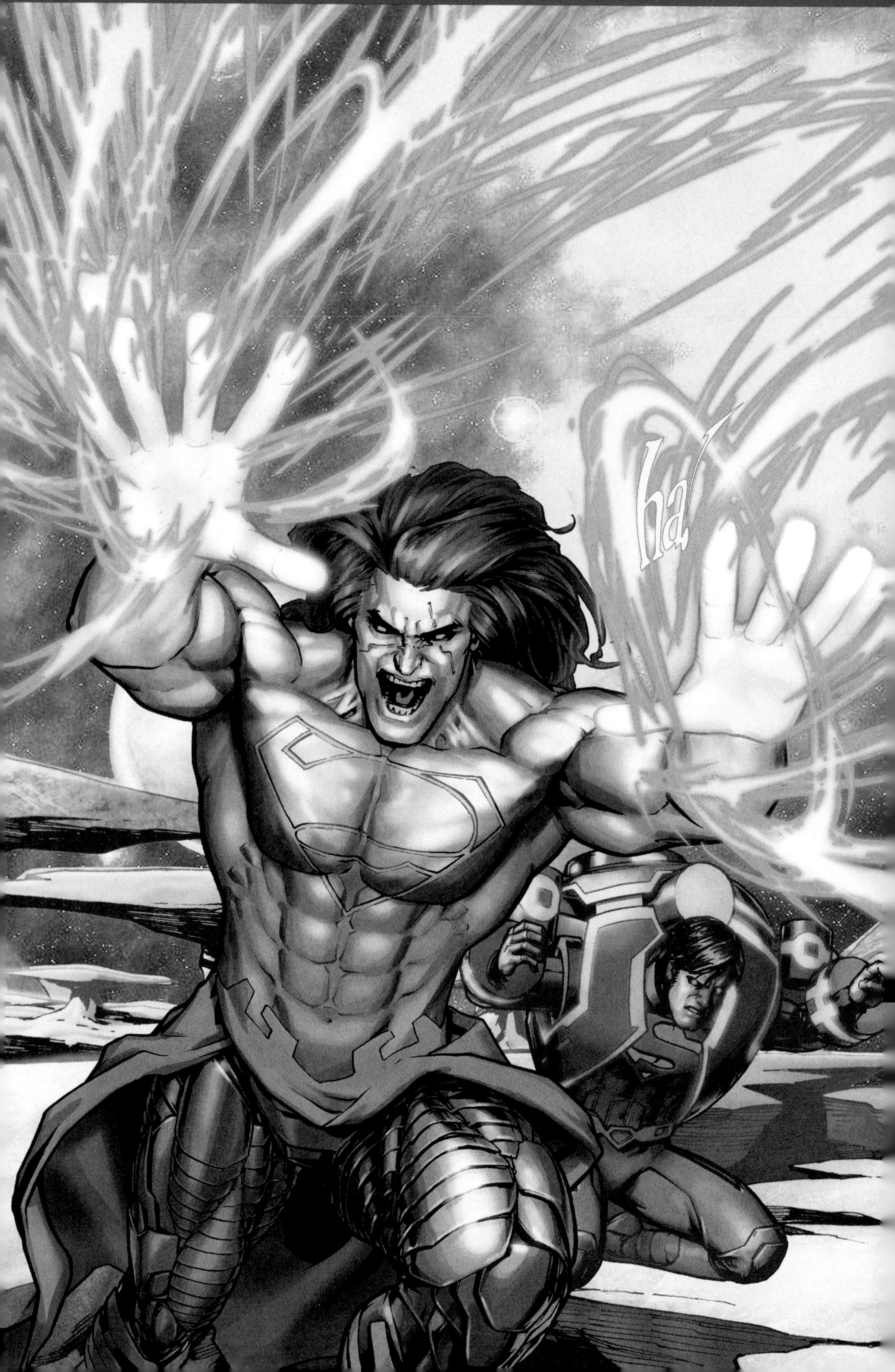
ha!

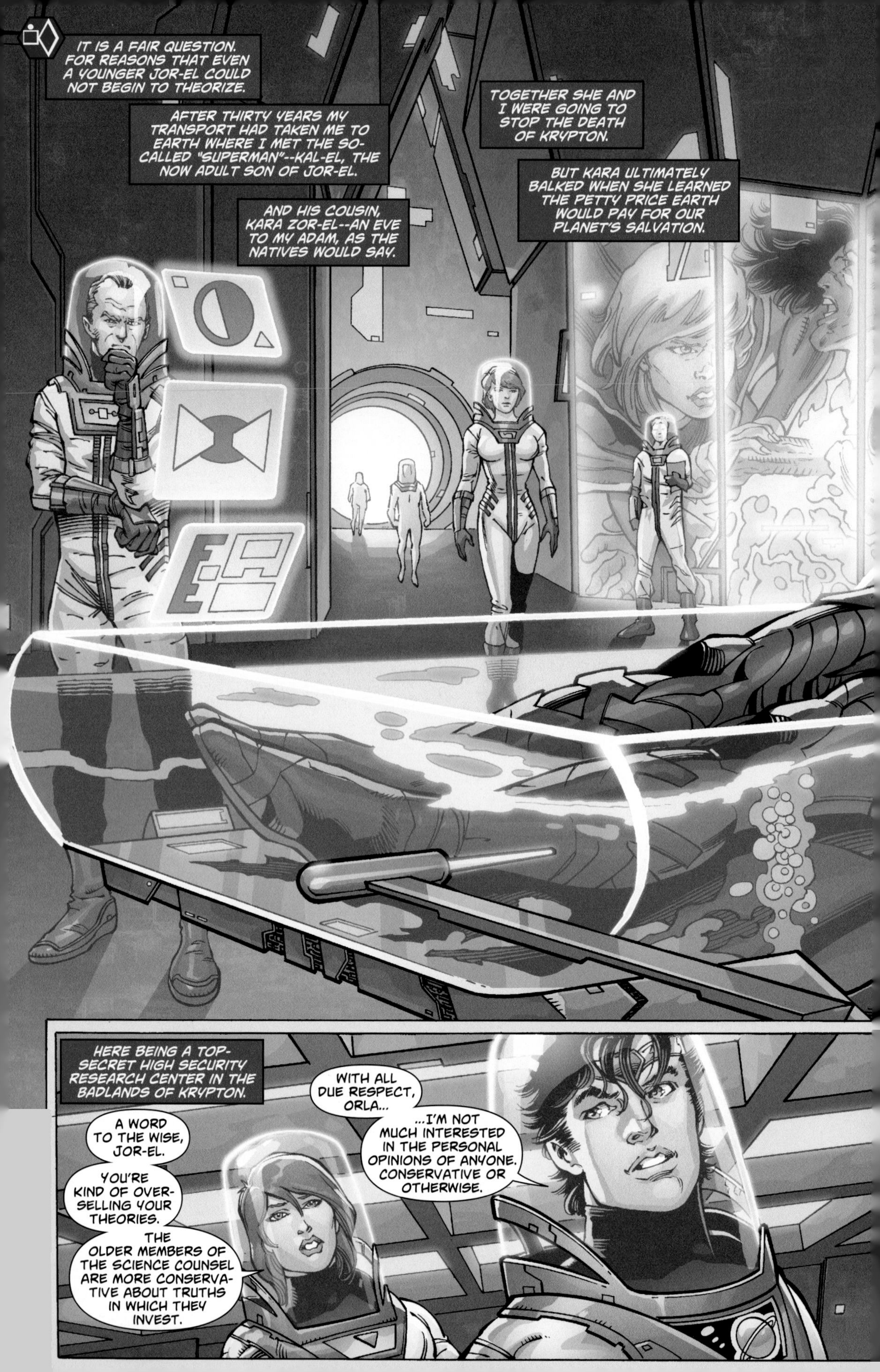
IT IS A FAIR QUESTION. FOR REASONS THAT EVEN A YOUNGER JOR-EL COULD NOT BEGIN TO THEORIZE.
AFTER THIRTY YEARS MY TRANSPORT HAD TAKEN ME TO EARTH WHERE I MET THE SO-CALLED "SUPERMAN"--KAL-EL, THE NOW ADULT SON OF JOR-EL.
AND HIS COUSIN, KARA ZOR-EL--AN EVE TO MY ADAM, AS THE NATIVES WOULD SAY.
TOGETHER SHE AND I WERE GOING TO STOP THE DEATH OF KRYPTON.
BUT KARA ULTIMATELY BALKED WHEN SHE LEARNED THE PETTY PRICE EARTH WOULD PAY FOR OUR PLANET'S SALVATION.
HERE BEING A TOP-SECRET HIGH SECURITY RESEARCH CENTER IN THE BADLANDS OF KRYPTON.
A WORD TO THE WISE, JOR-EL.
YOU'RE KIND OF OVER-SELLING YOUR THEORIES.
THE OLDER MEMBERS OF THE SCIENCE COUNSEL ARE MORE CONSERVA-TIVE ABOUT TRUTHS IN WHICH THEY INVEST.
WITH ALL DUE RESPECT, ORLA...
...I'M NOT MUCH INTERESTED IN THE PERSONAL OPINIONS OF ANYONE. CONSERVATIVE OR OTHERWISE.

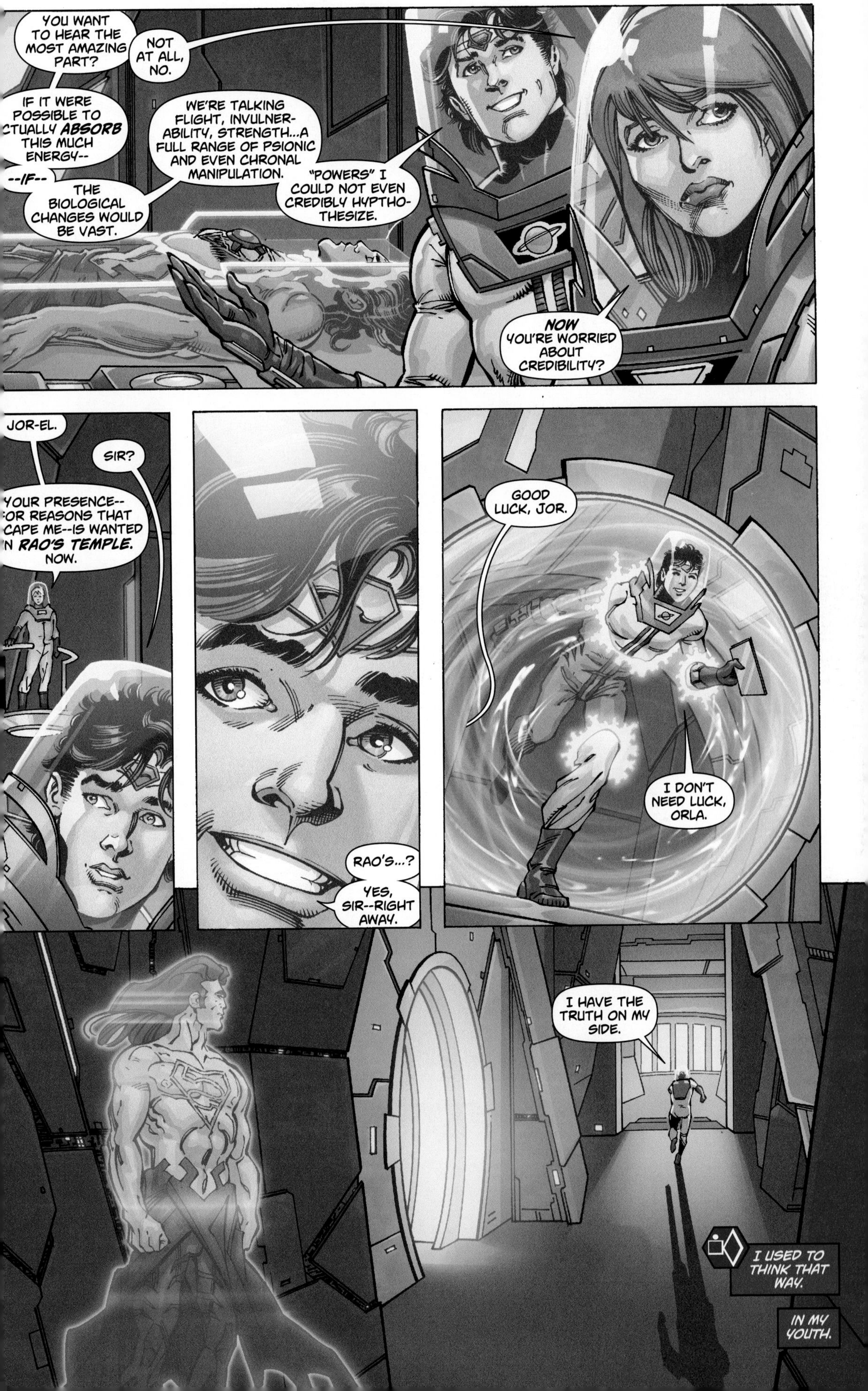
YOU WANT TO HEAR THE MOST AMAZING PART?
NOT AT ALL, NO.
IF IT WERE POSSIBLE TO ACTUALLY ***ABSORB*** THIS MUCH ENERGY--
--***IF***--
THE BIOLOGICAL CHANGES WOULD BE VAST.
WE'RE TALKING FLIGHT, INVULNER-ABILITY, STRENGTH...A FULL RANGE OF PSIONIC AND EVEN CHRONAL MANIPULATION.
"POWERS" I COULD NOT EVEN CREDIBLY HYPTHO-THESIZE.
NOW YOU'RE WORRIED ABOUT CREDIBILITY?
JOR-EL.
SIR?
YOUR PRESENCE-- FOR REASONS THAT ESCAPE ME--IS WANTED IN ***RAO'S TEMPLE***. NOW.
RAO'S...?
YES, SIR--RIGHT AWAY.
GOOD LUCK, JOR.
I DON'T NEED LUCK, ORLA.
I HAVE THE TRUTH ON MY SIDE.
I USED TO THINK THAT WAY.
IN MY YOUTH.

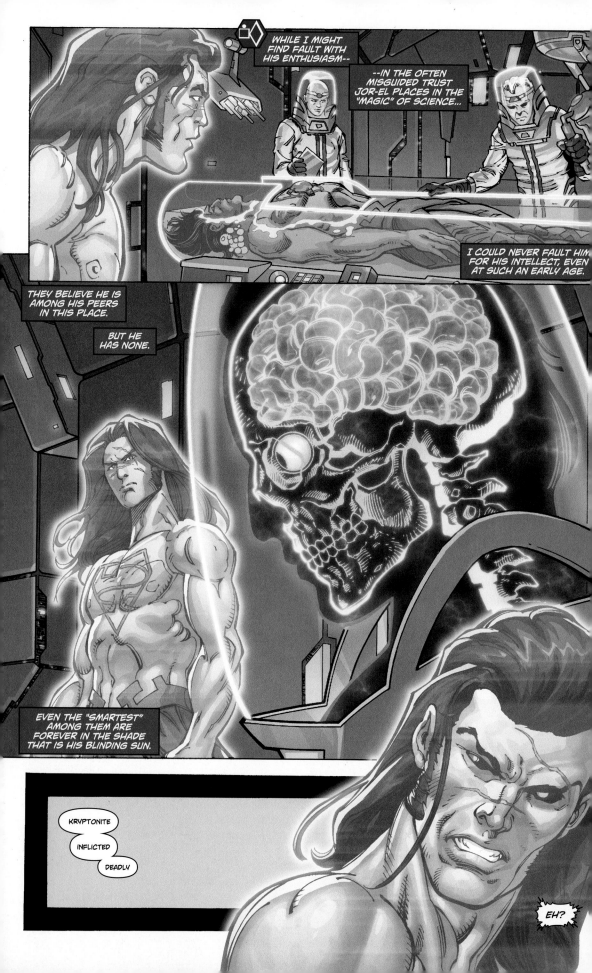

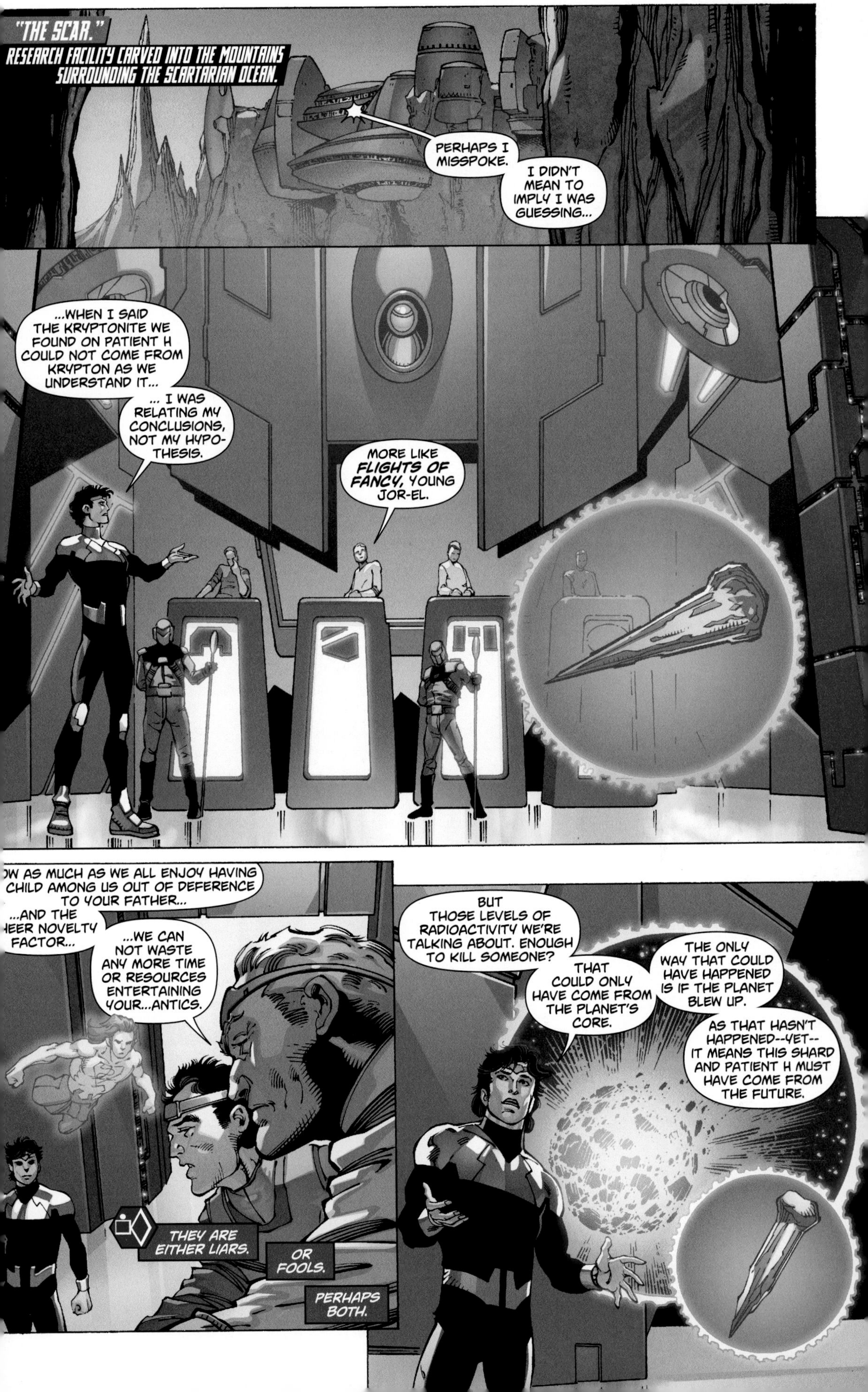
"THE SCAR."
RESEARCH FACILITY CARVED INTO THE MOUNTAINS SURROUNDING THE SCARTARIAN OCEAN.
PERHAPS I MISSPOKE.
I DIDN'T MEAN TO IMPLY I WAS GUESSING...
...WHEN I SAID THE KRYPTONITE WE FOUND ON PATIENT H COULD NOT COME FROM KRYPTON AS WE UNDERSTAND IT...
... I WAS RELATING MY CONCLUSIONS, NOT MY HYPO- THESIS.
MORE LIKE FLIGHTS OF FANCY, YOUNG JOR-EL.
OW AS MUCH AS WE ALL ENJOY HAVING CHILD AMONG US OUT OF DEFERENCE TO YOUR FATHER...
...AND THE HEER NOVELTY FACTOR...
...WE CAN NOT WASTE ANY MORE TIME OR RESOURCES ENTERTAINING YOUR...ANTICS.
THEY ARE EITHER LIARS.
OR FOOLS.
PERHAPS BOTH.
BUT THOSE LEVELS OF RADIOACTIVITY WE'RE TALKING ABOUT. ENOUGH TO KILL SOMEONE?
THAT COULD ONLY HAVE COME FROM THE PLANET'S CORE.
THE ONLY WAY THAT COULD HAVE HAPPENED IS IF THE PLANET BLEW UP.
AS THAT HASN'T HAPPENED--YET-- IT MEANS THIS SHARD AND PATIENT H MUST HAVE COME FROM THE FUTURE.

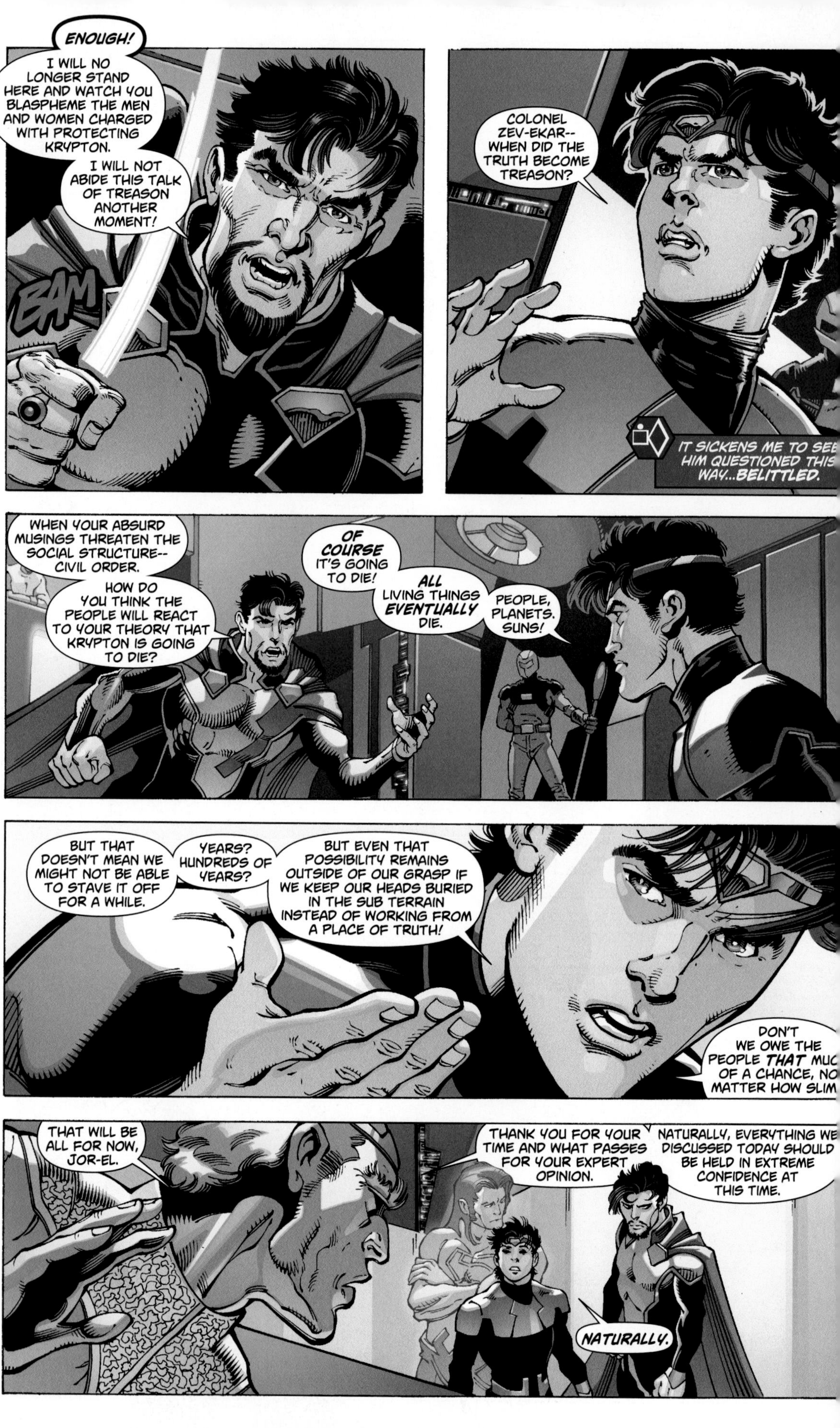
ENOUGH!
I WILL NO LONGER STAND HERE AND WATCH YOU BLASPHEME THE MEN AND WOMEN CHARGED WITH PROTECTING KRYPTON.
I WILL NOT ABIDE THIS TALK OF TREASON ANOTHER MOMENT!
BAM
COLONEL ZEV-EKAR-- WHEN DID THE TRUTH BECOME TREASON?
IT SICKENS ME TO SEE HIM QUESTIONED THIS WAY...BELITTLED.
WHEN YOUR ABSURD MUSINGS THREATEN THE SOCIAL STRUCTURE-- CIVIL ORDER.
HOW DO YOU THINK THE PEOPLE WILL REACT TO YOUR THEORY THAT KRYPTON IS GOING TO DIE?
OF COURSE IT'S GOING TO DIE!
ALL LIVING THINGS EVENTUALLY DIE.
PEOPLE, PLANETS. SUNS!
BUT THAT DOESN'T MEAN WE MIGHT NOT BE ABLE TO STAVE IT OFF FOR A WHILE.
YEARS? HUNDREDS OF YEARS?
BUT EVEN THAT POSSIBILITY REMAINS OUTSIDE OF OUR GRASP IF WE KEEP OUR HEADS BURIED IN THE SUB TERRAIN INSTEAD OF WORKING FROM A PLACE OF TRUTH!
DON'T WE OWE THE PEOPLE THAT MUC OF A CHANCE, NO MATTER HOW SLIM
THAT WILL BE ALL FOR NOW, JOR-EL.
THANK YOU FOR YOUR TIME AND WHAT PASSES FOR YOUR EXPERT OPINION.
NATURALLY, EVERYTHING WE DISCUSSED TODAY SHOULD BE HELD IN EXTREME CONFIDENCE AT THIS TIME.
NATURALLY.

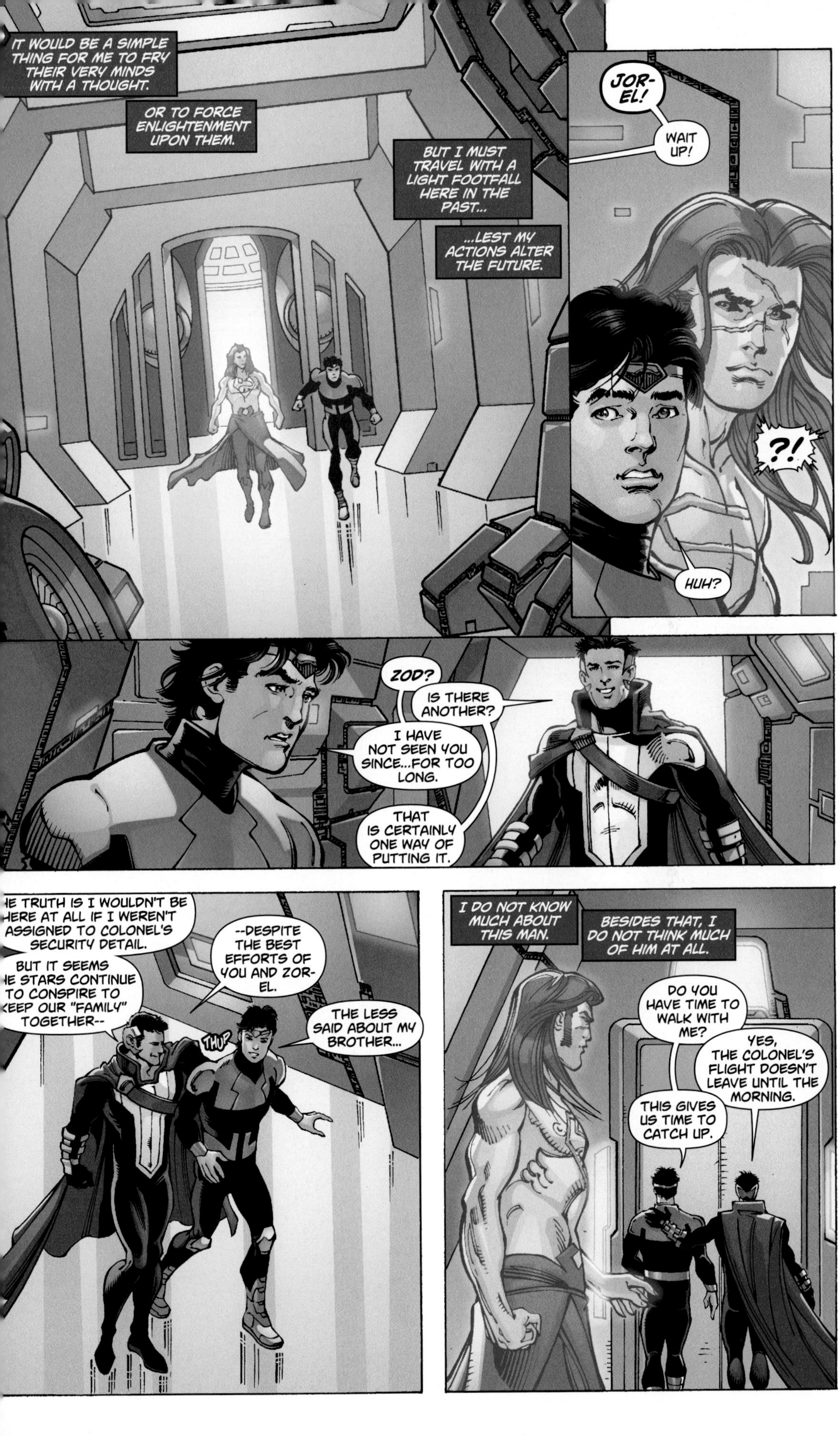
IT WOULD BE A SIMPLE THING FOR ME TO FRY THEIR VERY MINDS WITH A THOUGHT.
OR TO FORCE ENLIGHTENMENT UPON THEM.
BUT I MUST TRAVEL WITH A LIGHT FOOTFALL HERE IN THE PAST...
...LEST MY ACTIONS ALTER THE FUTURE.
JOR-EL!
WAIT UP!
?!
HUH?
ZOD?
IS THERE ANOTHER?
I HAVE NOT SEEN YOU SINCE...FOR TOO LONG.
THAT IS CERTAINLY ONE WAY OF PUTTING IT.
HE TRUTH IS I WOULDN'T BE HERE AT ALL IF I WEREN'T ASSIGNED TO COLONEL'S SECURITY DETAIL.
BUT IT SEEMS HE STARS CONTINUE TO CONSPIRE TO KEEP OUR "FAMILY" TOGETHER--
--DESPITE THE BEST EFFORTS OF YOU AND ZOR-EL.
THE LESS SAID ABOUT MY BROTHER...
THUP
I DO NOT KNOW MUCH ABOUT THIS MAN.
BESIDES THAT, I DO NOT THINK MUCH OF HIM AT ALL.
DO YOU HAVE TIME TO WALK WITH ME?
YES, THE COLONEL'S FLIGHT DOESN'T LEAVE UNTIL THE MORNING.
THIS GIVES US TIME TO CATCH UP.

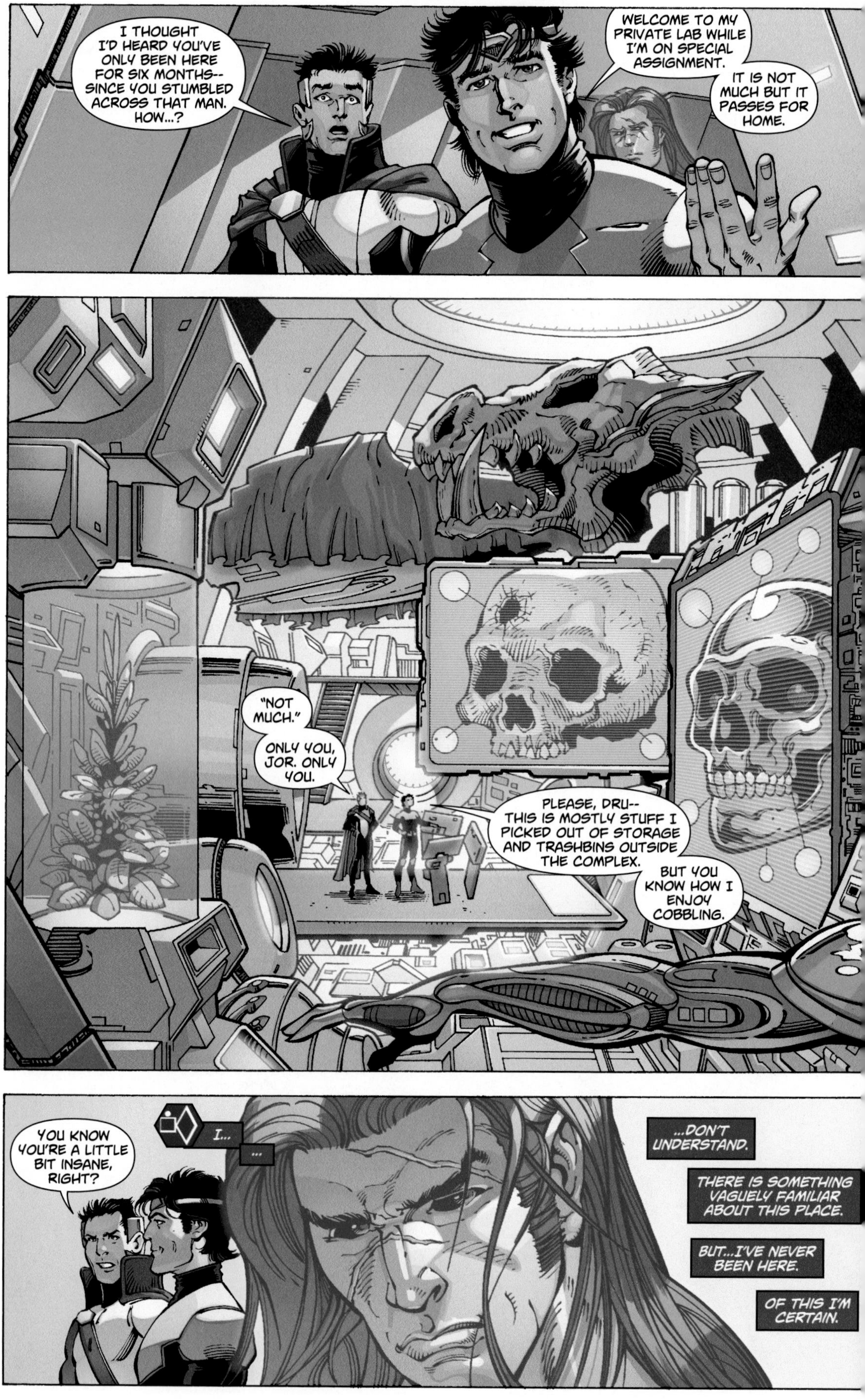
I THOUGHT I'D HEARD YOU'VE ONLY BEEN HERE FOR SIX MONTHS-- SINCE YOU STUMBLED ACROSS THAT MAN. HOW...?
WELCOME TO MY PRIVATE LAB WHILE I'M ON SPECIAL ASSIGNMENT.
IT IS NOT MUCH BUT IT PASSES FOR HOME.
"NOT MUCH."
ONLY YOU, JOR. ONLY YOU.
PLEASE, DRU-- THIS IS MOSTLY STUFF I PICKED OUT OF STORAGE AND TRASHBINS OUTSIDE THE COMPLEX.
BUT YOU KNOW HOW I ENJOY COBBLING.
YOU KNOW YOU'RE A LITTLE BIT INSANE, RIGHT?
I...
...
...DON'T UNDERSTAND.
THERE IS SOMETHING VAGUELY FAMILIAR ABOUT THIS PLACE.
BUT...I'VE NEVER BEEN HERE.
OF THIS I'M CERTAIN.

IN LIGHT OF RECENT DEVELOPMENTS...A PARTICULAR PROJECT OF MINE HAS TAKEN ON GREATER SIGNIFICANCE.

COMING FROM YOU THAT COULD MEAN ANYTHING FROM A PAN-DIMENSIONAL POWER SOURCE OR AN EVERLASTING BREATH MINT.

NOTHING SO AMBITIOUS.

I'VE BEEN CATALOGUING THE *HISTORY* OF KRYPTON--

--AS WELL AS MY OWN WILD PROJECTIONS ON THE FUTURE OF THE SAME--

--STARTING WITH THE BEGINNING OF THE PLANET UNTIL THE END.

HISTORY, GEOGRAPHY, MATH, SCIENCE, THE ARTS, ETHICS FROM ALL THREE ERAS AND ALL TWELVE COLONIES.

YEAH. *THAT* DOESN'T SOUND AMBITIOUS.

THAT HARD PART WASN'T THE MALE AND FEMALE OF OUR SPECIES.

IT WAS GETTING SOME OF THE ANCIENT, LONG-EXTINCT LIFE FORMS.

THAT'S...

THAT IS...

?!

THAT IS THE DRAGON I CLONED TO TEST SUPERMAN'S ABILITIES.

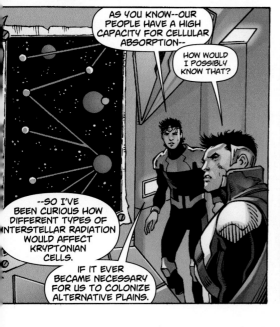

AS YOU KNOW--OUR PEOPLE HAVE A HIGH CAPACITY FOR CELLULAR ABSORPTION--

HOW WOULD I POSSIBLY KNOW THAT?

--SO I'VE BEEN CURIOUS HOW DIFFERENT TYPES OF INTERSTELLAR RADIATION WOULD AFFECT KRYPTONIAN CELLS.

IF IT EVER BECAME NECESSARY FOR US TO COLONIZE ALTERNATIVE PLAINS.

SO YOU'RE SKIRTING THE LAW AGAINST MANNED SPACE TRAVEL BUT DISGUISING YOUR CARGO INSIDE A TIME CAPSULE?

ONCE AROUND THE GALAXY AND BACK, YES.

I'M ALMOST IMPRESSED.

THESE SOLAR SYSTEMS.

I HAVE...BEEN THERE? BUT...

BUT HOW DO YOU EVEN INTEND TO GET YOUR PAYLOAD OUT OF ORBIT?

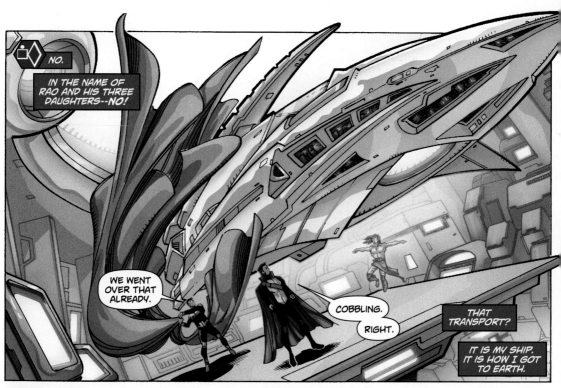

NO.

IN THE NAME OF RAO AND HIS THREE DAUGHTERS--NO!

WE WENT OVER THAT ALREADY.

COBBLING.

RIGHT.

THAT TRANSPORT?

IT IS MY SHIP. IT IS HOW I GOT TO EARTH.

BUT...HOW IS THAT POSSIBLE?!

I RECALL THE LAUNCH.

THE CHEERING OF THOUSANDS.

THE SACRED TRUST BETWEEN MYSELF AND MY MENTOR, JOR-EL.

"HOUSE OF EL."

NICE TOUCH.

A NOD TO HISTORY.

THE ARGONAUTS USED TO NAME THEIR AIRSKIFF FOR GOOD LUCK.

THE BOMBING OF KANDOR IN THE OLD WAR?

H'EL

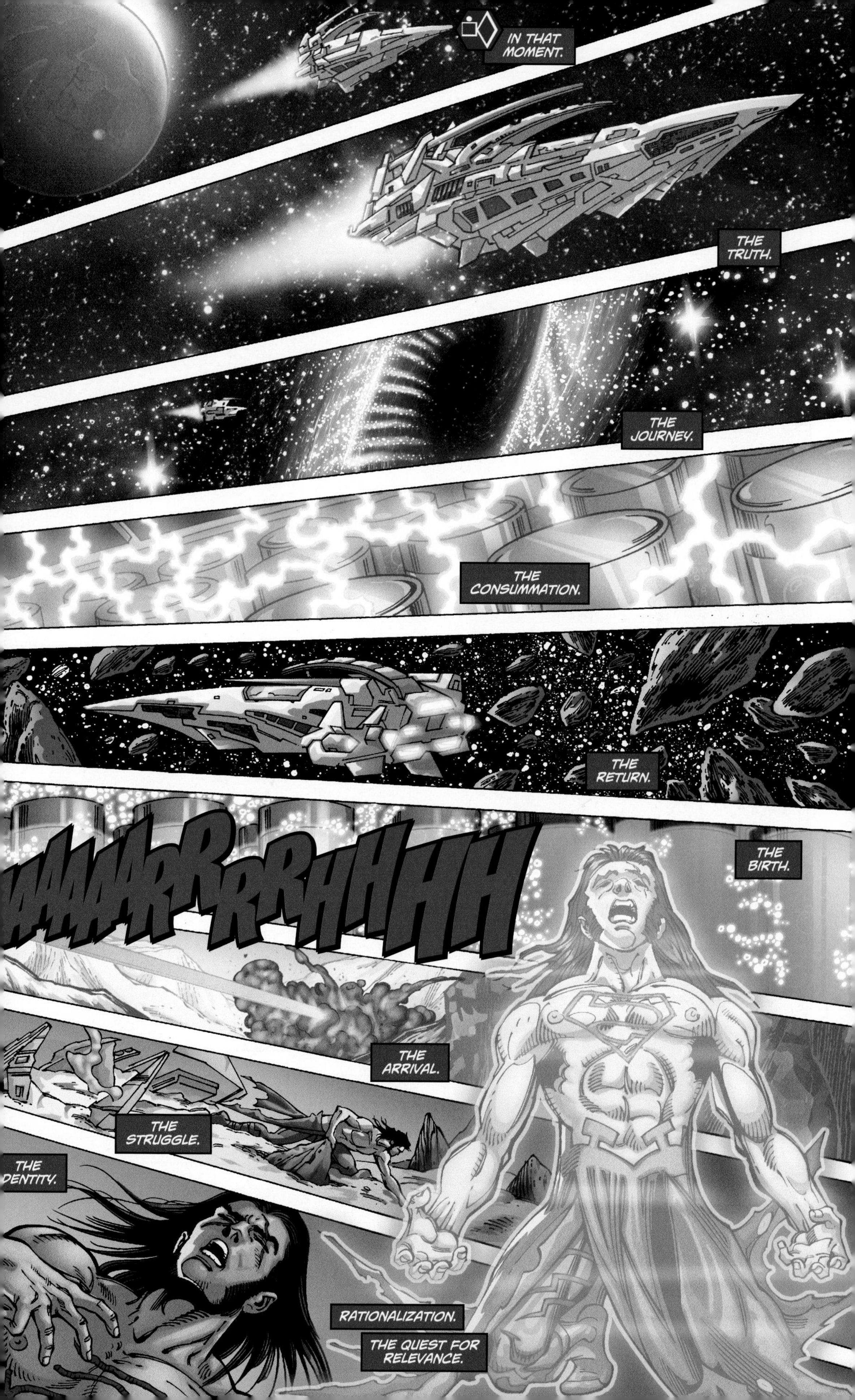

IN THAT MOMENT.
THE TRUTH.
THE JOURNEY.
THE CONSUMMATION.
THE RETURN.
AAAARRRRHHHHH
THE BIRTH.
THE ARRIVAL.
THE STRUGGLE.
THE DENTITY.
RATIONALIZATION.
THE QUEST FOR RELEVANCE.

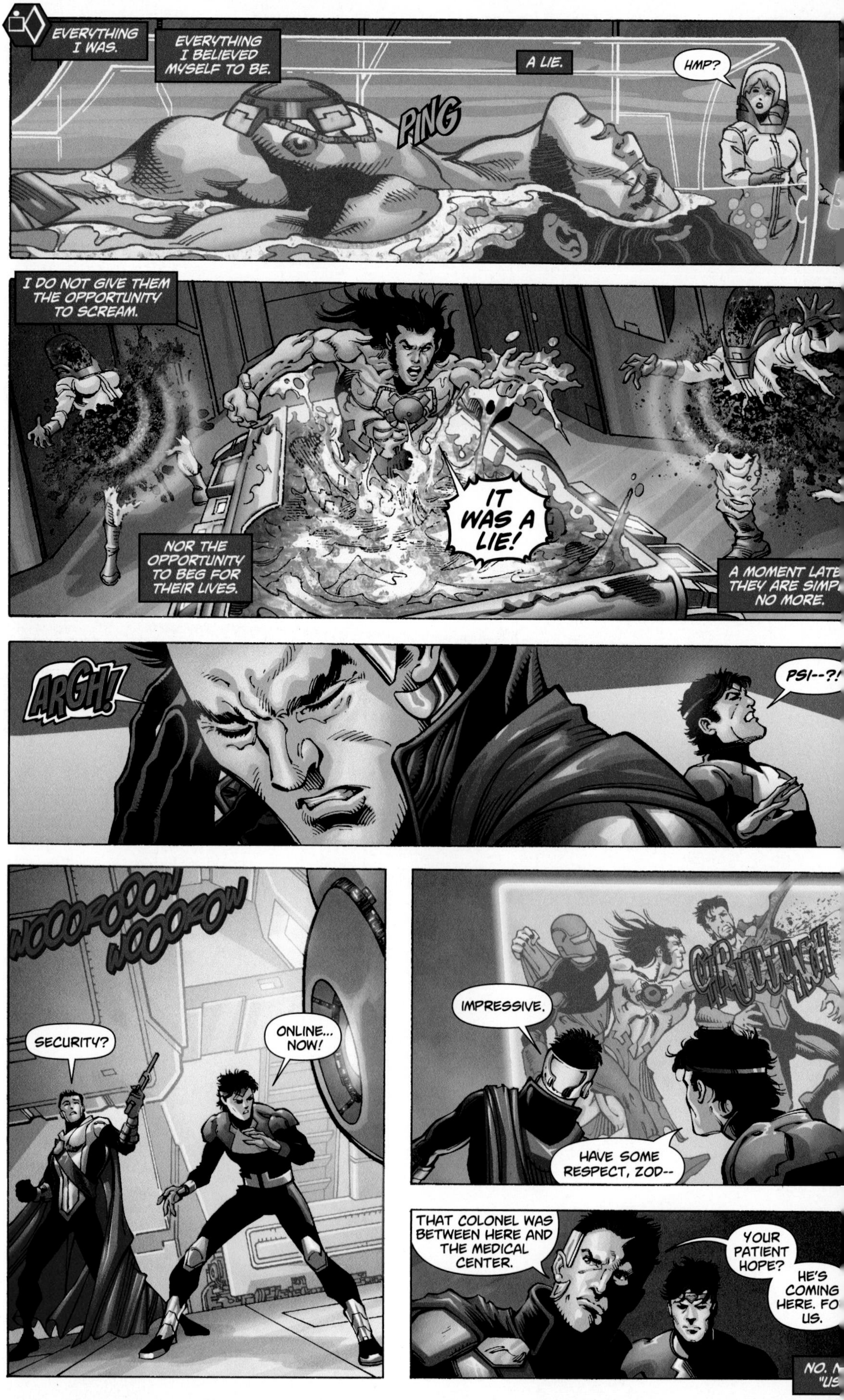
EVERYTHING I WAS.
EVERYTHING I BELIEVED MYSELF TO BE.
A LIE.
HMP?
PING
I DO NOT GIVE THEM THE OPPORTUNITY TO SCREAM.
IT WAS A LIE!
NOR THE OPPORTUNITY TO BEG FOR THEIR LIVES.
A MOMENT LATE THEY ARE SIMP NO MORE.
ARGH!
PSI--?!
WOOOROOOW WOOOROW
SECURITY?
ONLINE... NOW!
CRUUUNCH
IMPRESSIVE.
HAVE SOME RESPECT, ZOD--
THAT COLONEL WAS BETWEEN HERE AND THE MEDICAL CENTER.
YOUR PATIENT HOPE?
HE'S COMING HERE. FO US.
NO.

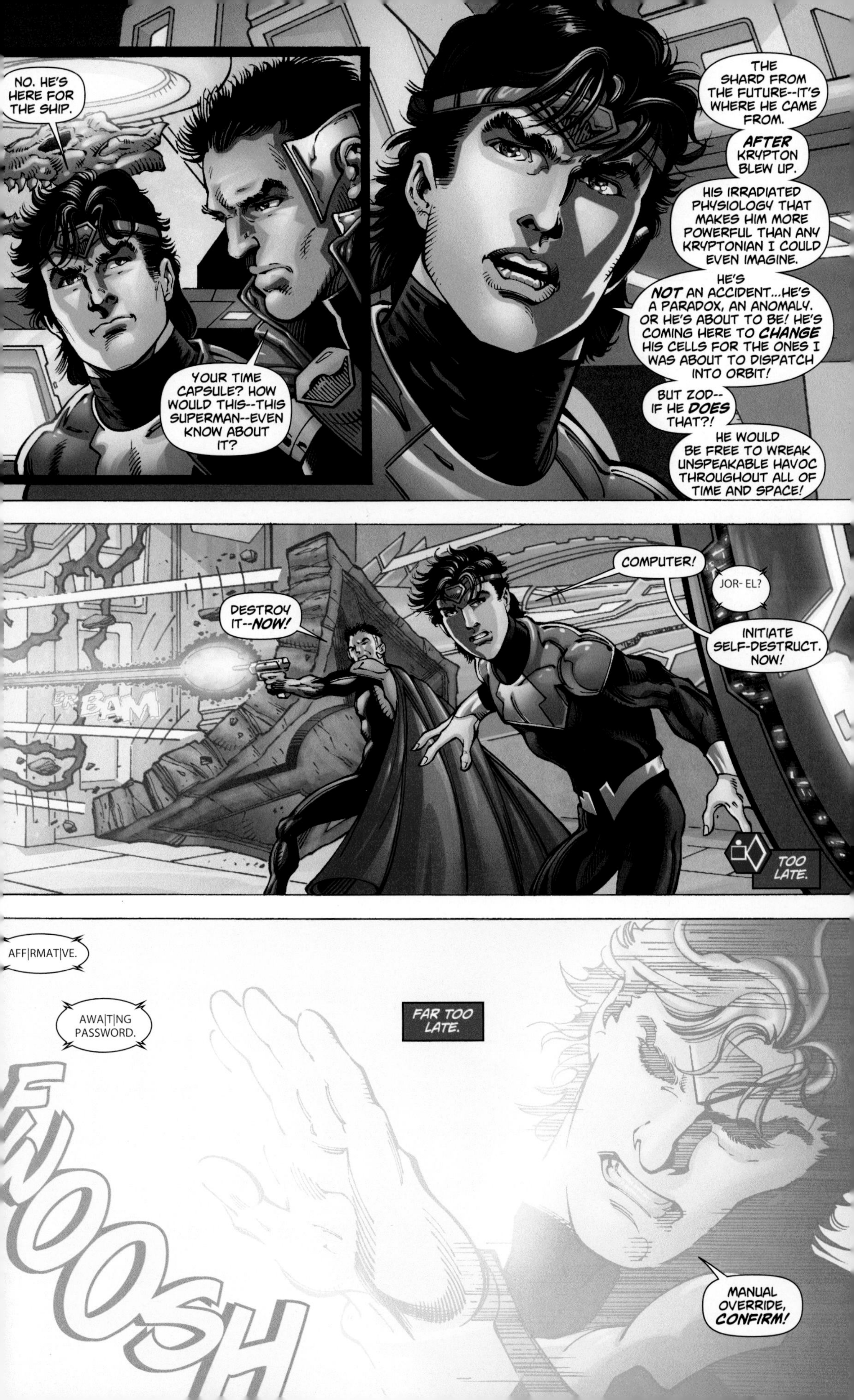
NO. HE'S HERE FOR THE SHIP.
YOUR TIME CAPSULE? HOW WOULD THIS--THIS SUPERMAN--EVEN KNOW ABOUT IT?
THE SHARD FROM THE FUTURE--IT'S WHERE HE CAME FROM.
AFTER KRYPTON BLEW UP.
HIS IRRADIATED PHYSIOLOGY THAT MAKES HIM MORE POWERFUL THAN ANY KRYPTONIAN I COULD EVEN IMAGINE.
HE'S NOT AN ACCIDENT...HE'S A PARADOX, AN ANOMALY. OR HE'S ABOUT TO BE! HE'S COMING HERE TO CHANGE HIS CELLS FOR THE ONES I WAS ABOUT TO DISPATCH INTO ORBIT!
BUT ZOD--IF HE DOES THAT?!
HE WOULD BE FREE TO WREAK UNSPEAKABLE HAVOC THROUGHOUT ALL OF TIME AND SPACE!
DESTROY IT--NOW!
BRBAM
COMPUTER!
JOR- EL?
INITIATE SELF-DESTRUCT. NOW!
TOO LATE.
AFF|RMAT|VE.
AWA|T|NG PASSWORD.
FAR TOO LATE.
FWOOOSH
MANUAL OVERRIDE, CONFIRM!

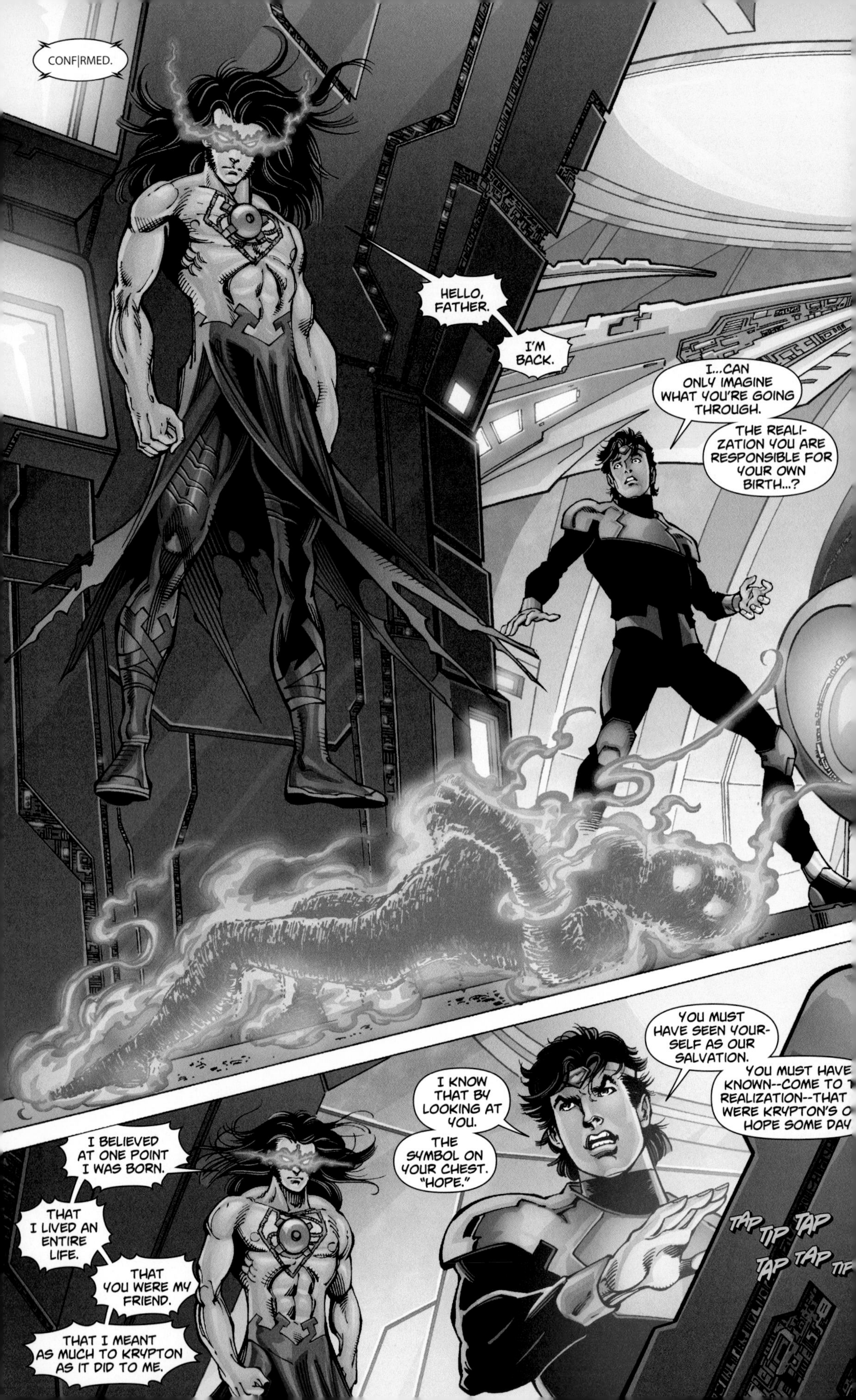
CONF|RMED.
HELLO, FATHER.
I'M BACK.
I...CAN ONLY IMAGINE WHAT YOU'RE GOING THROUGH.
THE REALIZATION YOU ARE RESPONSIBLE FOR YOUR OWN BIRTH...?
YOU MUST HAVE SEEN YOURSELF AS OUR SALVATION.
YOU MUST HAVE KNOWN--COME TO T REALIZATION--THAT WERE KRYPTON'S O HOPE SOME DAY
I KNOW THAT BY LOOKING AT YOU.
THE SYMBOL ON YOUR CHEST. "HOPE."
I BELIEVED AT ONE POINT I WAS BORN.
THAT I LIVED AN ENTIRE LIFE.
THAT YOU WERE MY FRIEND.
THAT I MEANT AS MUCH TO KRYPTON AS IT DID TO ME.
TAP TIP TAP
TAP TAP

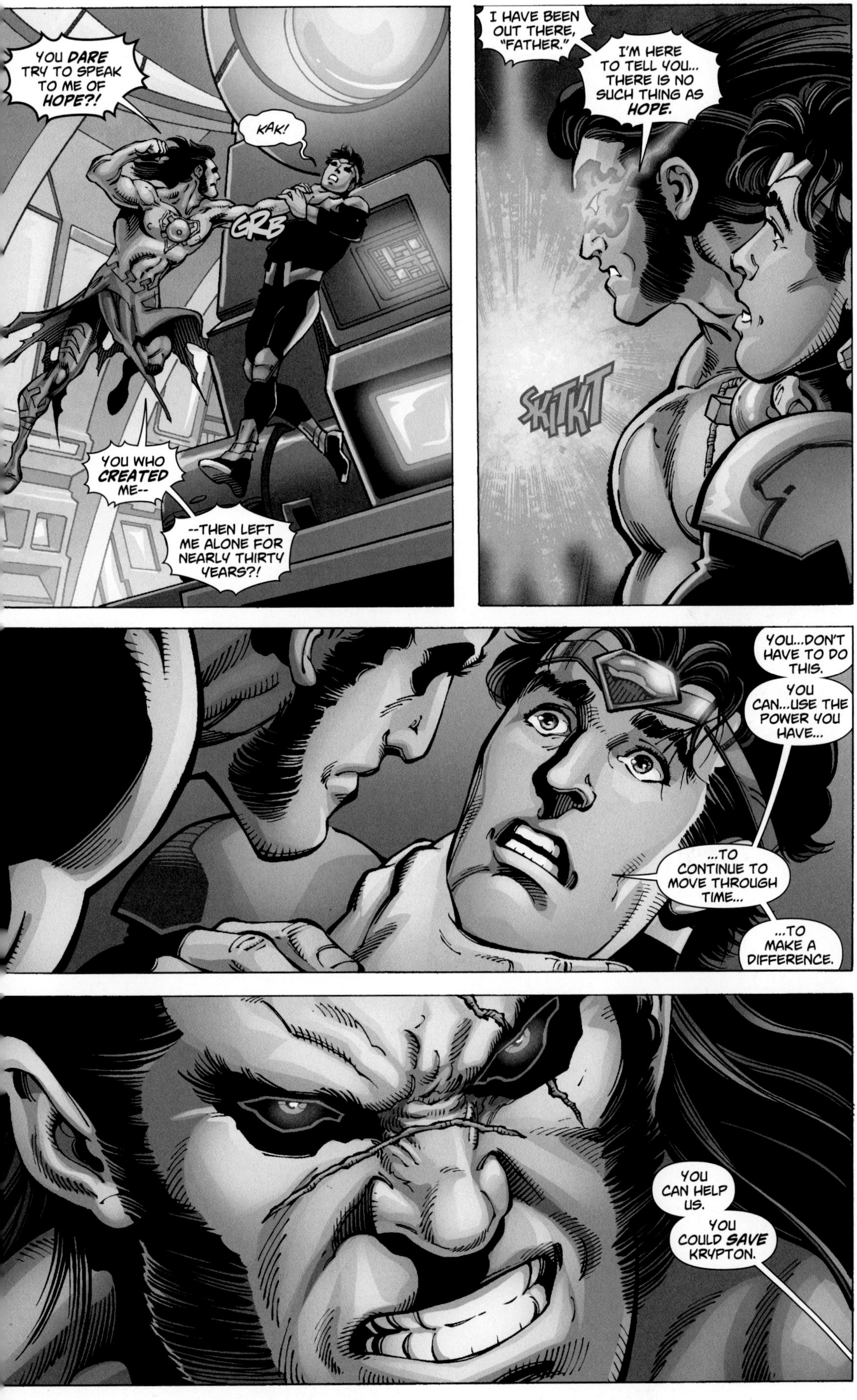
YOU DARE TRY TO SPEAK TO ME OF HOPE?!
KAK!
GRB
YOU WHO CREATED ME--
--THEN LEFT ME ALONE FOR NEARLY THIRTY YEARS?!
I HAVE BEEN OUT THERE, "FATHER."
I'M HERE TO TELL YOU... THERE IS NO SUCH THING AS HOPE.
SKITKT
YOU...DON'T HAVE TO DO THIS.
YOU CAN...USE THE POWER YOU HAVE...
...TO CONTINUE TO MOVE THROUGH TIME...
...TO MAKE A DIFFERENCE.
YOU CAN HELP US.
YOU COULD SAVE KRYPTON.

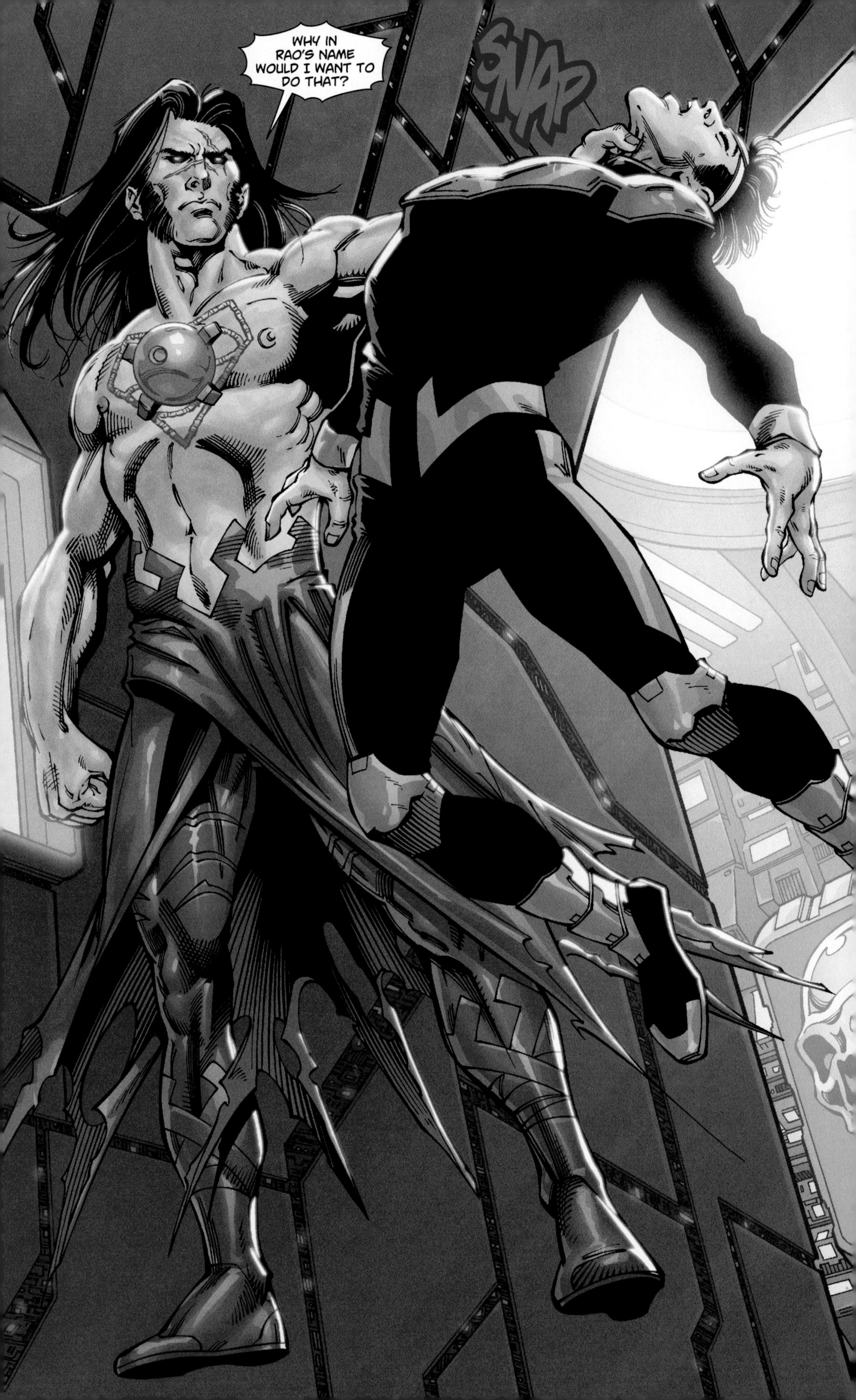
WHY IN RAO'S NAME WOULD I WANT TO DO THAT?
SNAP

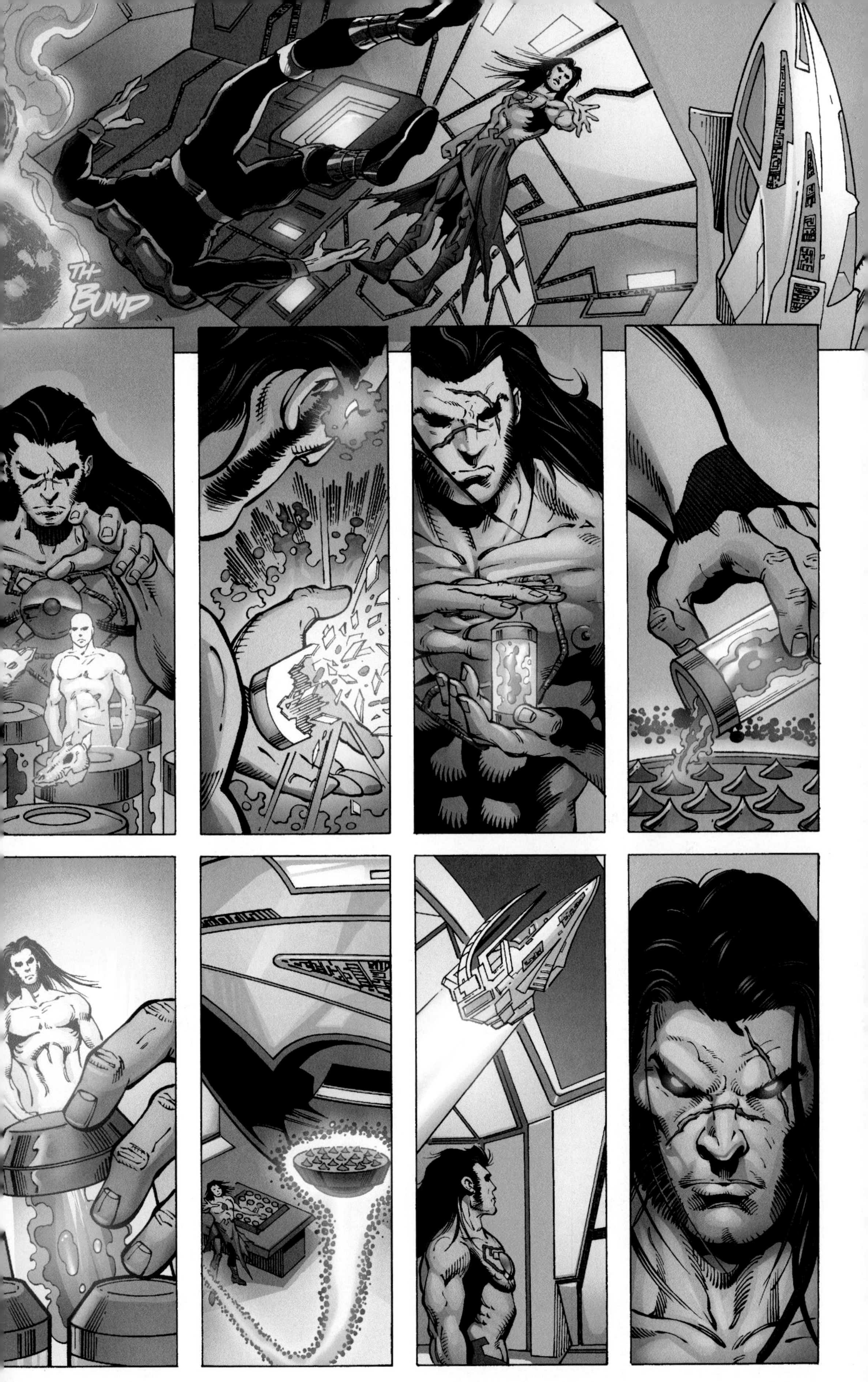
TH BUMP

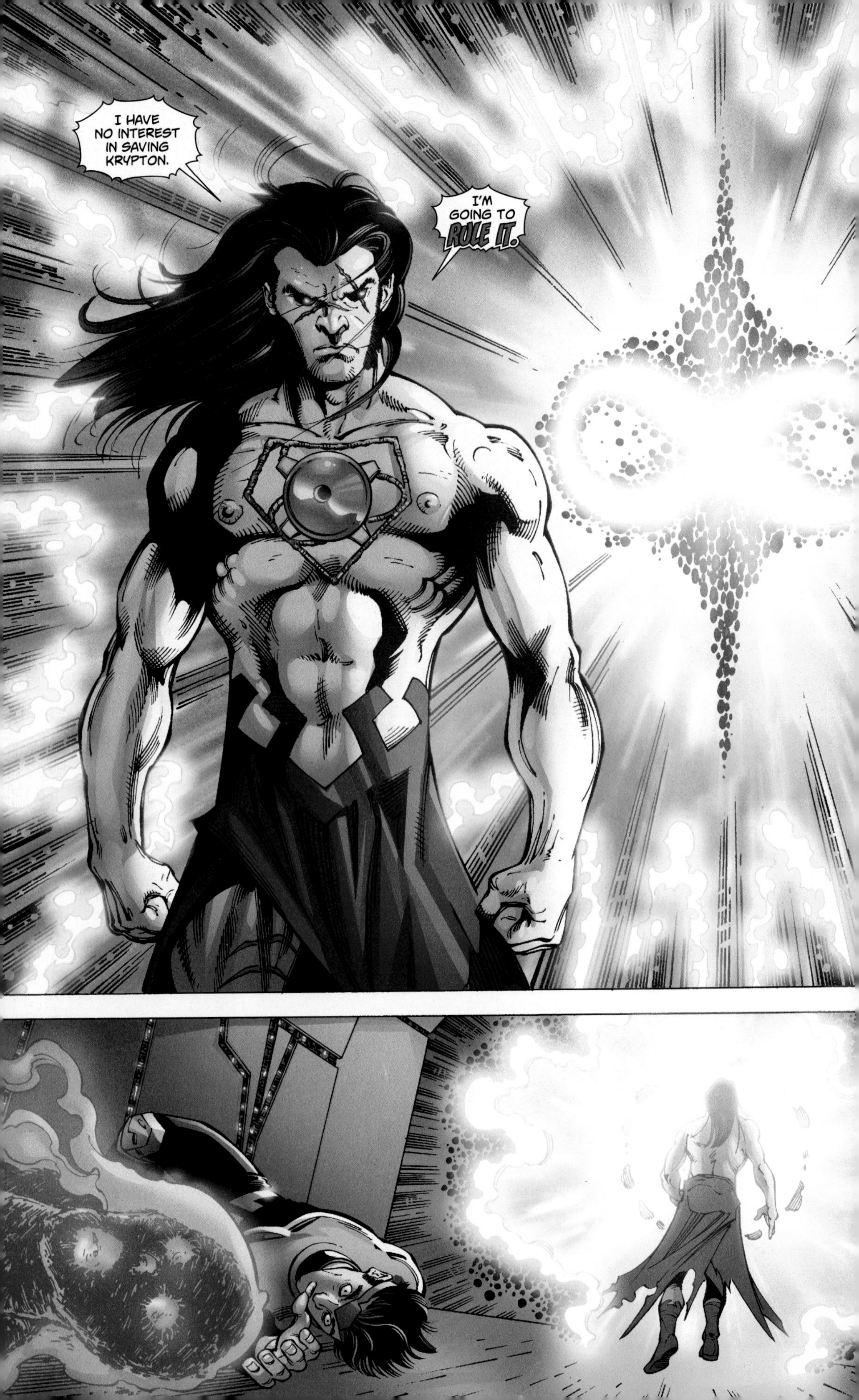
I HAVE NO INTEREST IN SAVING KRYPTON.
I'M GOING TO RULE IT.

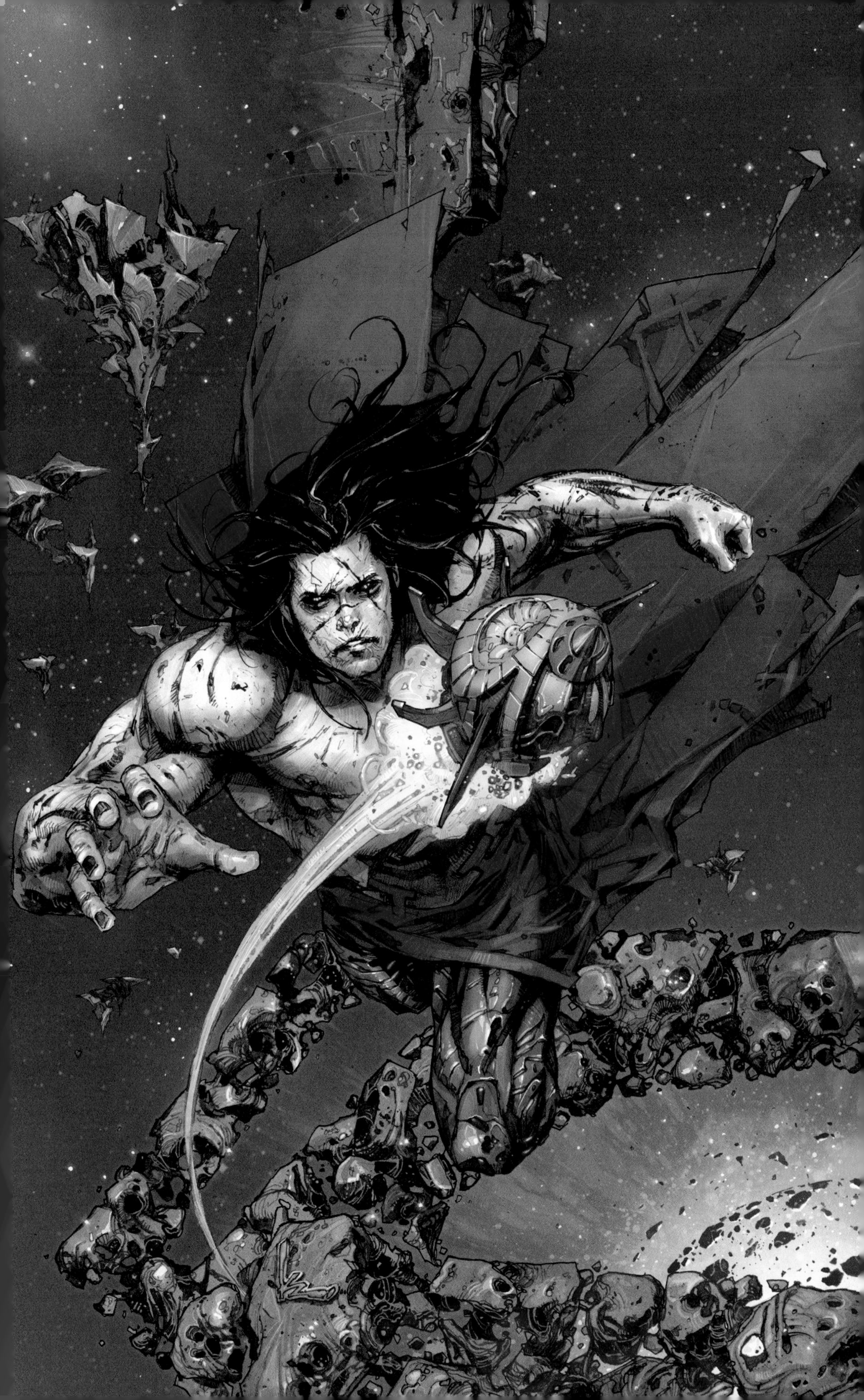

KRYPTON RETURNS PART ONE

SCOTT LOBDELL writer **KENNETH ROCAFORT DAN JURGENS** artists **TOMEU MOREY BLOND** colorists

cover art by **KENNETH ROCAFORT**

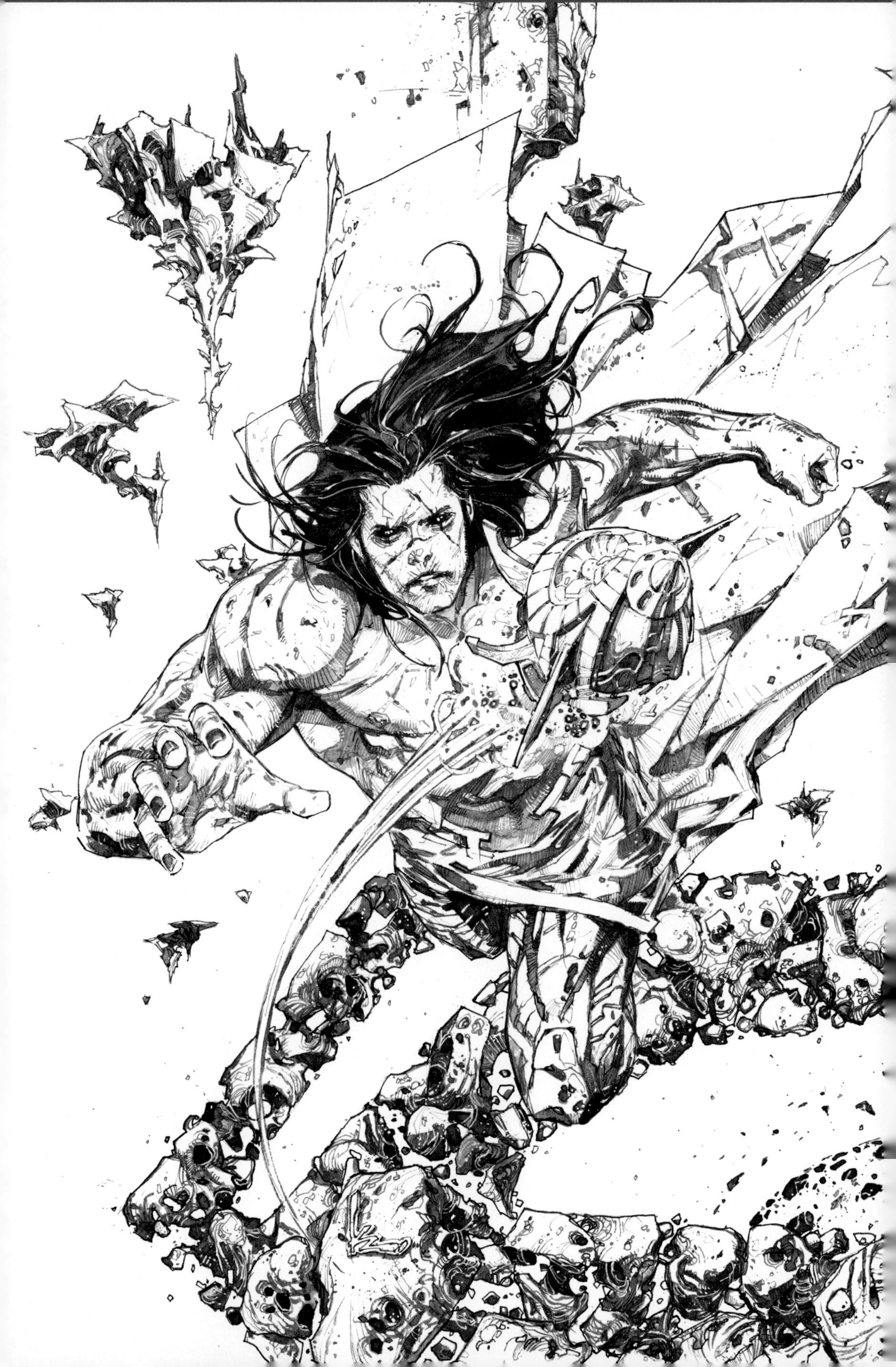

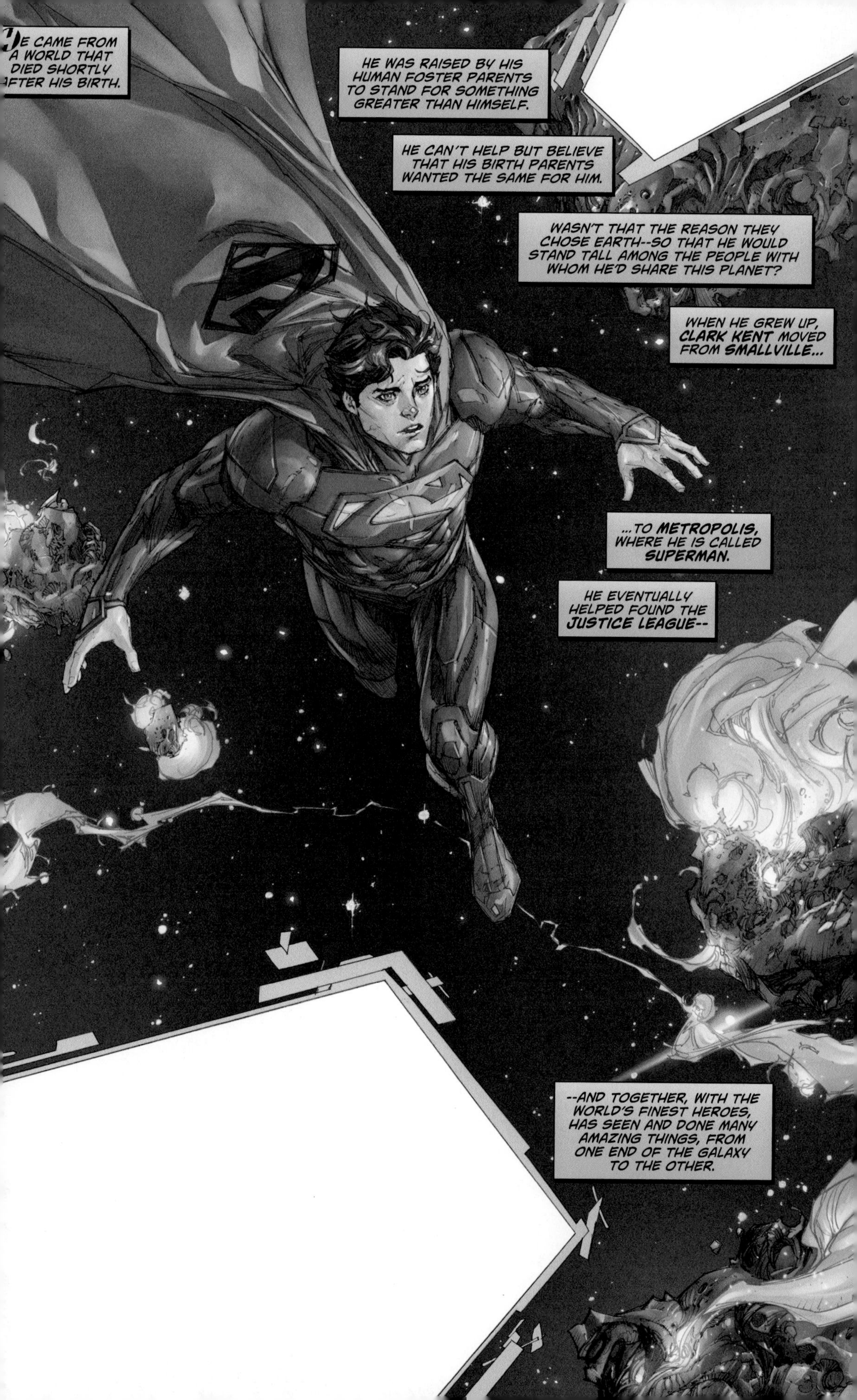
HE CAME FROM A WORLD THAT DIED SHORTLY AFTER HIS BIRTH.
HE WAS RAISED BY HIS HUMAN FOSTER PARENTS TO STAND FOR SOMETHING GREATER THAN HIMSELF.
HE CAN'T HELP BUT BELIEVE THAT HIS BIRTH PARENTS WANTED THE SAME FOR HIM.
WASN'T THAT THE REASON THEY CHOSE EARTH--SO THAT HE WOULD STAND TALL AMONG THE PEOPLE WITH WHOM HE'D SHARE THIS PLANET?
WHEN HE GREW UP, CLARK KENT MOVED FROM SMALLVILLE...
...TO METROPOLIS, WHERE HE IS CALLED SUPERMAN.
HE EVENTUALLY HELPED FOUND THE JUSTICE LEAGUE--
--AND TOGETHER, WITH THE WORLD'S FINEST HEROES, HAS SEEN AND DONE MANY AMAZING THINGS, FROM ONE END OF THE GALAXY TO THE OTHER.

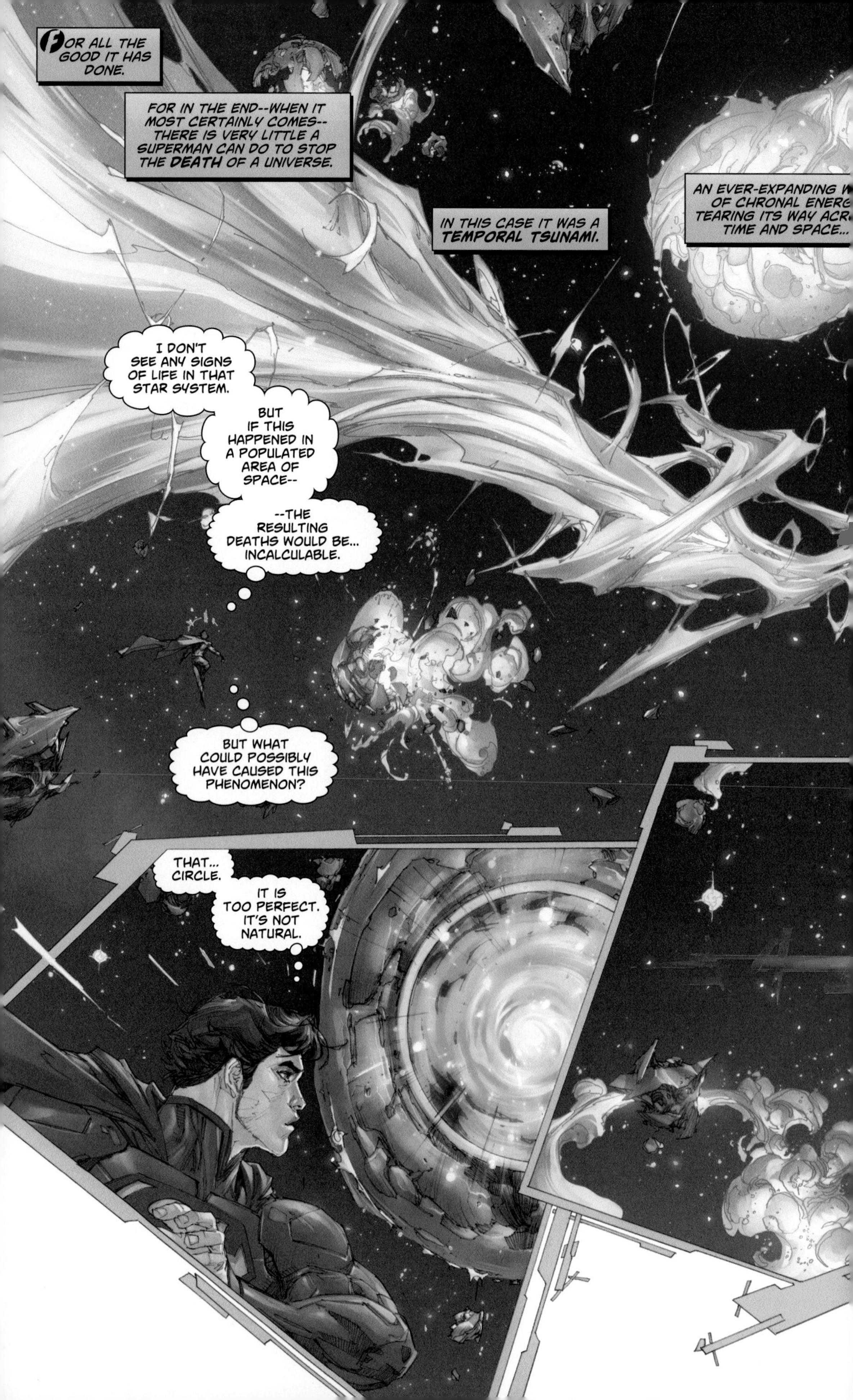
FOR ALL THE GOOD IT HAS DONE.
FOR IN THE END--WHEN IT MOST CERTAINLY COMES--THERE IS VERY LITTLE A SUPERMAN CAN DO TO STOP THE DEATH OF A UNIVERSE.
IN THIS CASE IT WAS A TEMPORAL TSUNAMI.
I DON'T SEE ANY SIGNS OF LIFE IN THAT STAR SYSTEM.
BUT IF THIS HAPPENED IN A POPULATED AREA OF SPACE--
--THE RESULTING DEATHS WOULD BE... INCALCULABLE.
BUT WHAT COULD POSSIBLY HAVE CAUSED THIS PHENOMENON?
THAT... CIRCLE.
IT IS TOO PERFECT. IT'S NOT NATURAL.

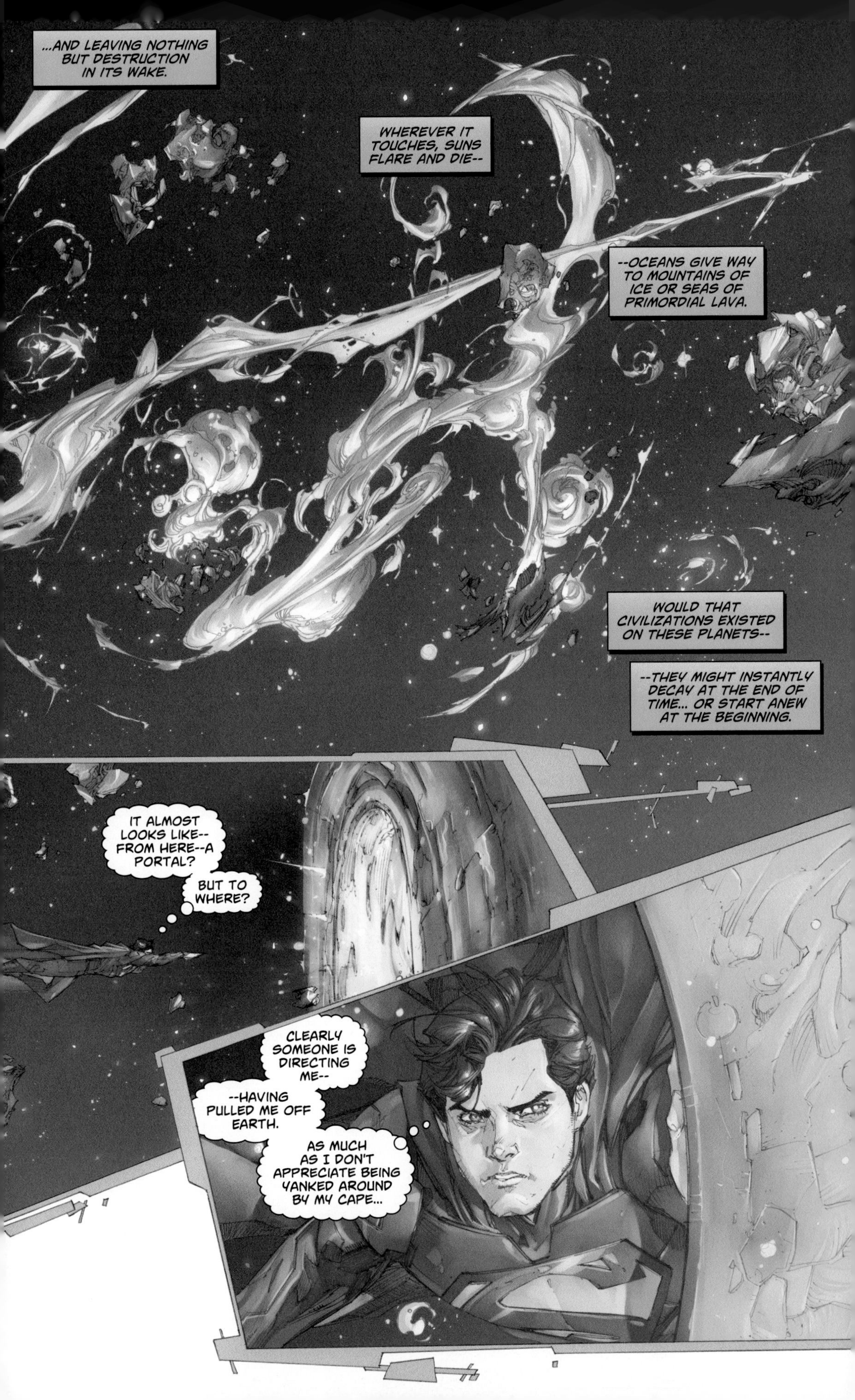
...AND LEAVING NOTHING BUT DESTRUCTION IN ITS WAKE.
WHEREVER IT TOUCHES, SUNS FLARE AND DIE--
--OCEANS GIVE WAY TO MOUNTAINS OF ICE OR SEAS OF PRIMORDIAL LAVA.
WOULD THAT CIVILIZATIONS EXISTED ON THESE PLANETS--
--THEY MIGHT INSTANTLY DECAY AT THE END OF TIME... OR START ANEW AT THE BEGINNING.
IT ALMOST LOOKS LIKE--FROM HERE--A PORTAL?
BUT TO WHERE?
CLEARLY SOMEONE IS DIRECTING ME--
--HAVING PULLED ME OFF EARTH.
AS MUCH AS I DON'T APPRECIATE BEING YANKED AROUND BY MY CAPE...

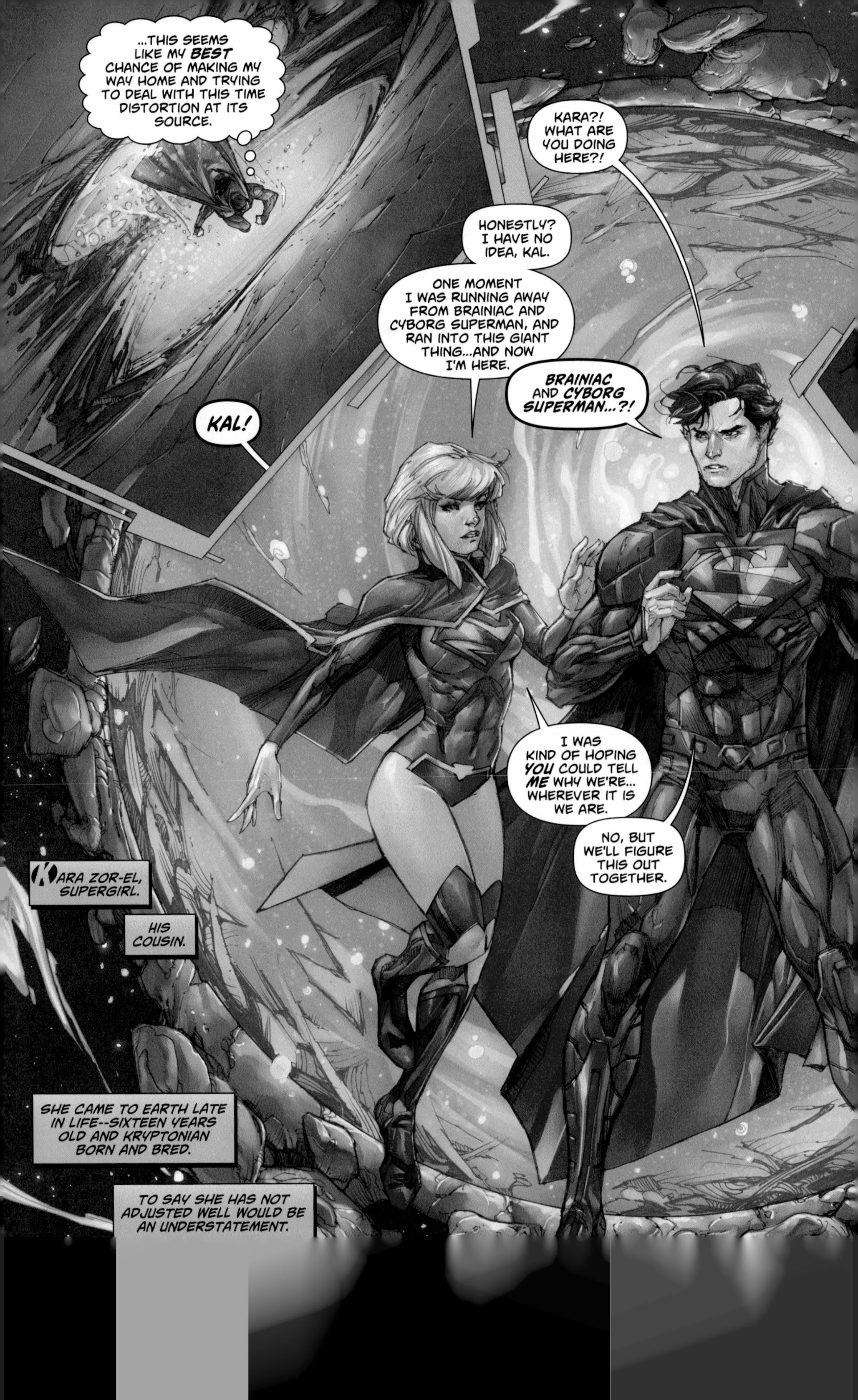

...THIS SEEMS LIKE MY BEST CHANCE OF MAKING MY WAY HOME AND TRYING TO DEAL WITH THIS TIME DISTORTION AT ITS SOURCE.
KARA?! WHAT ARE YOU DOING HERE?!
HONESTLY? I HAVE NO IDEA, KAL.
ONE MOMENT I WAS RUNNING AWAY FROM BRAINIAC AND CYBORG SUPERMAN, AND RAN INTO THIS GIANT THING...AND NOW I'M HERE.
KAL!
BRAINIAC AND CYBORG SUPERMAN...?!
I WAS KIND OF HOPING YOU COULD TELL ME WHY WE'RE... WHEREVER IT IS WE ARE.
NO, BUT WE'LL FIGURE THIS OUT TOGETHER.
KARA ZOR-EL, SUPERGIRL.
HIS COUSIN.
SHE CAME TO EARTH LATE IN LIFE--SIXTEEN YEARS OLD AND KRYPTONIAN BORN AND BRED.
TO SAY SHE HAS NOT ADJUSTED WELL WOULD BE AN UNDERSTATEMENT.

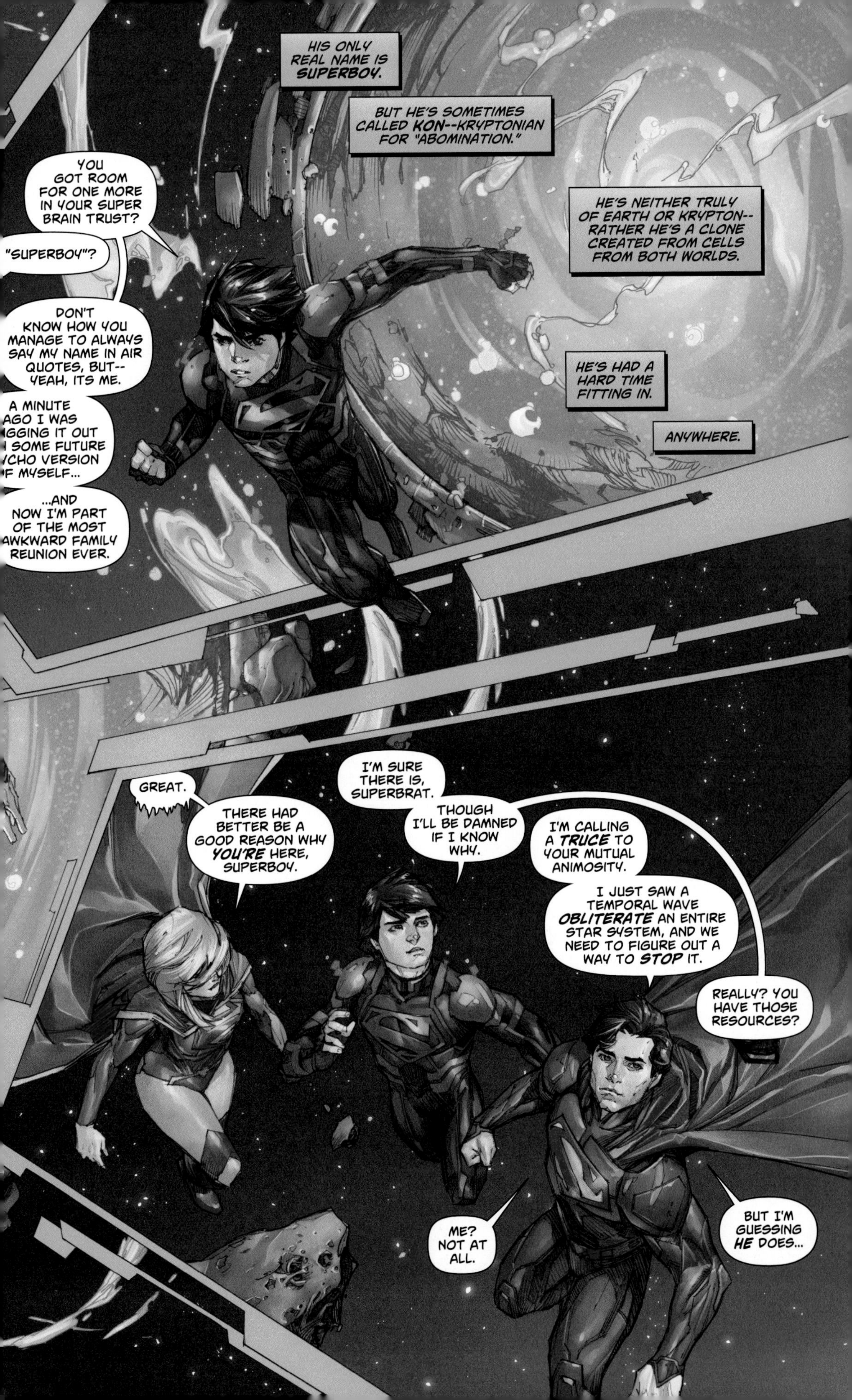

HIS ONLY REAL NAME IS SUPERBOY.
BUT HE'S SOMETIMES CALLED KON--KRYPTONIAN FOR "ABOMINATION."
YOU GOT ROOM FOR ONE MORE IN YOUR SUPER BRAIN TRUST?
"SUPERBOY"?
DON'T KNOW HOW YOU MANAGE TO ALWAYS SAY MY NAME IN AIR QUOTES, BUT-- YEAH, ITS ME.
A MINUTE AGO I WAS
...AND NOW I'M PART OF THE MOST AWKWARD FAMILY REUNION EVER.
HE'S NEITHER TRULY OF EARTH OR KRYPTON-- RATHER HE'S A CLONE CREATED FROM CELLS FROM BOTH WORLDS.
HE'S HAD A HARD TIME FITTING IN.
ANYWHERE.
GREAT.
THERE HAD BETTER BE A GOOD REASON WHY YOU'RE HERE, SUPERBOY.
I'M SURE THERE IS, SUPERBRAT.
THOUGH I'LL BE DAMNED IF I KNOW WHY.
I'M CALLING A TRUCE TO YOUR MUTUAL ANIMOSITY.
I JUST SAW A TEMPORAL WAVE OBLITERATE AN ENTIRE STAR SYSTEM, AND WE NEED TO FIGURE OUT A WAY TO STOP IT.
REALLY? YOU HAVE THOSE RESOURCES?
ME? NOT AT ALL.
BUT I'M GUESSING HE DOES...

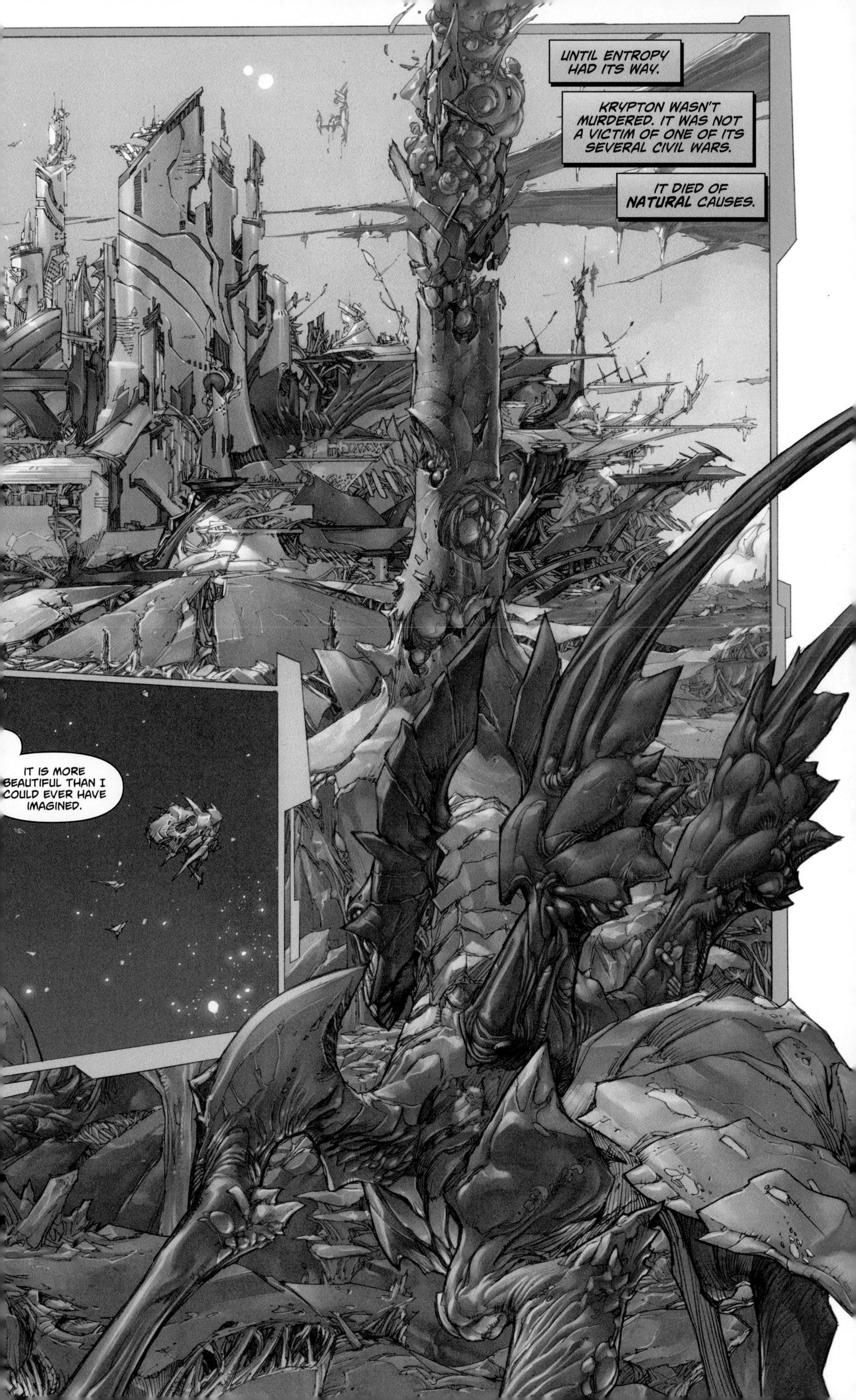
UNTIL ENTROPY HAD ITS WAY.
KRYPTON WASN'T MURDERED. IT WAS NOT A VICTIM OF ONE OF ITS SEVERAL CIVIL WARS.
IT DIED OF NATURAL CAUSES.
IT IS MORE BEAUTIFUL THAN I COULD EVER HAVE IMAGINED.

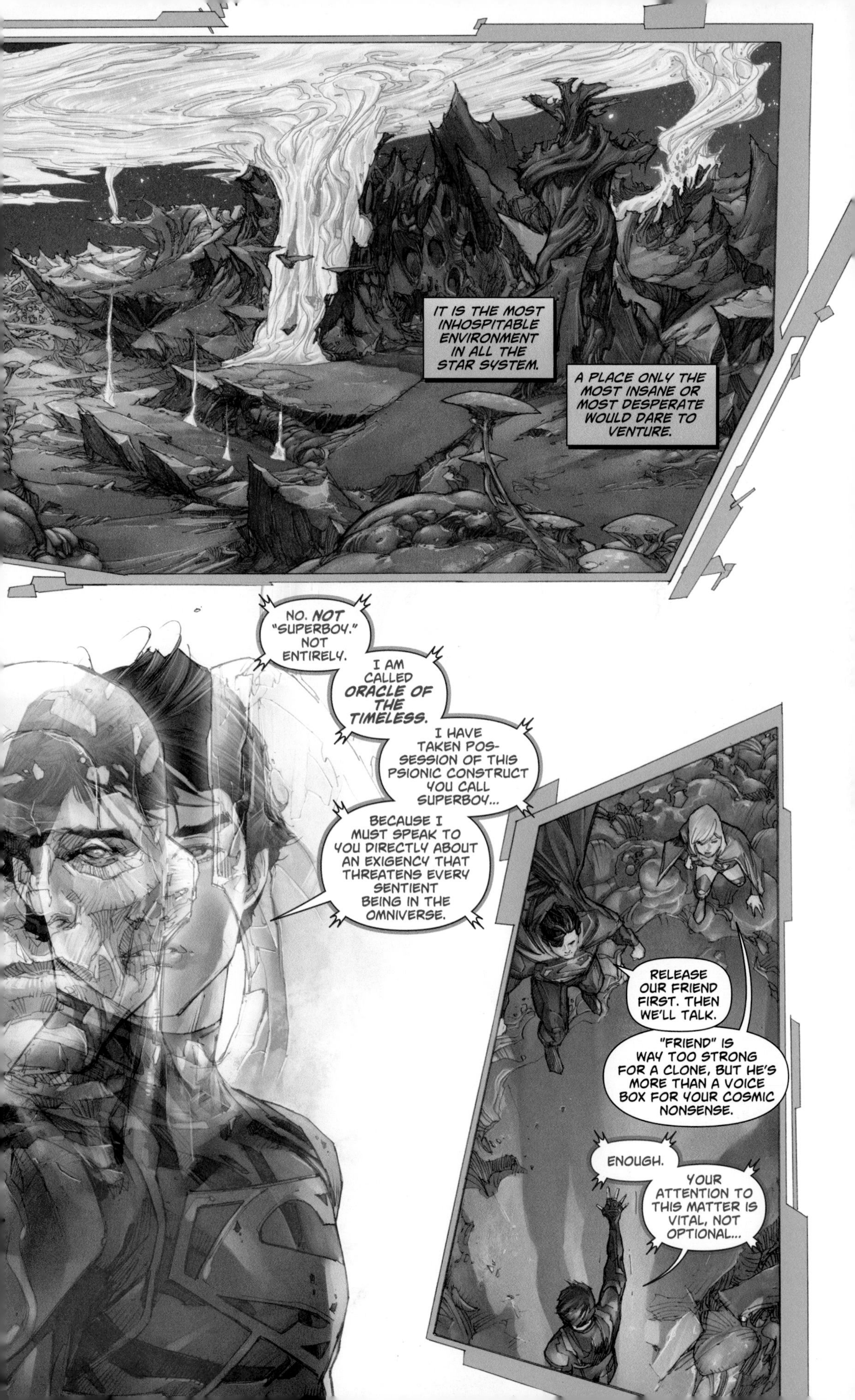
IT IS THE MOST INHOSPITABLE ENVIRONMENT IN ALL THE STAR SYSTEM.
A PLACE ONLY THE MOST INSANE OR MOST DESPERATE WOULD DARE TO VENTURE.
NO. NOT "SUPERBOY." NOT ENTIRELY.
I AM CALLED ORACLE OF THE TIMELESS.
I HAVE TAKEN POSSESSION OF THIS PSIONIC CONSTRUCT YOU CALL SUPERBOY...
BECAUSE I MUST SPEAK TO YOU DIRECTLY ABOUT AN EXIGENCY THAT THREATENS EVERY SENTIENT BEING IN THE OMNIVERSE.
RELEASE OUR FRIEND FIRST. THEN WE'LL TALK.
"FRIEND" IS WAY TOO STRONG FOR A CLONE, BUT HE'S MORE THAN A VOICE BOX FOR YOUR COSMIC NONSENSE.
ENOUGH.
YOUR ATTENTION TO THIS MATTER IS VITAL, NOT OPTIONAL...

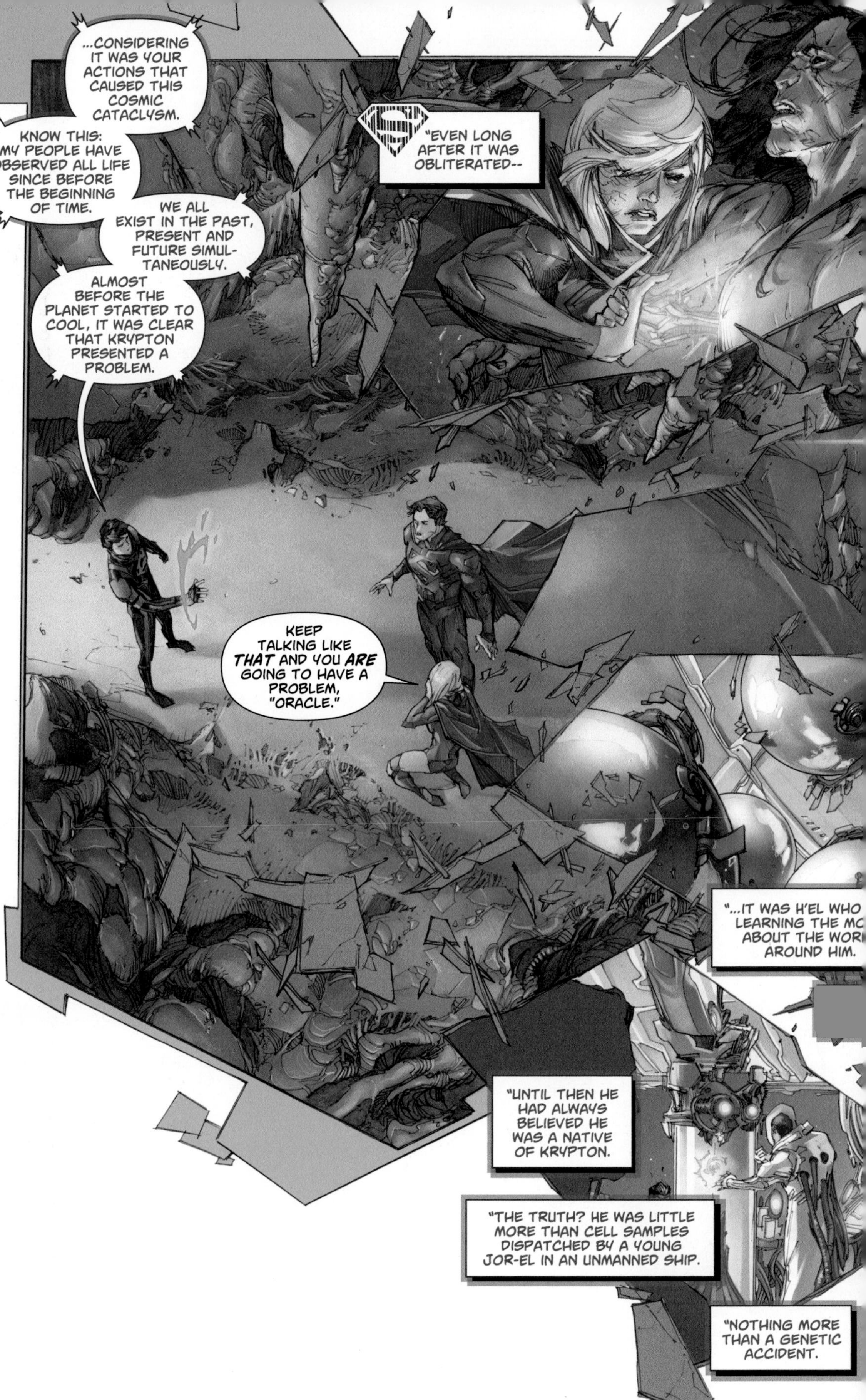
...CONSIDERING IT WAS YOUR ACTIONS THAT CAUSED THIS COSMIC CATACLYSM.
"EVEN LONG AFTER IT WAS OBLITERATED--
KNOW THIS: MY PEOPLE HAVE OBSERVED ALL LIFE SINCE BEFORE THE BEGINNING OF TIME.
WE ALL EXIST IN THE PAST, PRESENT AND FUTURE SIMUL- TANEOUSLY.
ALMOST BEFORE THE PLANET STARTED TO COOL, IT WAS CLEAR THAT KRYPTON PRESENTED A PROBLEM.
KEEP TALKING LIKE THAT AND YOU ARE GOING TO HAVE A PROBLEM, "ORACLE."
"...IT WAS H'EL WHO
"UNTIL THEN HE HAD ALWAYS BELIEVED HE WAS A NATIVE OF KRYPTON.
"THE TRUTH? HE WAS LITTLE MORE THAN CELL SAMPLES DISPATCHED BY A YOUNG JOR-EL IN AN UNMANNED SHIP.
"NOTHING MORE THAN A GENETIC ACCIDENT.

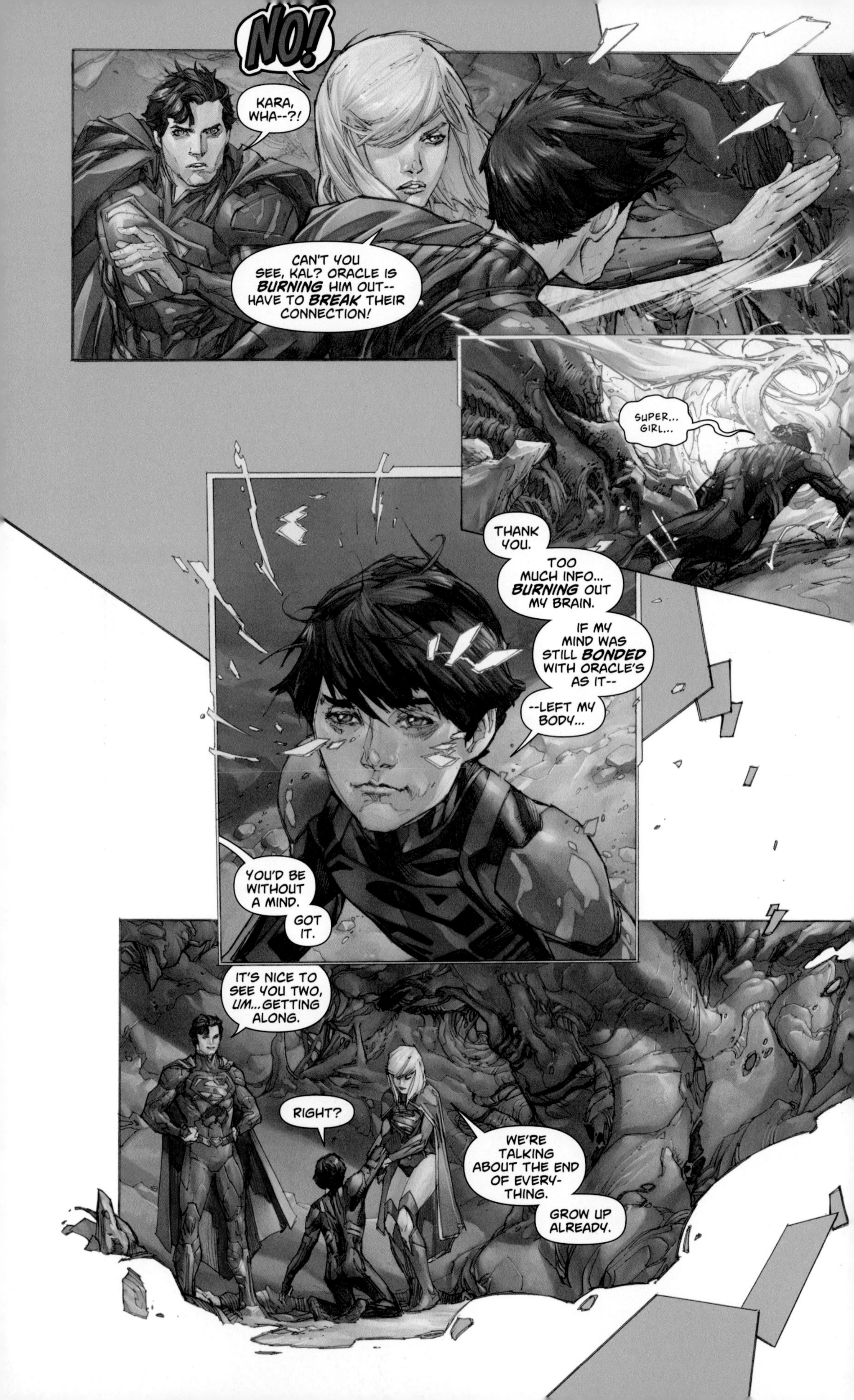
NO!
KARA, WHA--?!
CAN'T YOU SEE, KAL? ORACLE IS BURNING HIM OUT-- HAVE TO BREAK THEIR CONNECTION!
SUPER... GIRL...
THANK YOU.
TOO MUCH INFO... BURNING OUT MY BRAIN.
IF MY MIND WAS STILL BONDED WITH ORACLE'S AS IT--
--LEFT MY BODY...
YOU'D BE WITHOUT A MIND.
GOT IT.
IT'S NICE TO SEE YOU TWO, UM...GETTING ALONG.
RIGHT?
WE'RE TALKING ABOUT THE END OF EVERY-THING.
GROW UP ALREADY.

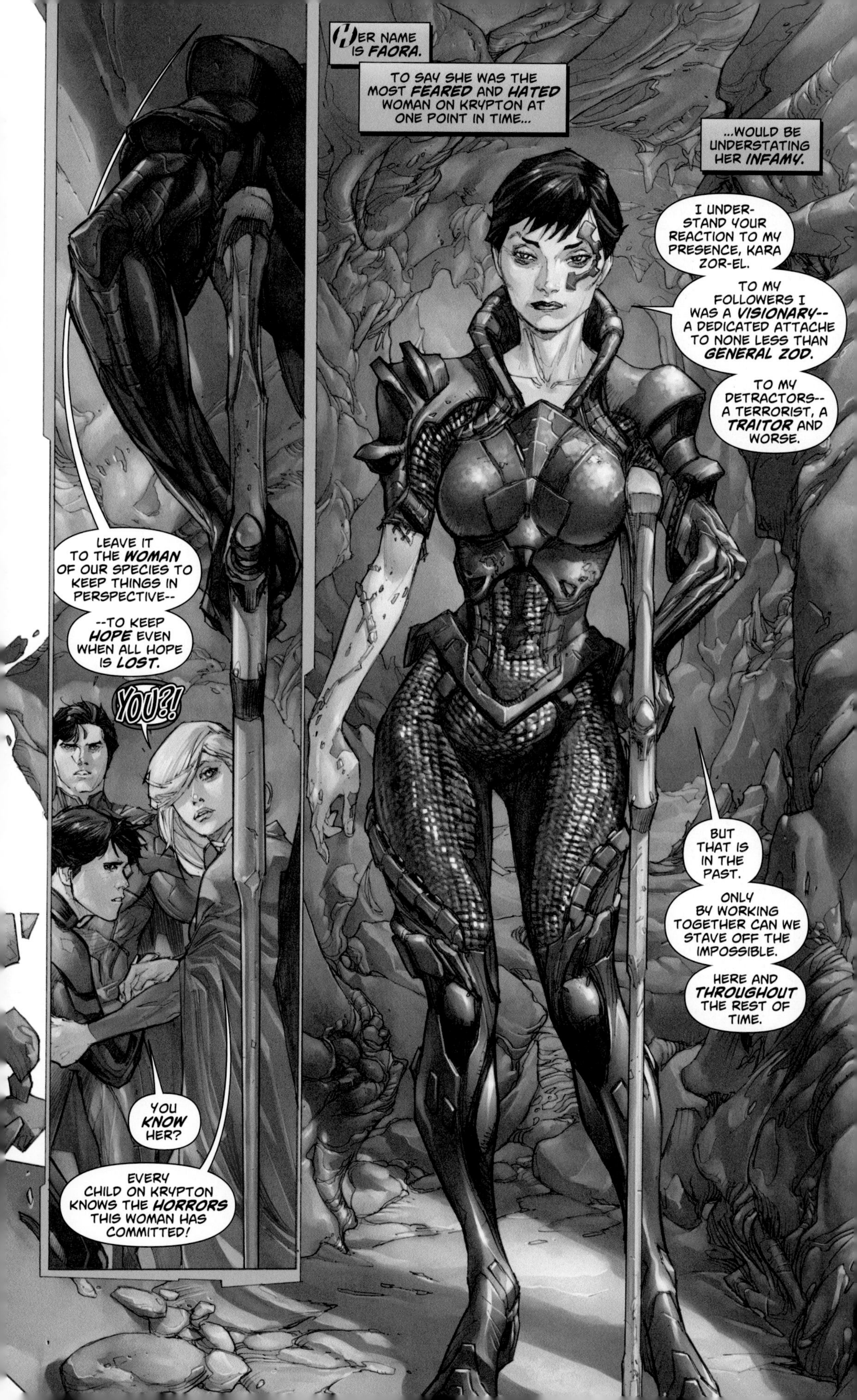
HER NAME IS FAORA.
TO SAY SHE WAS THE MOST FEARED AND HATED WOMAN ON KRYPTON AT ONE POINT IN TIME...
...WOULD BE UNDERSTATING HER INFAMY.
I UNDERSTAND YOUR REACTION TO MY PRESENCE, KARA ZOR-EL.
TO MY FOLLOWERS I WAS A VISIONARY-- A DEDICATED ATTACHE TO NONE LESS THAN GENERAL ZOD.
TO MY DETRACTORS-- A TERRORIST, A TRAITOR AND WORSE.
YOU?!
YOU KNOW HER?
EVERY CHILD ON KRYPTON KNOWS THE HORRORS THIS WOMAN HAS COMMITTED!
LEAVE IT TO THE WOMAN OF OUR SPECIES TO KEEP THINGS IN PERSPECTIVE--
--TO KEEP HOPE EVEN WHEN ALL HOPE IS LOST.
BUT THAT IS IN THE PAST.
ONLY BY WORKING TOGETHER CAN WE STAVE OFF THE IMPOSSIBLE.
HERE AND THROUGHOUT THE REST OF TIME.

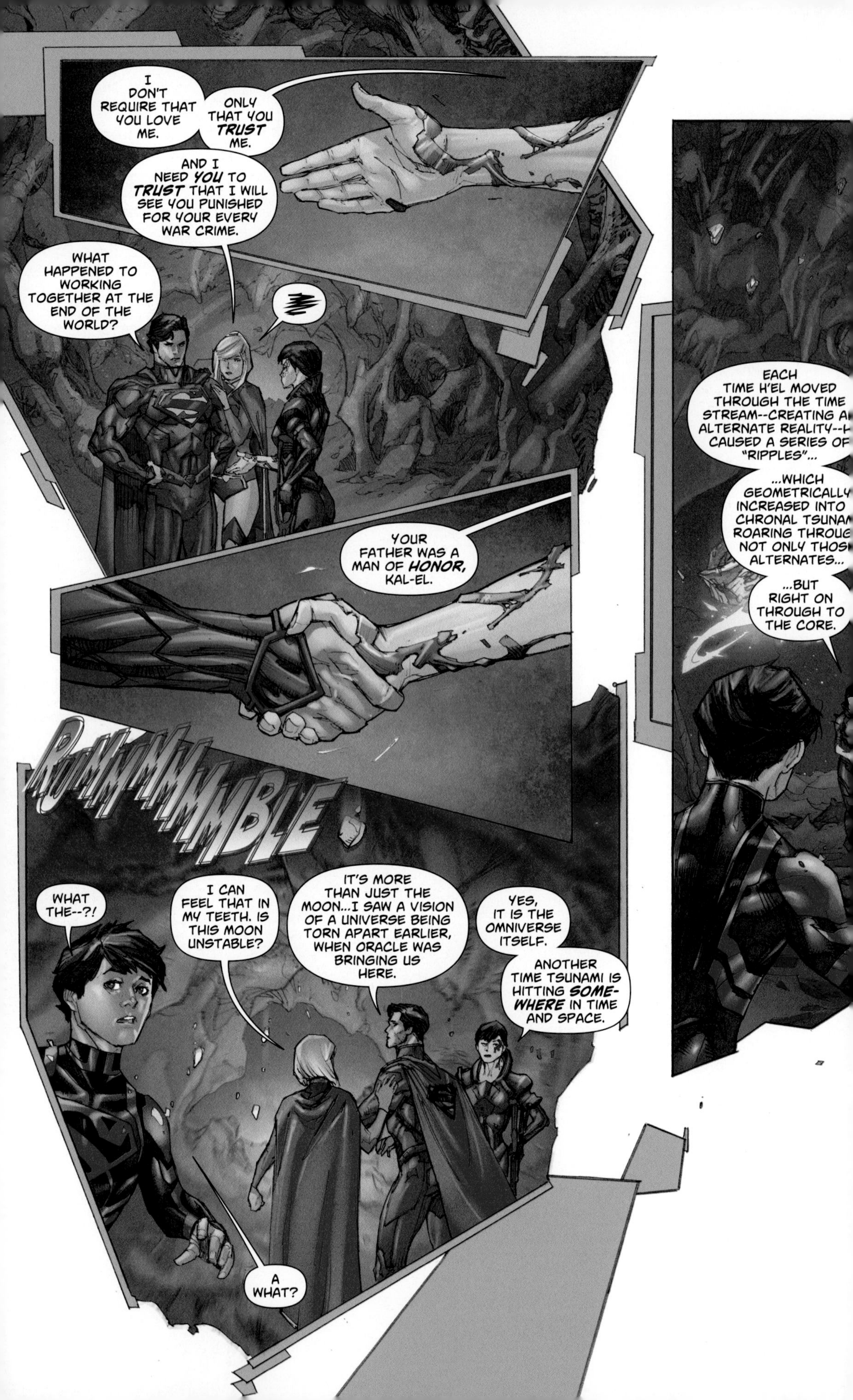
I DON'T REQUIRE THAT YOU LOVE ME.
ONLY THAT YOU TRUST ME.
AND I NEED YOU TO TRUST THAT I WILL SEE YOU PUNISHED FOR YOUR EVERY WAR CRIME.
WHAT HAPPENED TO WORKING TOGETHER AT THE END OF THE WORLD?
YOUR FATHER WAS A MAN OF HONOR, KAL-EL.
RUMMMMMBLE
WHAT THE--?!
I CAN FEEL THAT IN MY TEETH. IS THIS MOON UNSTABLE?
IT'S MORE THAN JUST THE MOON...I SAW A VISION OF A UNIVERSE BEING TORN APART EARLIER, WHEN ORACLE WAS BRINGING US HERE.
YES, IT IS THE OMNIVERSE ITSELF.
ANOTHER TIME TSUNAMI IS HITTING SOMEWHERE IN TIME AND SPACE.
A WHAT?
EACH TIME H'EL MOVED THROUGH THE TIME STREAM--CREATING A ALTERNATE REALITY-- CAUSED A SERIES OF "RIPPLES"...
...WHICH GEOMETRICALLY INCREASED INTO CHRONAL TSUNAM ROARING THROUG NOT ONLY THOS ALTERNATES...
...BUT RIGHT ON THROUGH TO THE CORE.

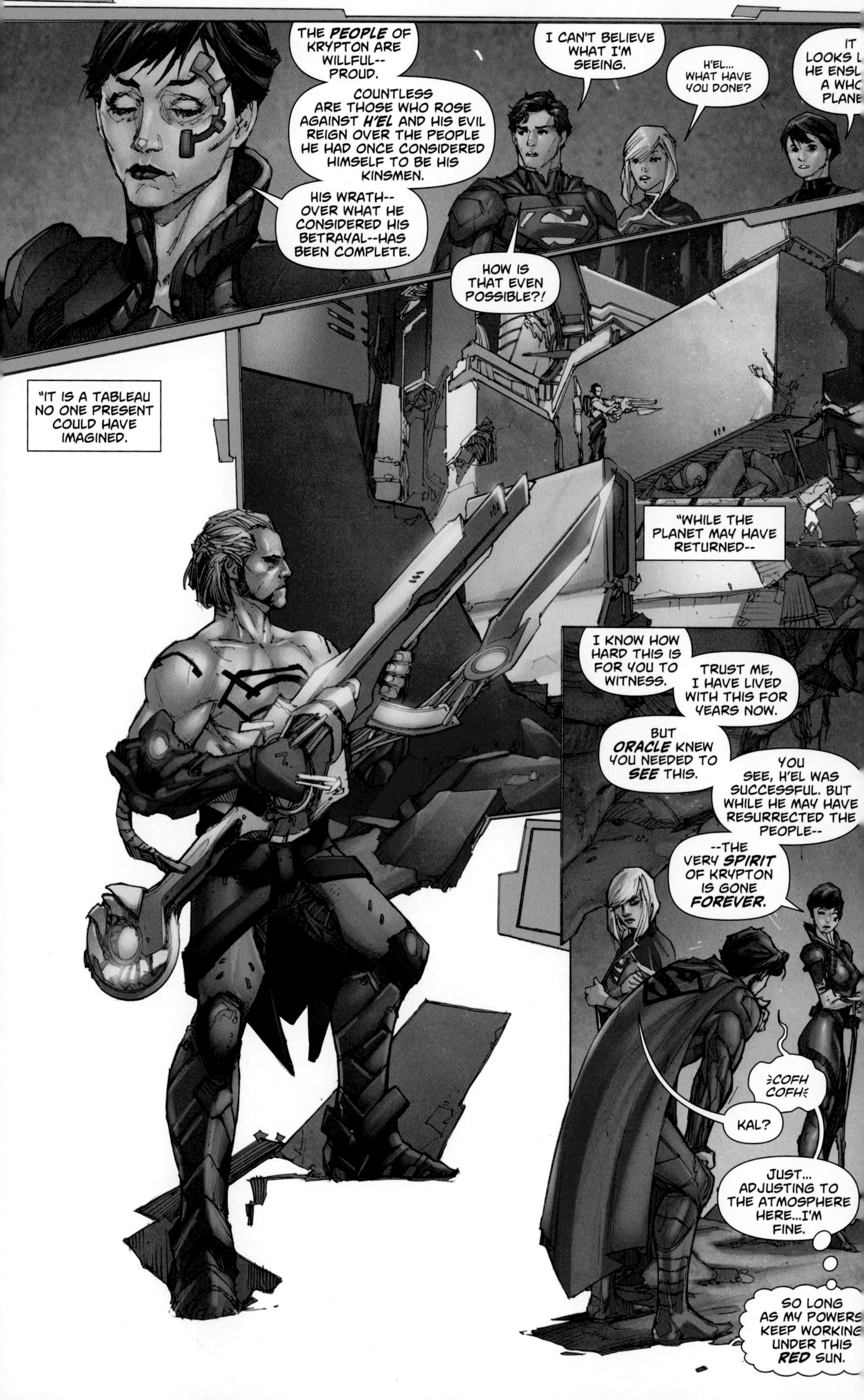
THE PEOPLE OF KRYPTON ARE WILLFUL-- PROUD.
COUNTLESS ARE THOSE WHO ROSE AGAINST H'EL AND HIS EVIL REIGN OVER THE PEOPLE HE HAD ONCE CONSIDERED HIMSELF TO BE HIS KINSMEN.
HIS WRATH-- OVER WHAT HE CONSIDERED HIS BETRAYAL--HAS BEEN COMPLETE.
I CAN'T BELIEVE WHAT I'M SEEING.
H'EL... WHAT HAVE YOU DONE?
IT LOOKS L HE ENSL A WHO PLANE
HOW IS THAT EVEN POSSIBLE?!
"IT IS A TABLEAU NO ONE PRESENT COULD HAVE IMAGINED.
"WHILE THE PLANET MAY HAVE RETURNED--
I KNOW HOW HARD THIS IS FOR YOU TO WITNESS.
TRUST ME, I HAVE LIVED WITH THIS FOR YEARS NOW.
BUT ORACLE KNEW YOU NEEDED TO SEE THIS.
YOU SEE, H'EL WAS SUCCESSFUL. BUT WHILE HE MAY HAVE RESURRECTED THE PEOPLE--
--THE VERY SPIRIT OF KRYPTON IS GONE FOREVER.
COFH COFH
KAL?
JUST... ADJUSTING TO THE ATMOSPHERE HERE...I'M FINE.
SO LONG AS MY POWERS KEEP WORKING UNDER THIS RED SUN.

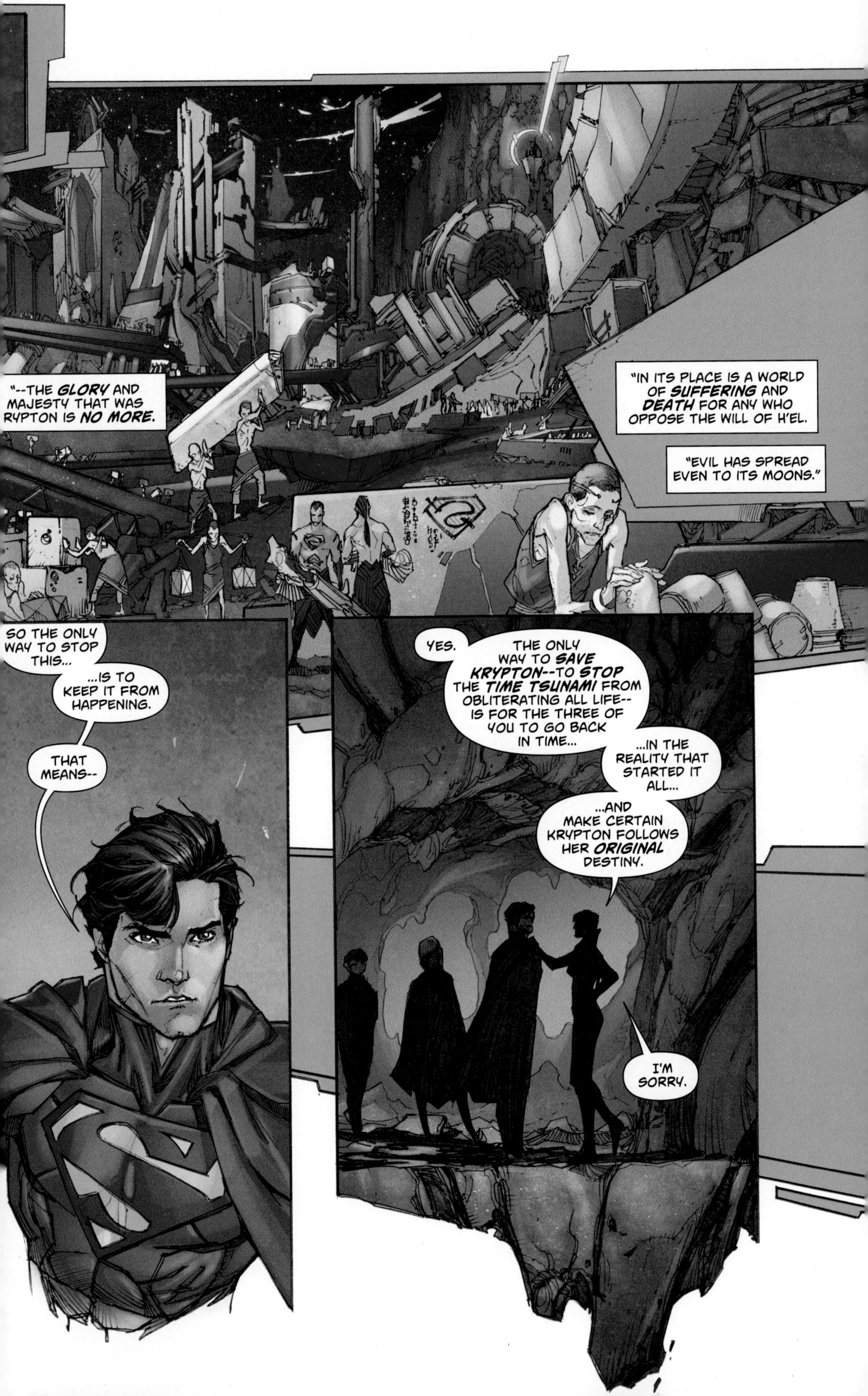
"--THE GLORY AND MAJESTY THAT WAS KRYPTON IS NO MORE.
"IN ITS PLACE IS A WORLD OF SUFFERING AND DEATH FOR ANY WHO OPPOSE THE WILL OF H'EL.
"EVIL HAS SPREAD EVEN TO ITS MOONS."
SO THE ONLY WAY TO STOP THIS...
...IS TO KEEP IT FROM HAPPENING.
THAT MEANS--
YES.
THE ONLY WAY TO SAVE KRYPTON--TO STOP THE TIME TSUNAMI FROM OBLITERATING ALL LIFE--IS FOR THE THREE OF YOU TO GO BACK IN TIME...
...IN THE REALITY THAT STARTED IT ALL...
...AND MAKE CERTAIN KRYPTON FOLLOWS HER ORIGINAL DESTINY.
I'M SORRY.

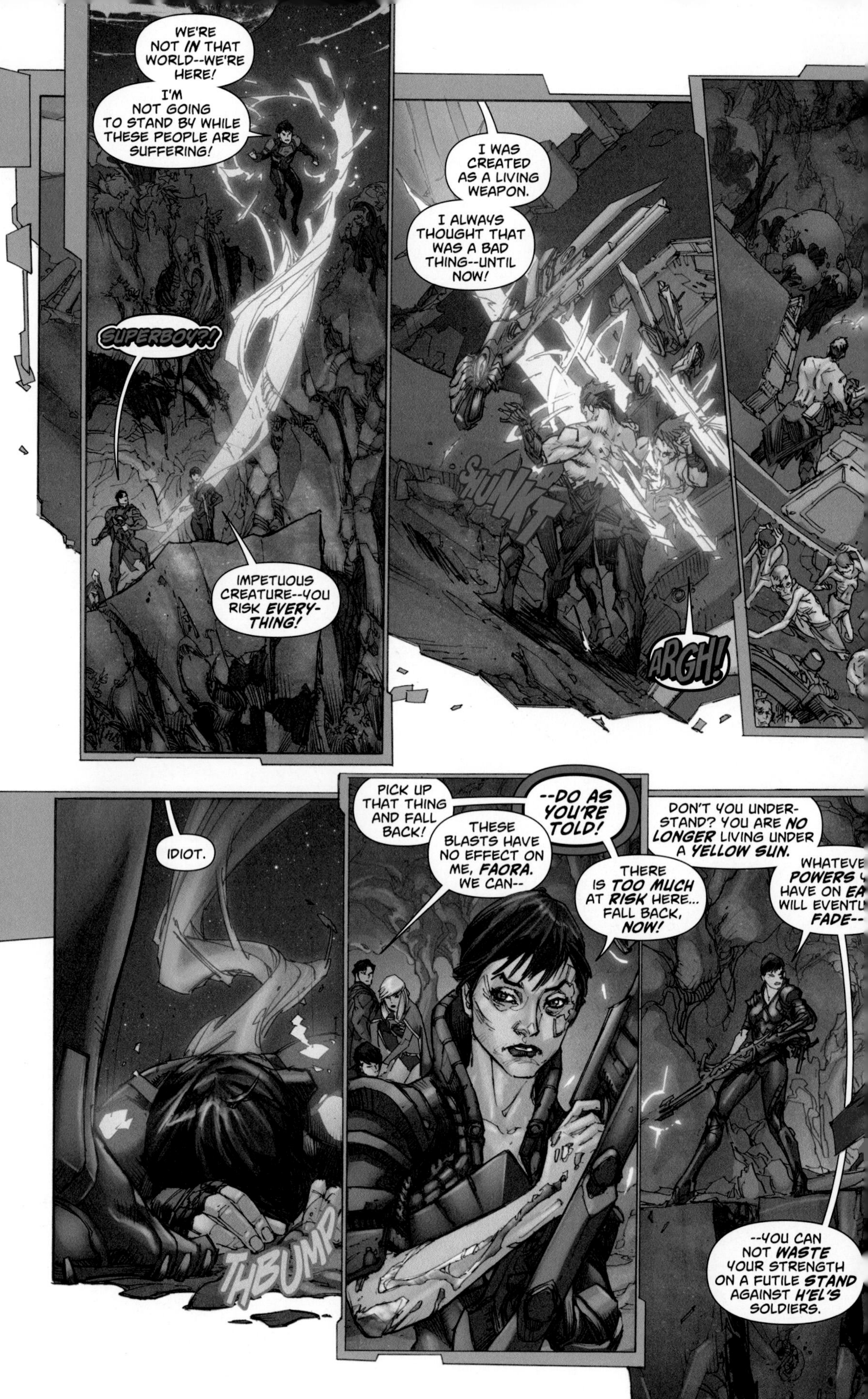
WE'RE NOT IN THAT WORLD--WE'RE HERE!
I'M NOT GOING TO STAND BY WHILE THESE PEOPLE ARE SUFFERING!
SUPERBOY?!
IMPETUOUS CREATURE--YOU RISK EVERY-THING!
I WAS CREATED AS A LIVING WEAPON.
I ALWAYS THOUGHT THAT WAS A BAD THING--UNTIL NOW!
SHUNKT
ARGH!
IDIOT.
THBUMP
PICK UP THAT THING AND FALL BACK!
--DO AS YOU'RE TOLD!
THESE BLASTS HAVE NO EFFECT ON ME, FAORA. WE CAN--
THERE IS TOO MUCH AT RISK HERE... FALL BACK, NOW!
DON'T YOU UNDER-STAND? YOU ARE NO LONGER LIVING UNDER A YELLOW SUN.
WHATEVE POWERS Y HAVE ON EA WILL EVENTU FADE--
--YOU CAN NOT WASTE YOUR STRENGTH ON A FUTILE STAND AGAINST H'EL'S SOLDIERS.

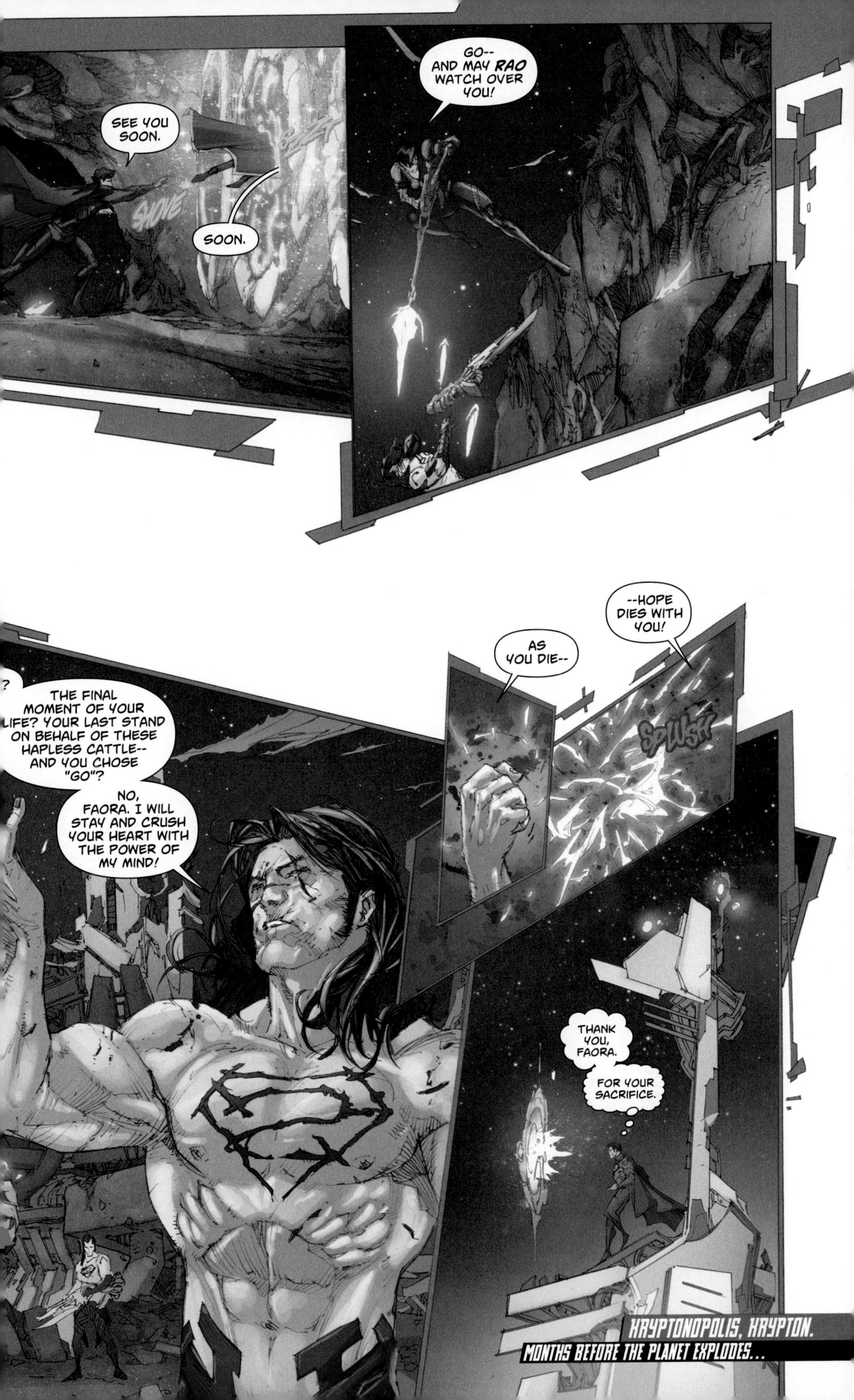
SEE YOU SOON.
SHOVE
SOON.
GO-- AND MAY RAO WATCH OVER YOU!
THE FINAL MOMENT OF YOUR LIFE? YOUR LAST STAND ON BEHALF OF THESE HAPLESS CATTLE-- AND YOU CHOSE "GO"?
NO, FAORA. I WILL STAY AND CRUSH YOUR HEART WITH THE POWER OF MY MIND!
AS YOU DIE--
--HOPE DIES WITH YOU!
SPLUSH
THANK YOU, FAORA.
FOR YOUR SACRIFICE.
KRYPTONOPOLIS, KRYPTON.
MONTHS BEFORE THE PLANET EXPLODES...

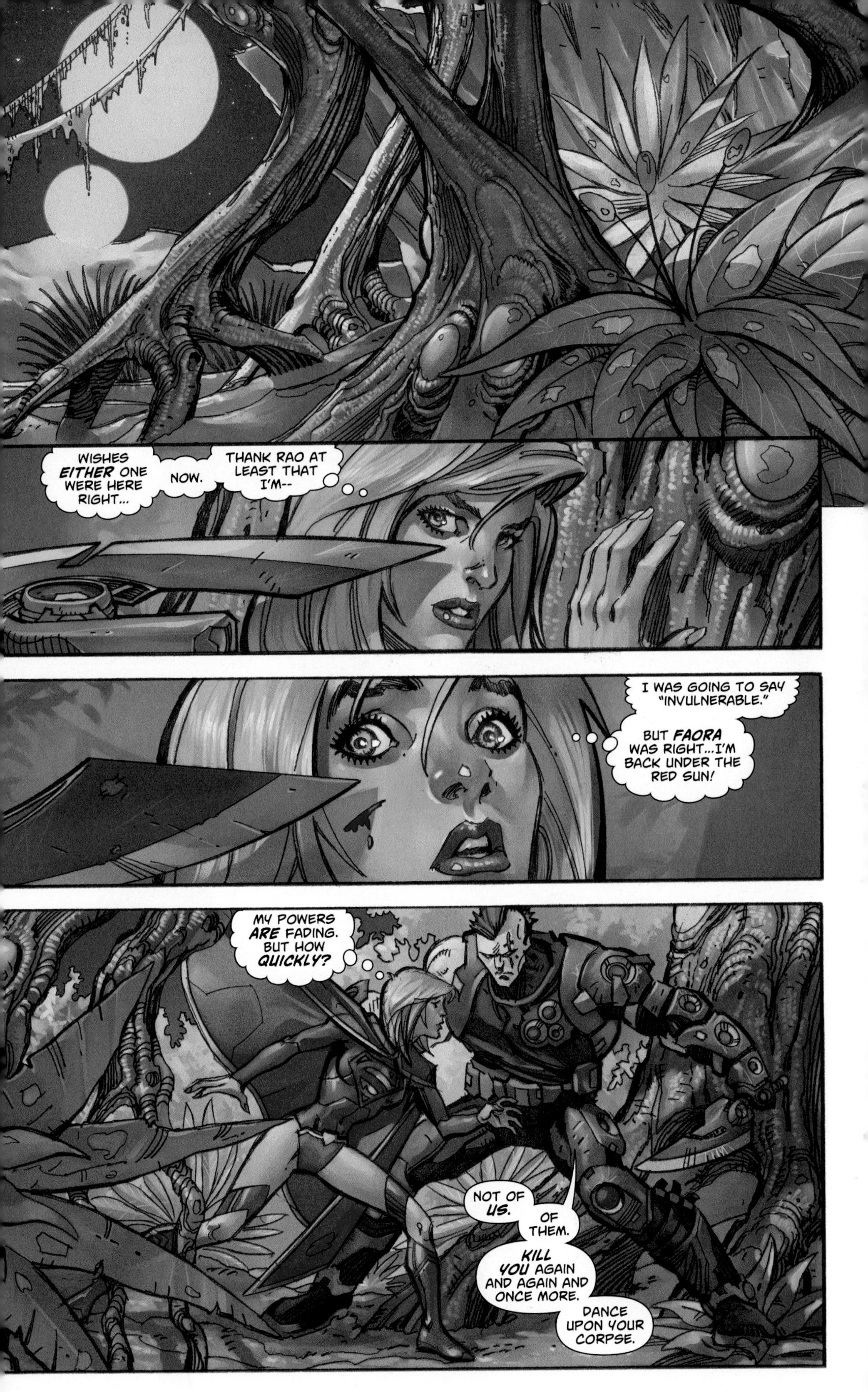
WISHES EITHER ONE WERE HERE RIGHT...
NOW.
THANK RAO AT LEAST THAT I'M--
I WAS GOING TO SAY "INVULNERABLE."
BUT FAORA WAS RIGHT...I'M BACK UNDER THE RED SUN!
MY POWERS ARE FADING. BUT HOW QUICKLY?
NOT OF US.
OF THEM.
KILL YOU AGAIN AND AGAIN AND ONCE MORE.
DANCE UPON YOUR CORPSE.

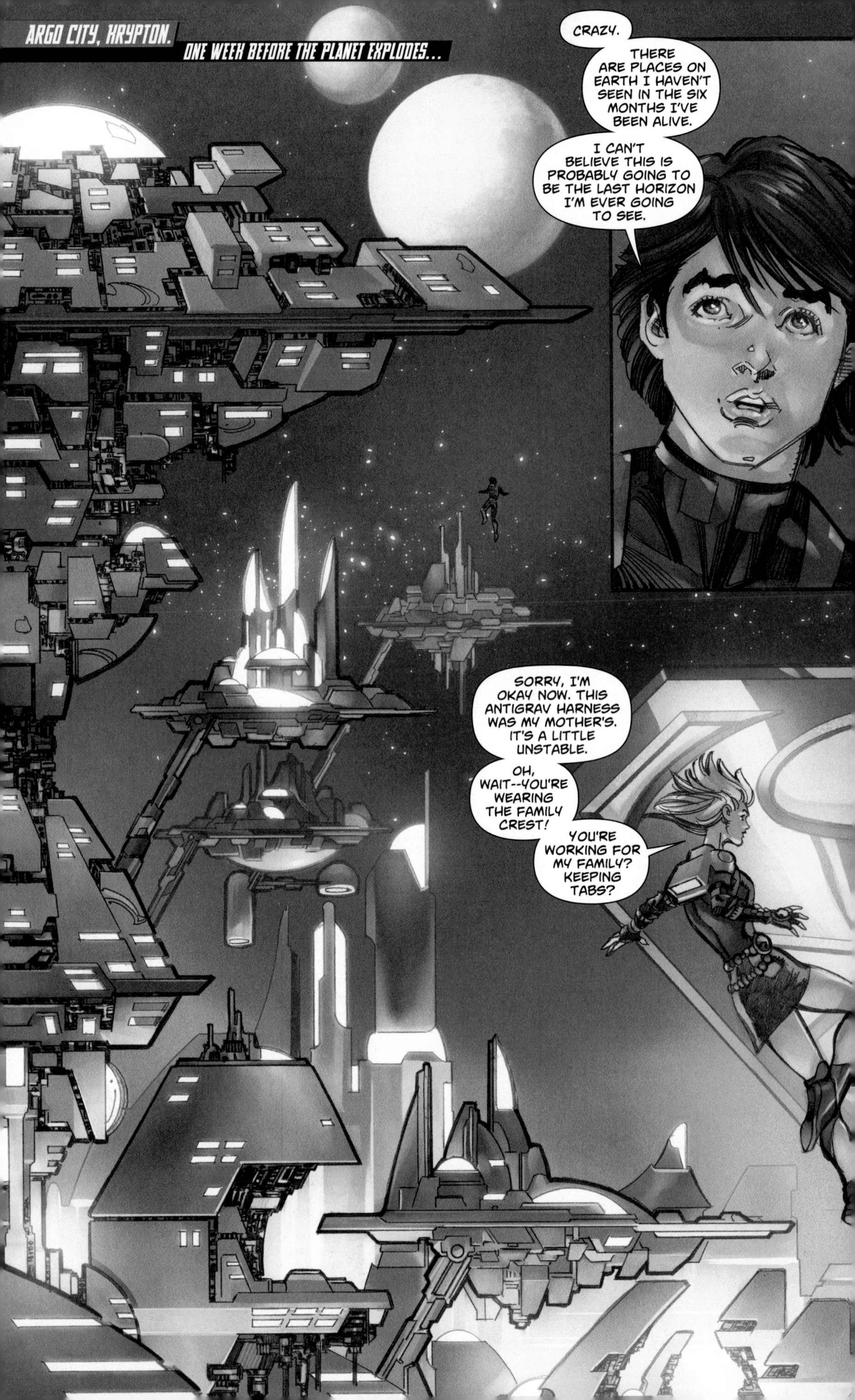
ARGO CITY, KRYPTON.
ONE WEEK BEFORE THE PLANET EXPLODES...
CRAZY.
THERE ARE PLACES ON EARTH I HAVEN'T SEEN IN THE SIX MONTHS I'VE BEEN ALIVE.
I CAN'T BELIEVE THIS IS PROBABLY GOING TO BE THE LAST HORIZON I'M EVER GOING TO SEE.
SORRY, I'M OKAY NOW. THIS ANTIGRAV HARNESS WAS MY MOTHER'S. IT'S A LITTLE UNSTABLE.
OH, WAIT--YOU'RE WEARING THE FAMILY CREST!
YOU'RE WORKING FOR MY FAMILY? KEEPING TABS?

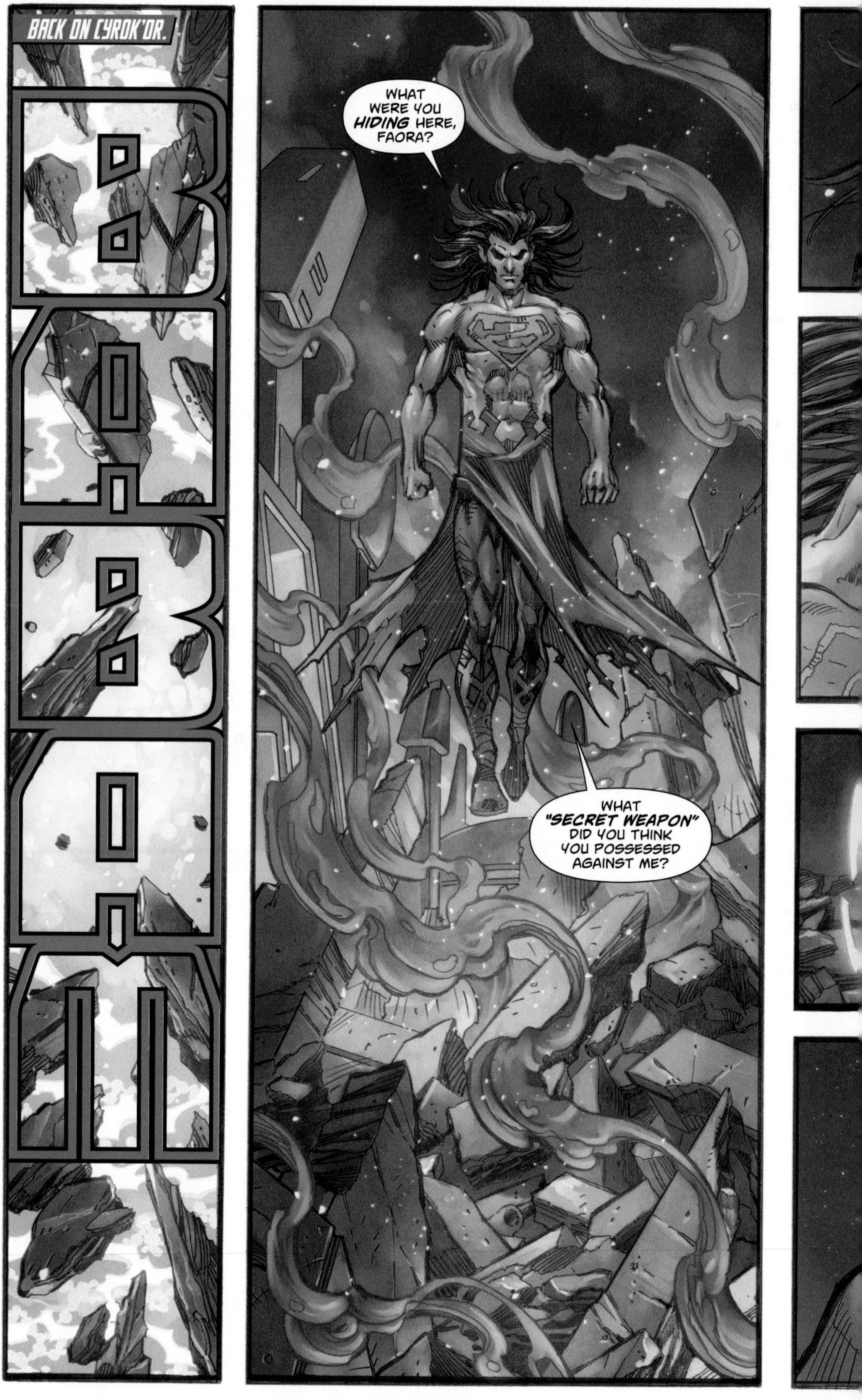
BACK ON CYROK'DR.
WHAT WERE YOU HIDING HERE, FAORA?
WHAT "SECRET WEAPON" DID YOU THINK YOU POSSESSED AGAINST ME?

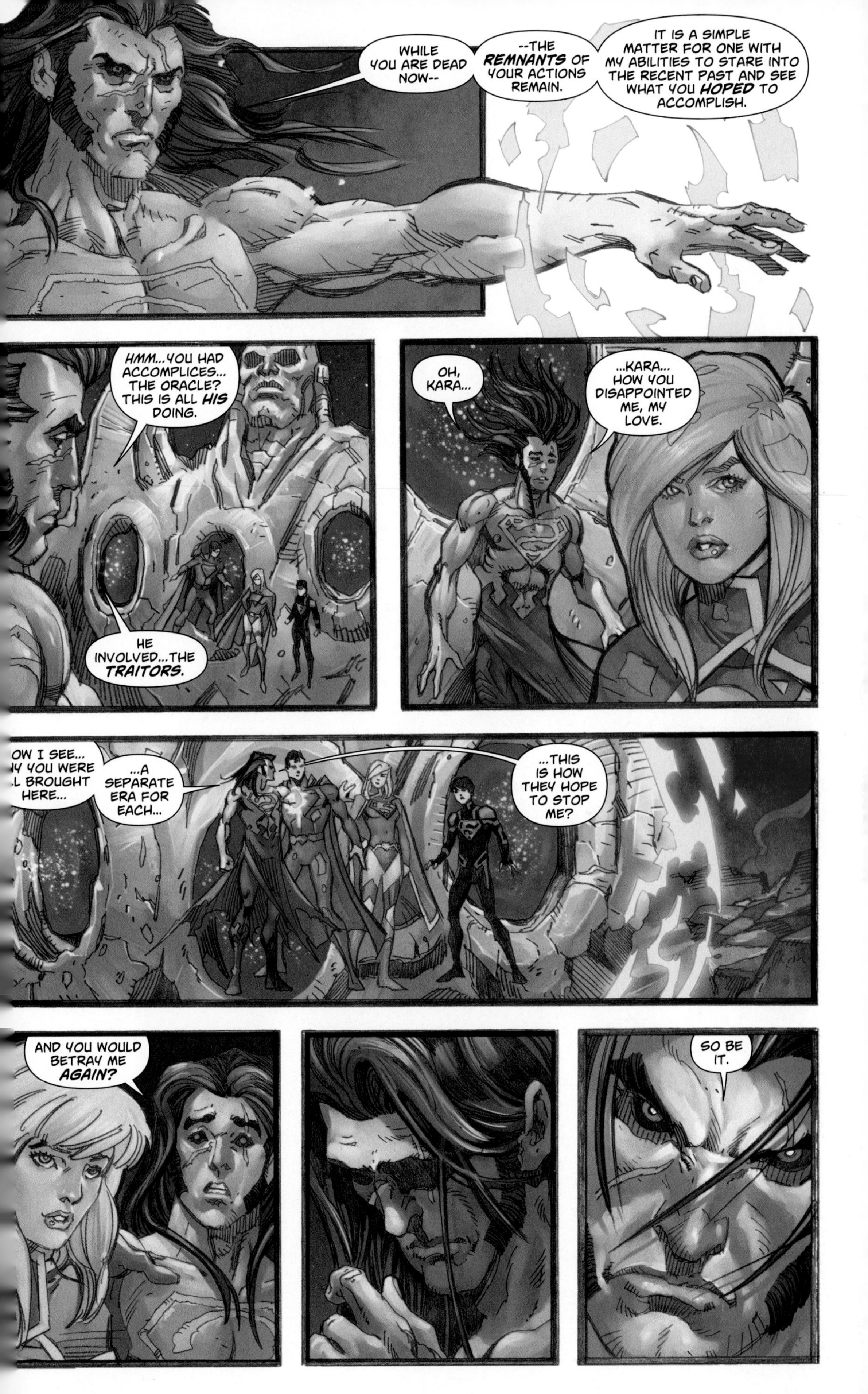
WHILE YOU ARE DEAD NOW--
--THE REMNANTS OF YOUR ACTIONS REMAIN.
IT IS A SIMPLE MATTER FOR ONE WITH MY ABILITIES TO STARE INTO THE RECENT PAST AND SEE WHAT YOU HOPED TO ACCOMPLISH.
HMM...YOU HAD ACCOMPLICES... THE ORACLE? THIS IS ALL HIS DOING.
HE INVOLVED...THE TRAITORS.
OH, KARA...
...KARA... HOW YOU DISAPPOINTED ME, MY LOVE.
OW I SEE... Y YOU WERE L BROUGHT HERE...
...A SEPARATE ERA FOR EACH...
...THIS IS HOW THEY HOPE TO STOP ME?
AND YOU WOULD BETRAY ME AGAIN?
SO BE IT.

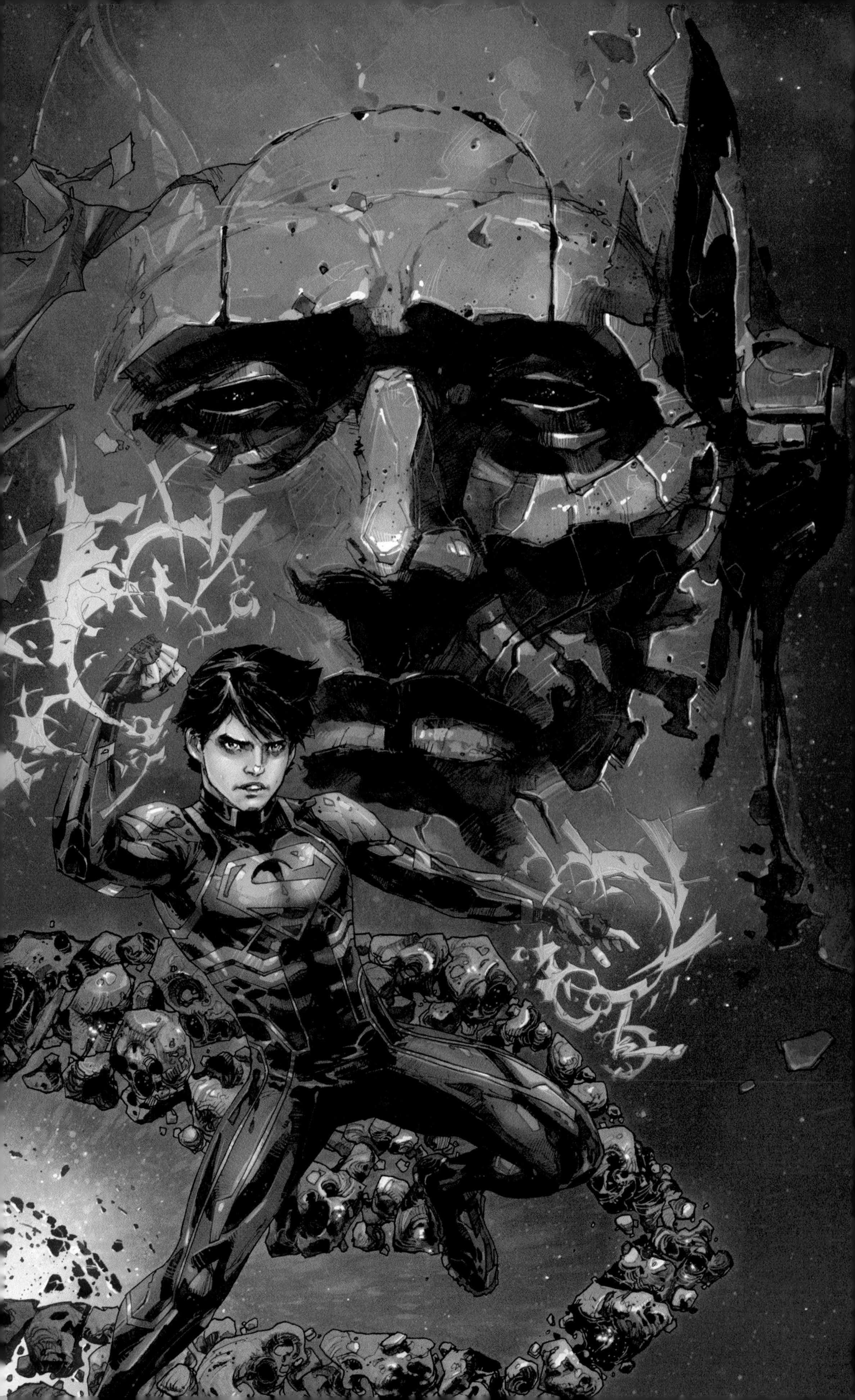

KRYPTON RETURNS PART TWO

SCOTT LOBDELL plot **SCOTT LOBDELL JUSTIN JORDAN MICHAEL ALAN NELSON** dialogue **ED BENES** artist
TANYA HORIE RICHARD HORIE colorists cover art by **KENNETH ROCAFORT**

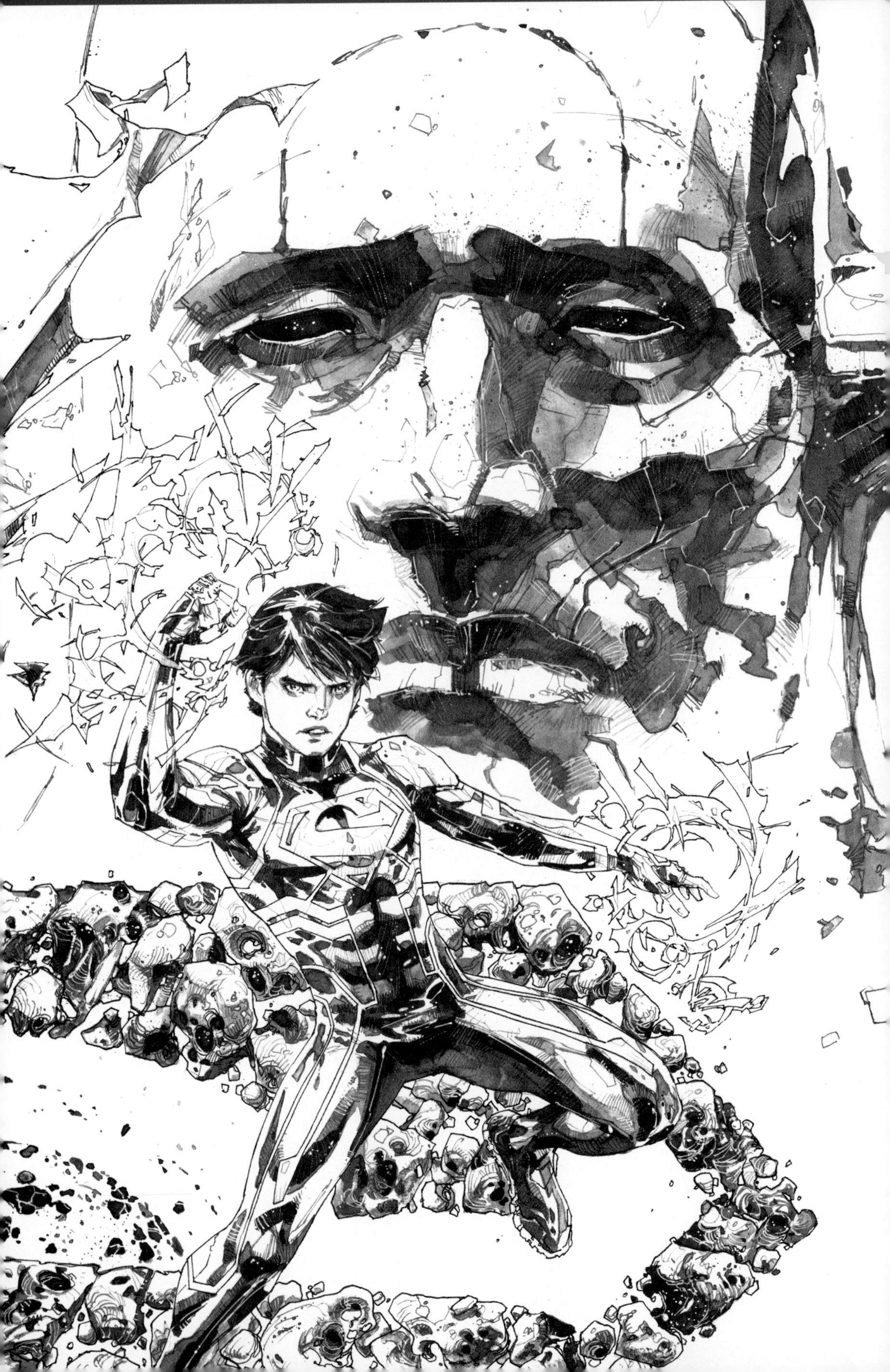

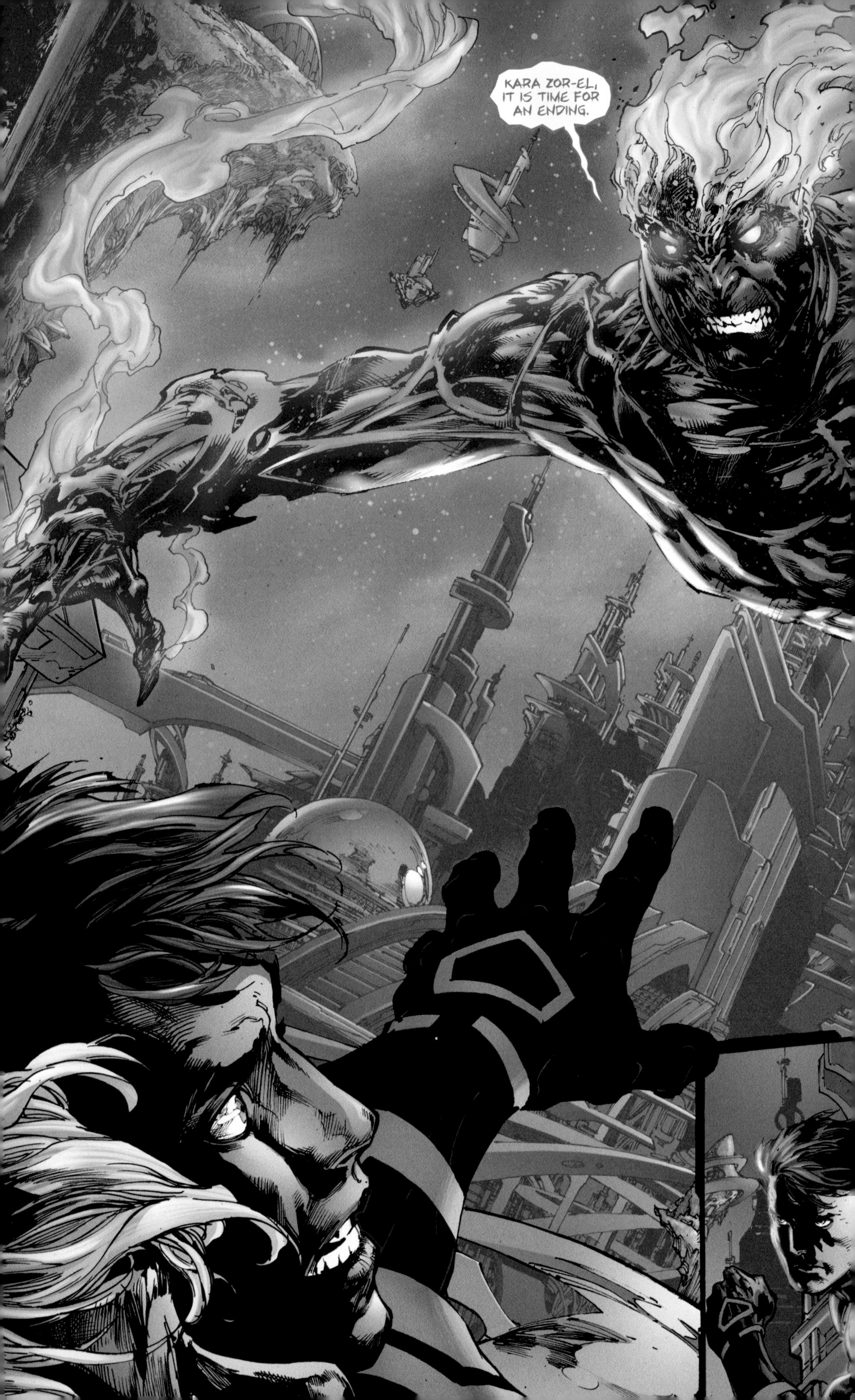
KARA ZOR-EL, IT IS TIME FOR AN ENDING.

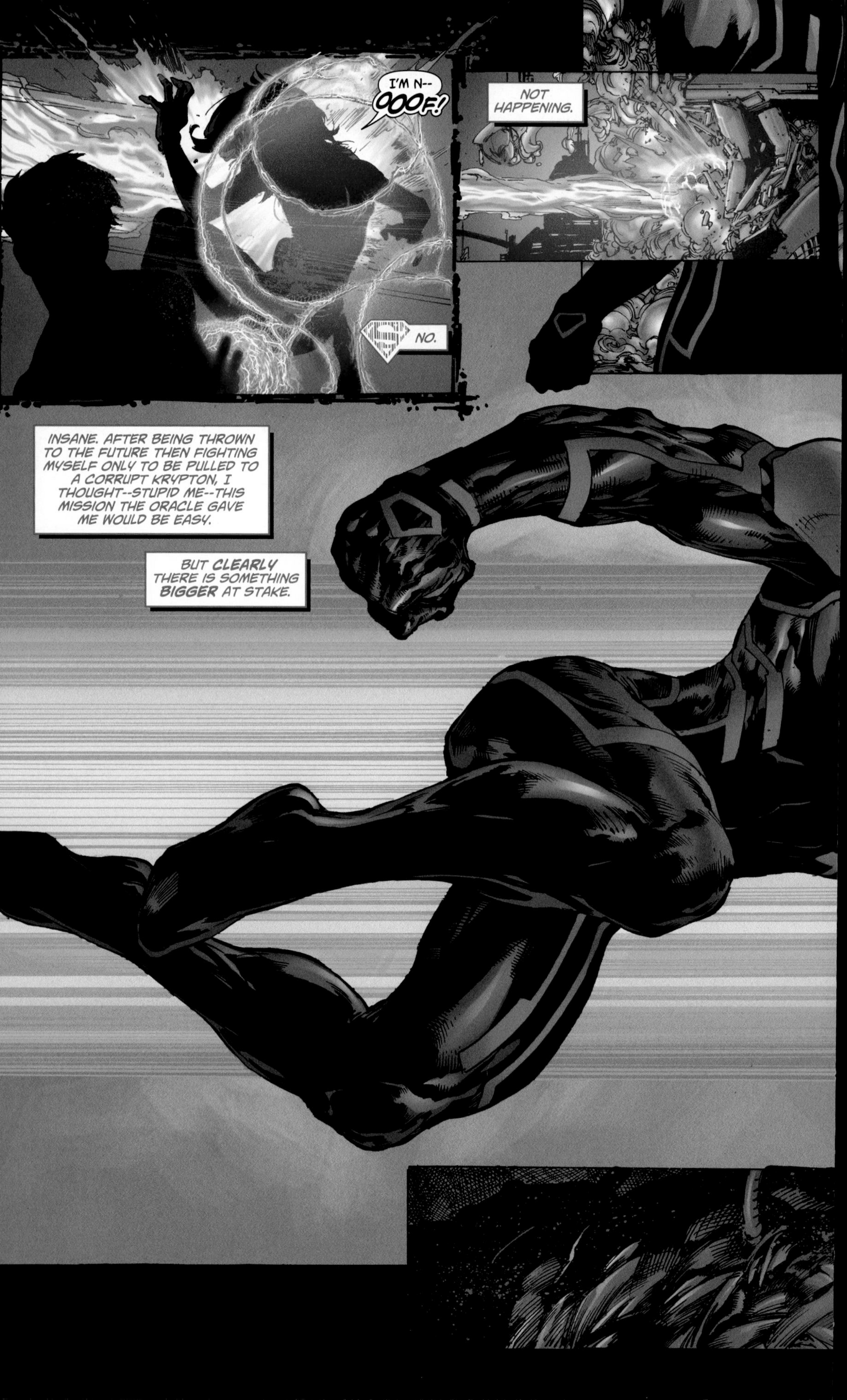
I'M N--
OOOF!
NOT HAPPENING.
NO.
INSANE. AFTER BEING THROWN TO THE FUTURE THEN FIGHTING MYSELF ONLY TO BE PULLED TO A CORRUPT KRYPTON, I THOUGHT--STUPID ME--THIS MISSION THE ORACLE GAVE ME WOULD BE EASY.
BUT CLEARLY THERE IS SOMETHING BIGGER AT STAKE.

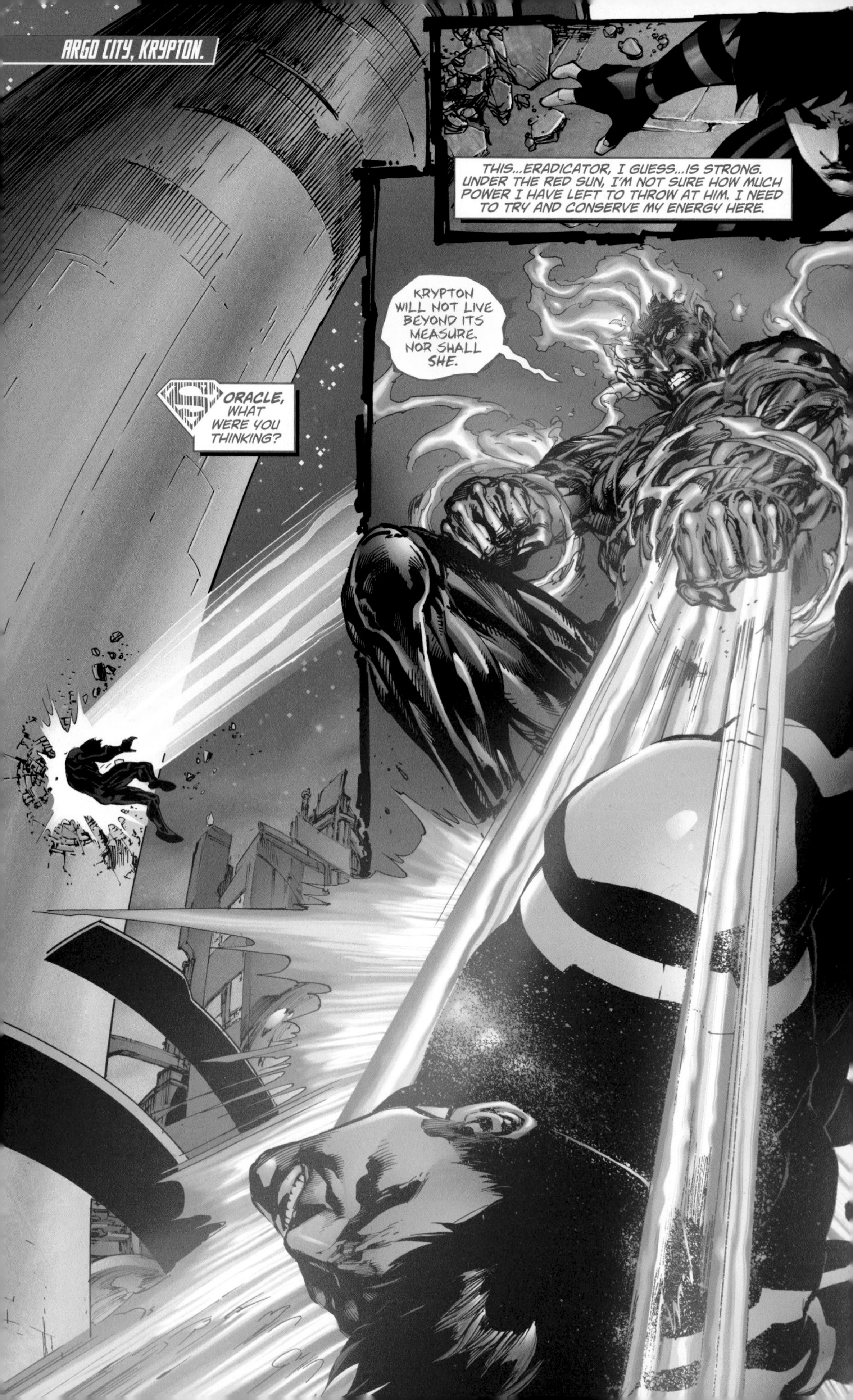
ARGO CITY, KRYPTON.
THIS...ERADICATOR, I GUESS...IS STRONG. UNDER THE RED SUN, I'M NOT SURE HOW MUCH POWER I HAVE LEFT TO THROW AT HIM. I NEED TO TRY AND CONSERVE MY ENERGY HERE.
KRYPTON WILL NOT LIVE BEYOND ITS MEASURE. NOR SHALL SHE.
ORACLE, WHAT WERE YOU THINKING?

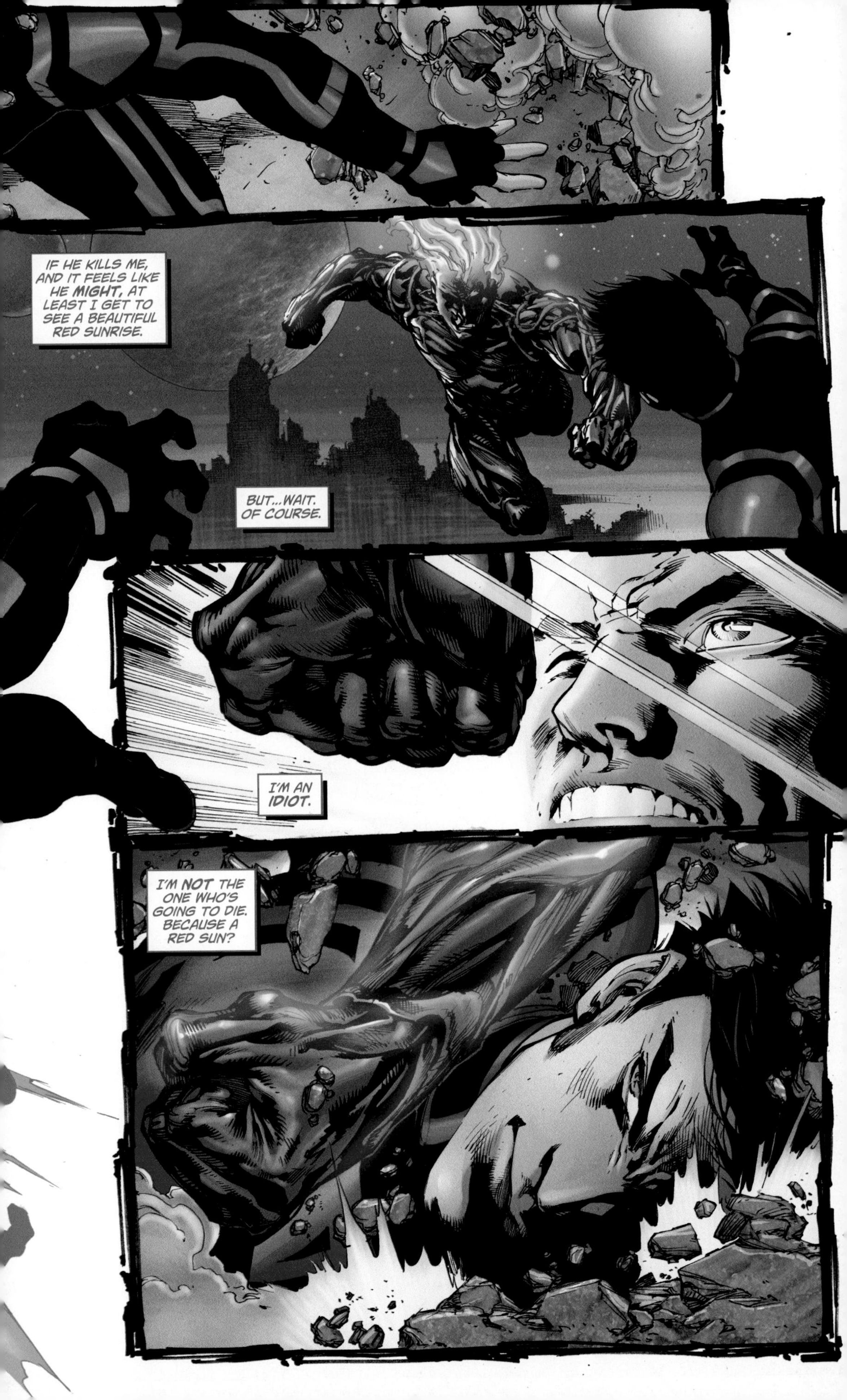
IF HE KILLS ME, AND IT FEELS LIKE HE MIGHT, AT LEAST I GET TO SEE A BEAUTIFUL RED SUNRISE.
BUT...WAIT. OF COURSE.
I'M AN IDIOT.
I'M NOT THE ONE WHO'S GOING TO DIE. BECAUSE A RED SUN?

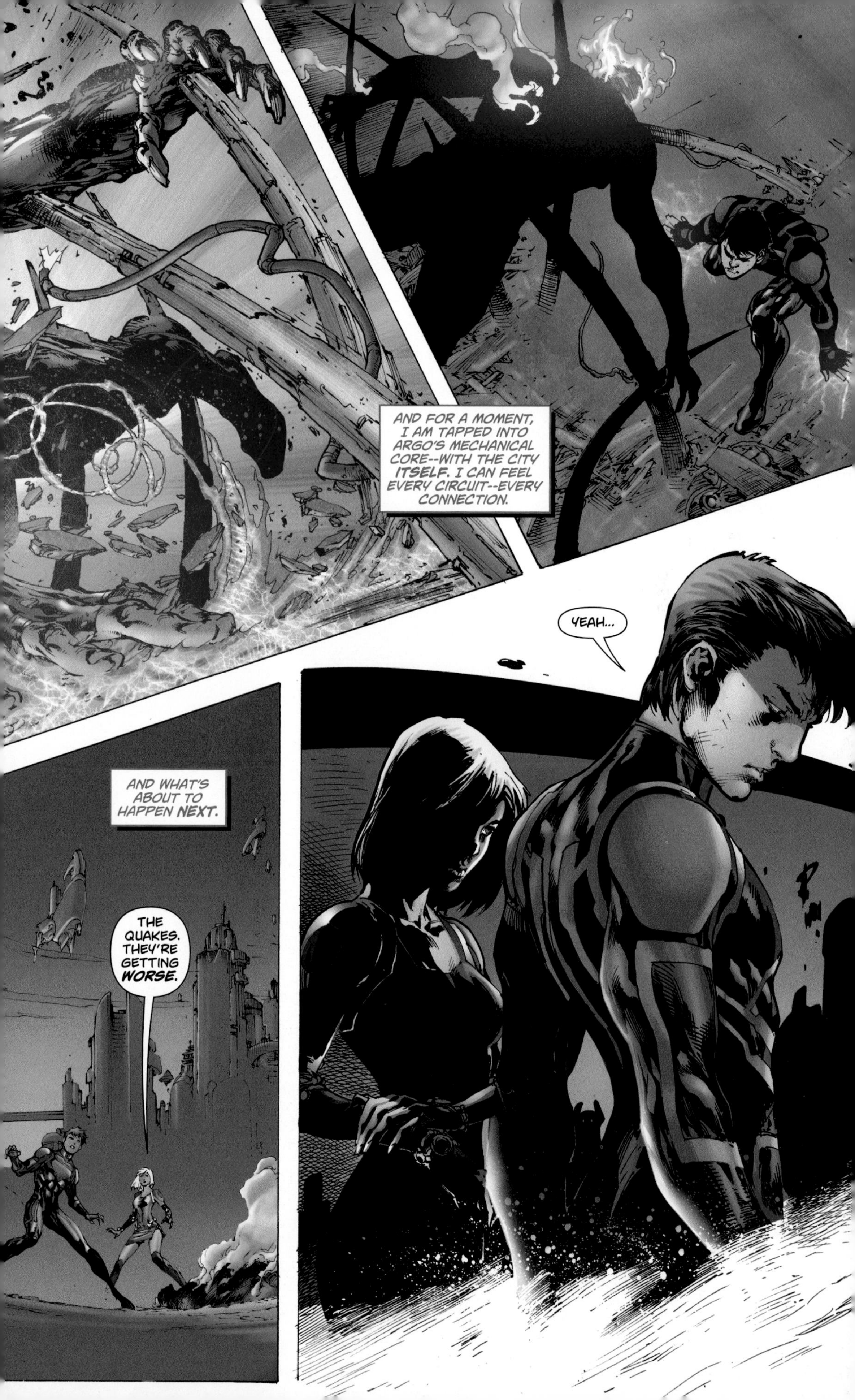
AND FOR A MOMENT, I AM TAPPED INTO ARGO'S MECHANICAL CORE--WITH THE CITY ITSELF. I CAN FEEL EVERY CIRCUIT--EVERY CONNECTION.
AND WHAT'S ABOUT TO HAPPEN NEXT.
THE QUAKES. THEY'RE GETTING WORSE.
YEAH...

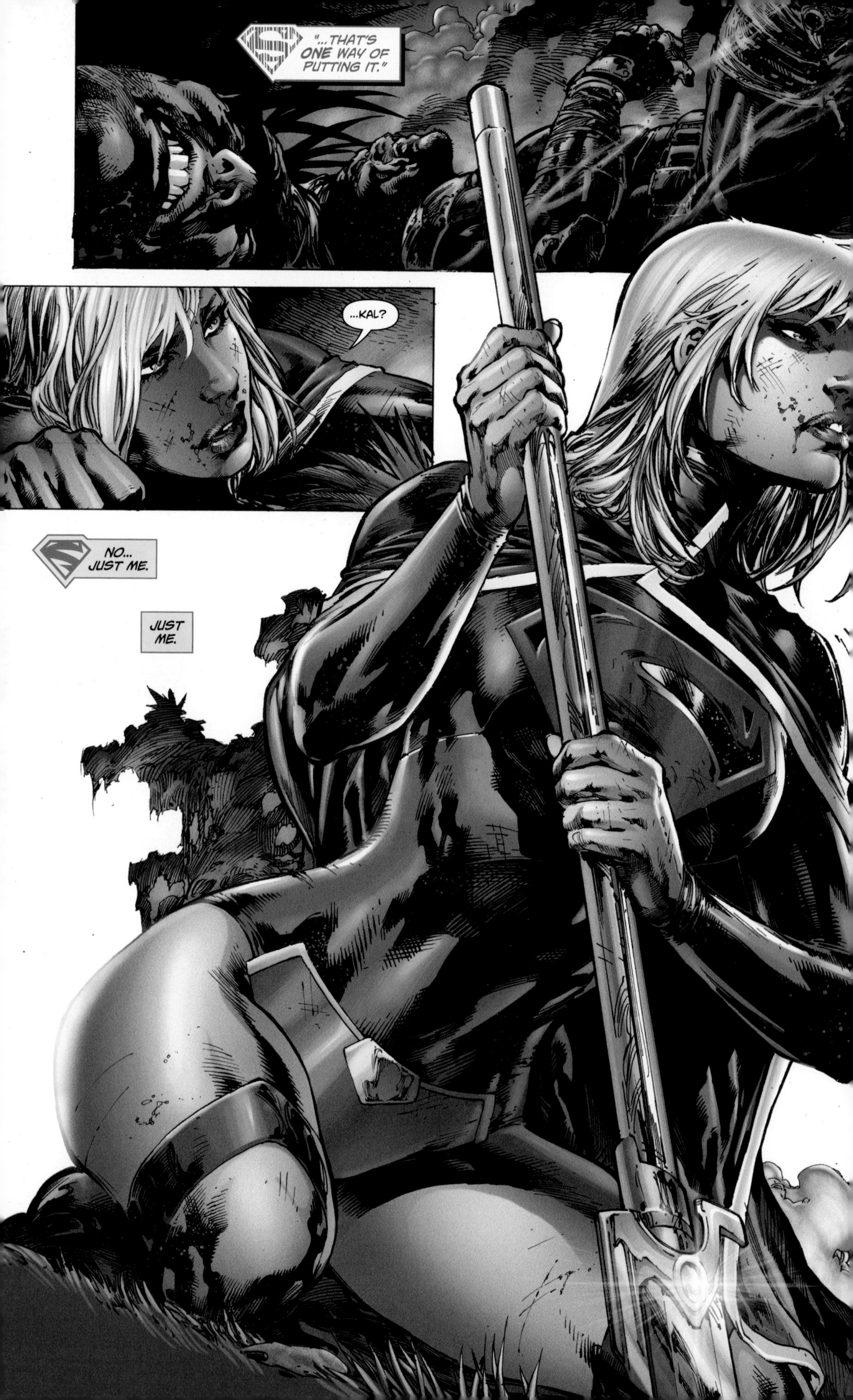
"...THAT'S ONE WAY OF PUTTING IT."
...KAL?
NO... JUST ME.
JUST ME.

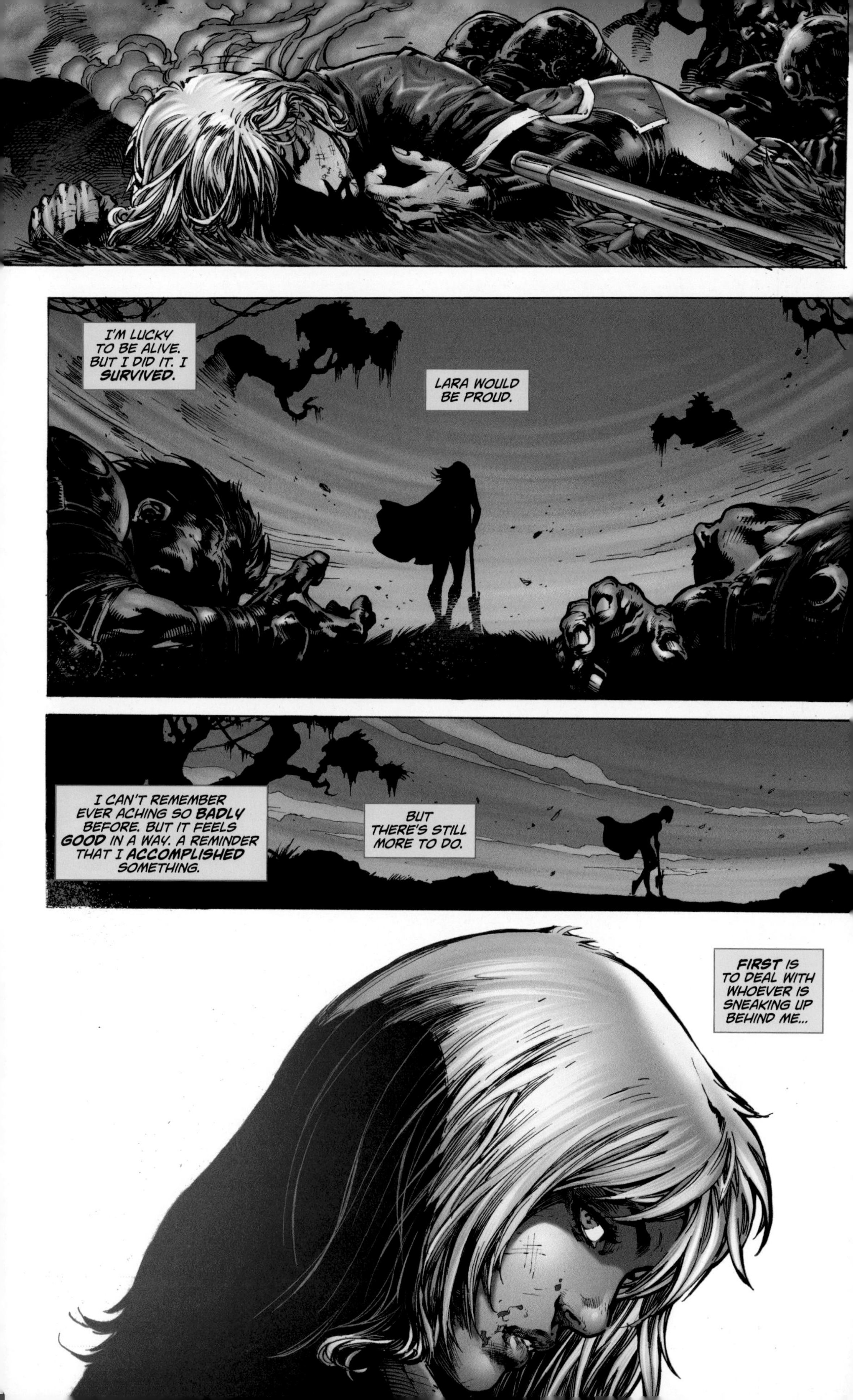
I'M LUCKY TO BE ALIVE. BUT I DID IT. I SURVIVED.
LARA WOULD BE PROUD.
I CAN'T REMEMBER EVER ACHING SO BADLY BEFORE. BUT IT FEELS GOOD IN A WAY. A REMINDER THAT I ACCOMPLISHED SOMETHING.
BUT THERE'S STILL MORE TO DO.
FIRST IS TO DEAL WITH WHOEVER IS SNEAKING UP BEHIND ME...

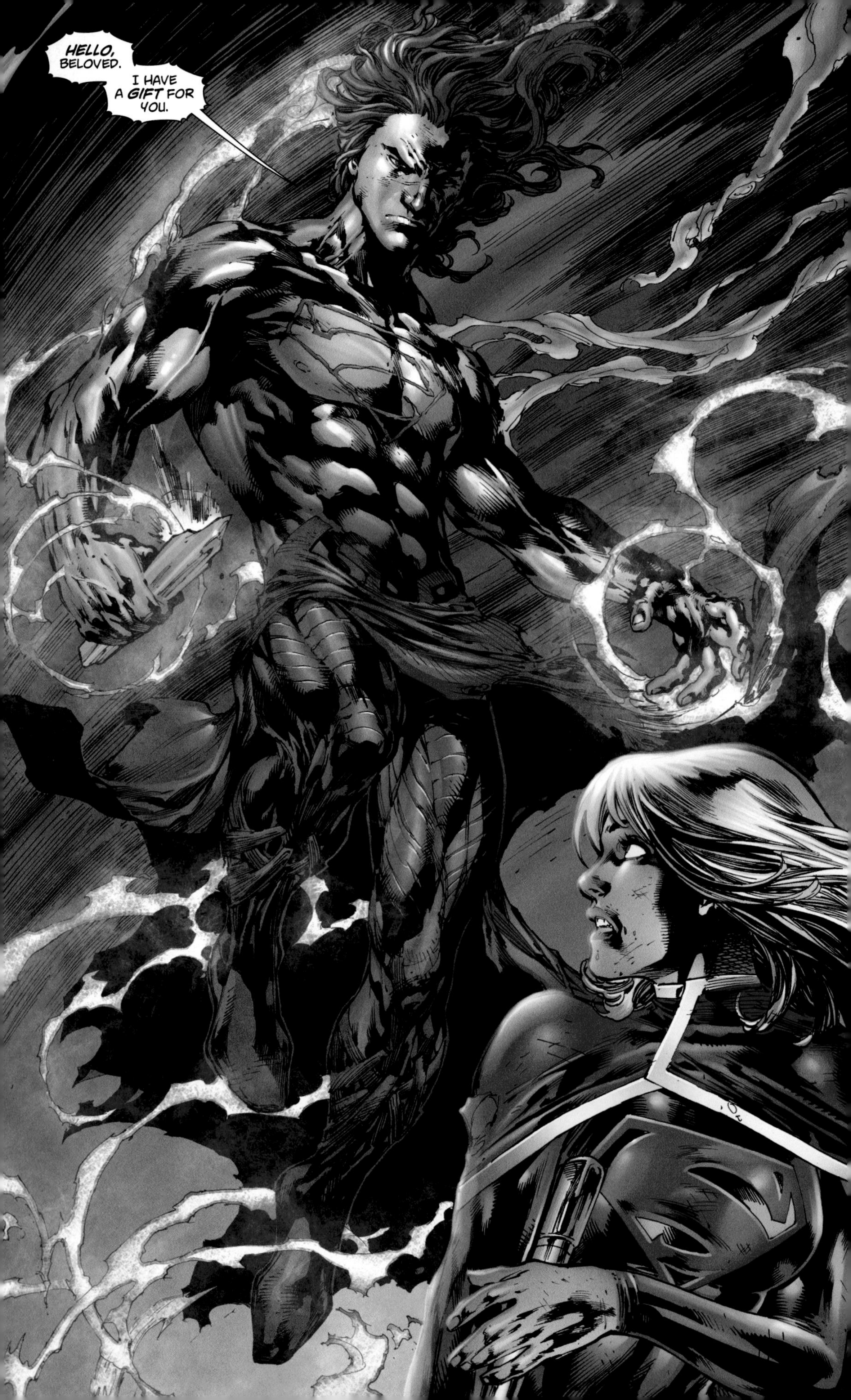
HELLO, BELOVED.
I HAVE A GIFT FOR YOU.

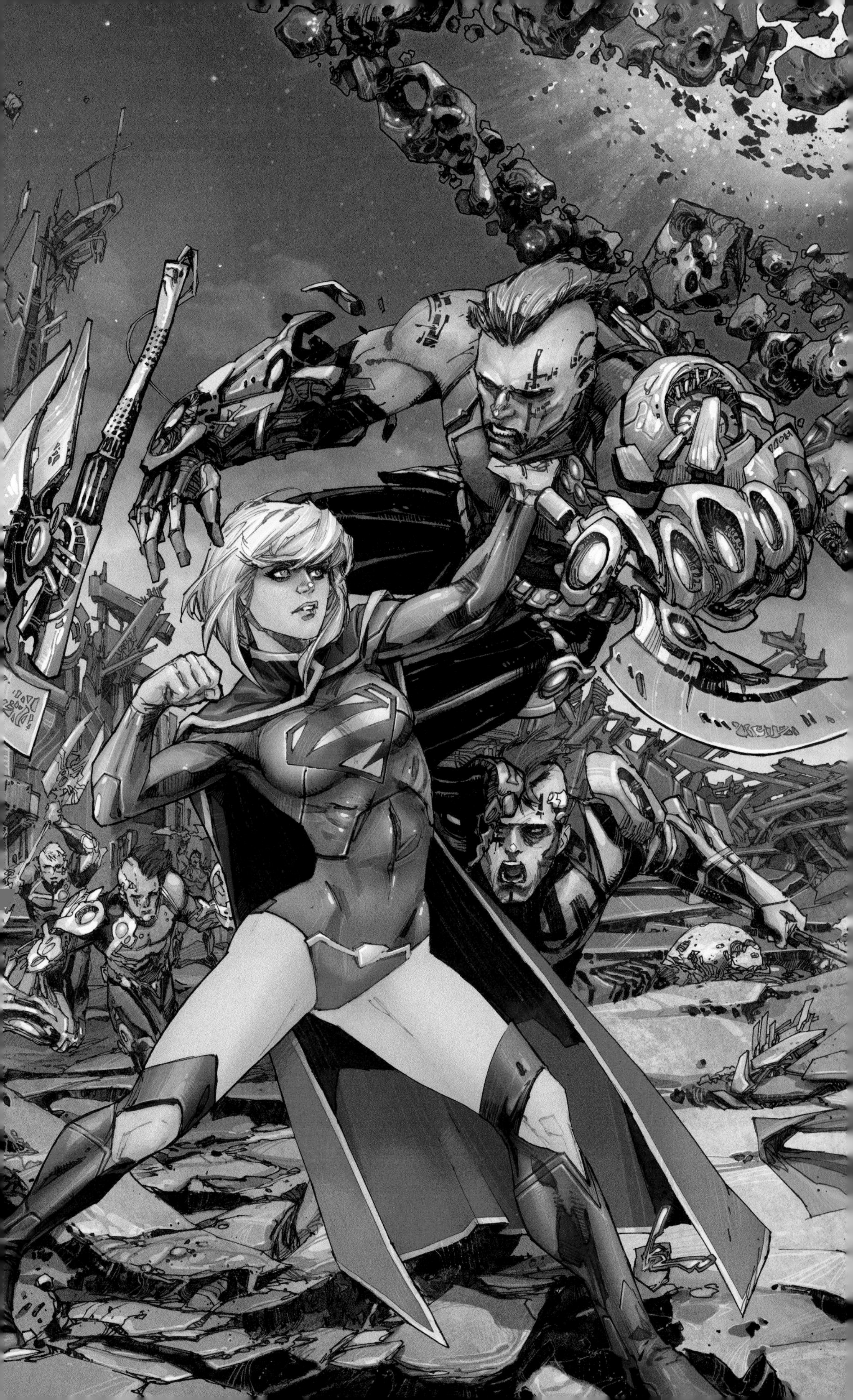

KRYPTON RETURNS PART THREE

SCOTT LOBDELL plot **SCOTT LOBDELL JUSTIN JORDAN MICHAEL ALAN NELSON** dialogue **PAULO SIQUEIRA** artist

HI-FI colorist cover art by **KENNETH ROCAFORT**

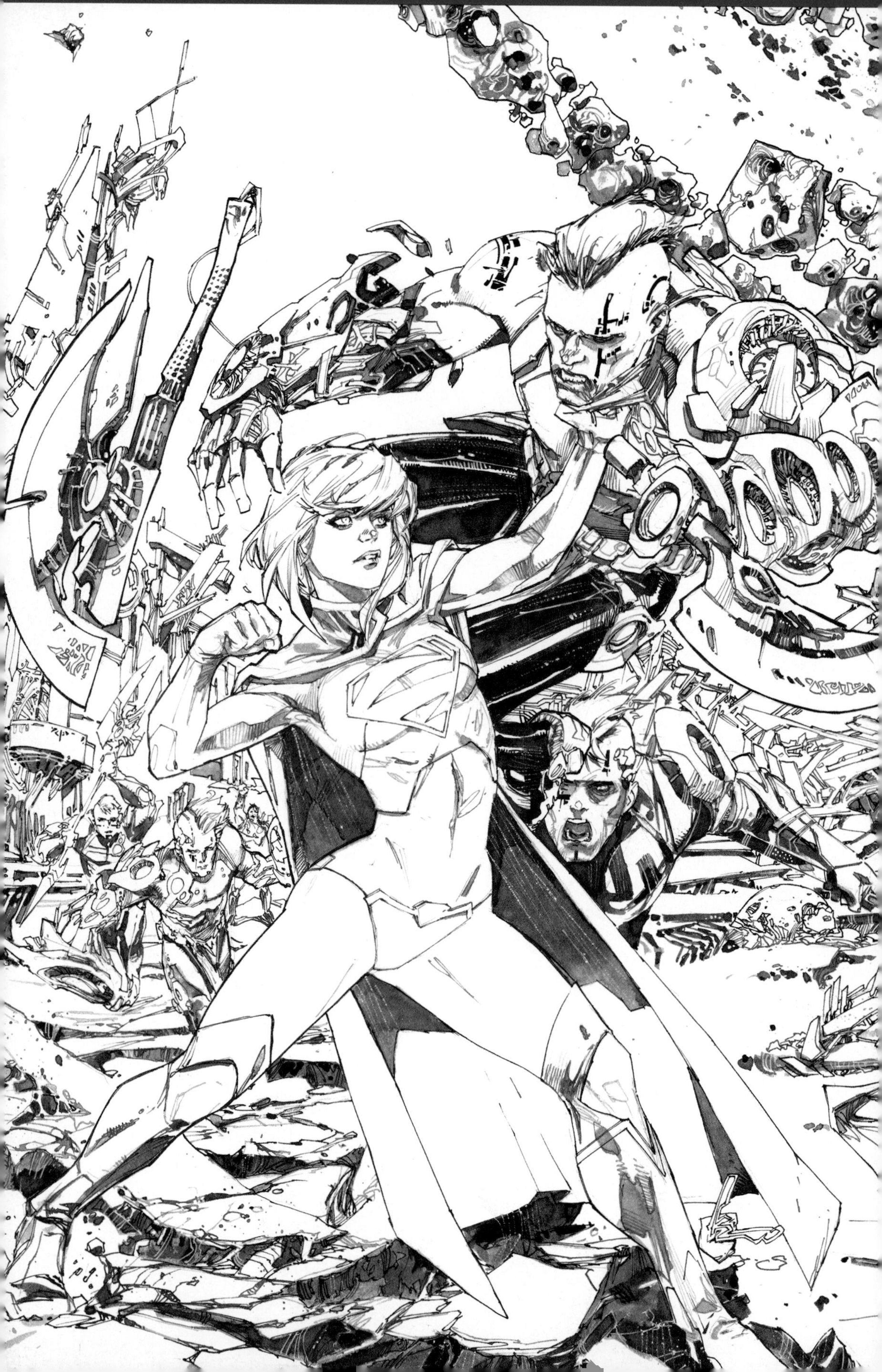

ALL THE OMNIVERSE IS THREATENED...

A TIME TSUNAMI-- A WAVE OF TIME DISTORTION-- HAS BEGUN WASHING AWAY ALL THAT IS.

BROUGHT ABOUT BY THE MACHINATIONS OF THE FAUX KRYPTONIAN KNOWN AS H'EL.

BUT EVEN AS THE COSMIC ENTITY THAT IS ORACLE BEARS SILENT WITNESS TO THE CHRONAL CATACLYSM--HIS MIND IS ELSEWHERE.

HE IS OBSERVING THE THREE CHAMPIONS HE DISPATCHED THROUGH TIME IN ORDER TO PREVENT THE INEVITABLE.

SUPERBOY.

SUPERGIRL.

AND EARTH'S GREATEST DEFENDER, SUPERMAN

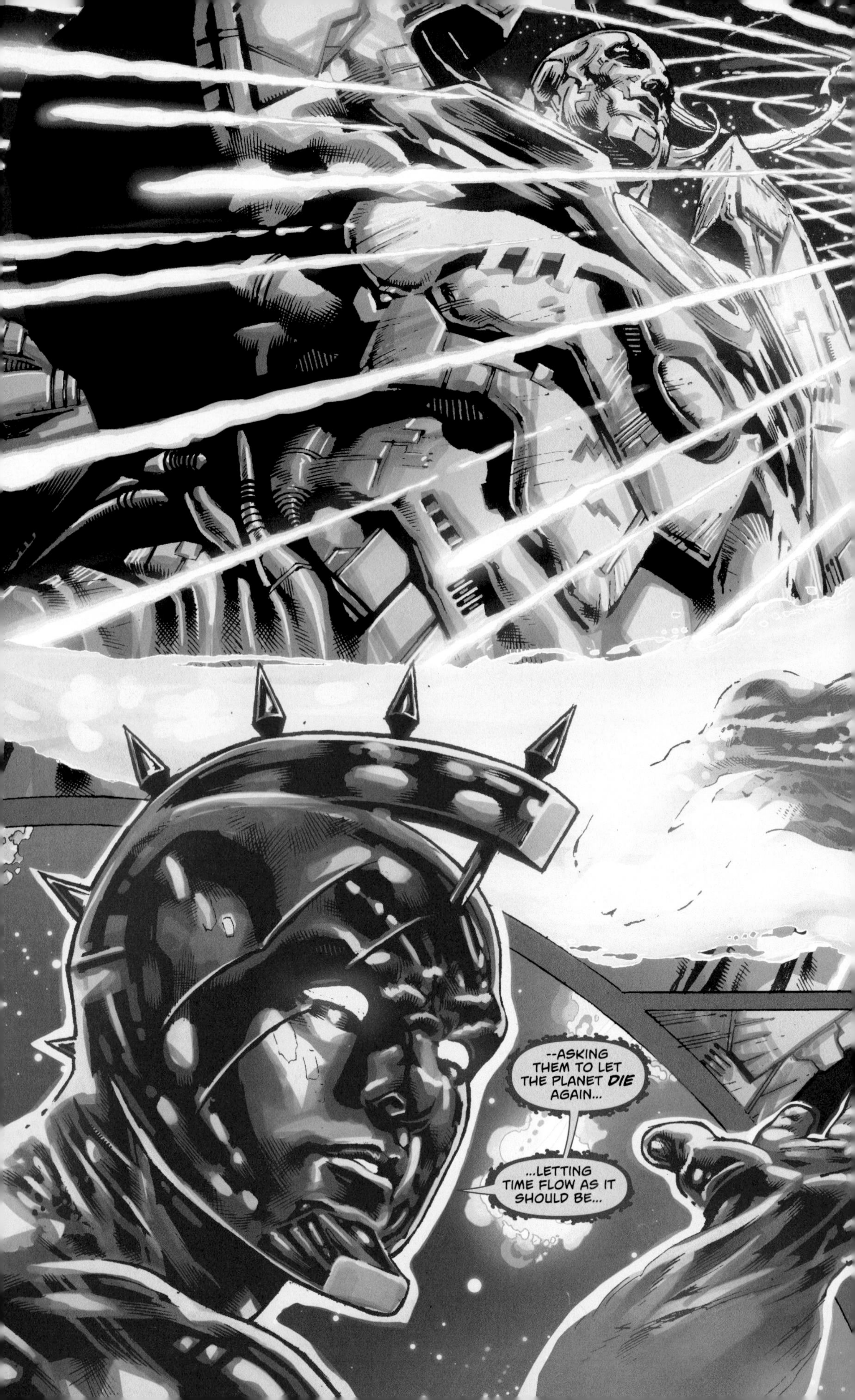
--ASKING THEM TO LET THE PLANET DIE AGAIN...
...LETTING TIME FLOW AS IT SHOULD BE...

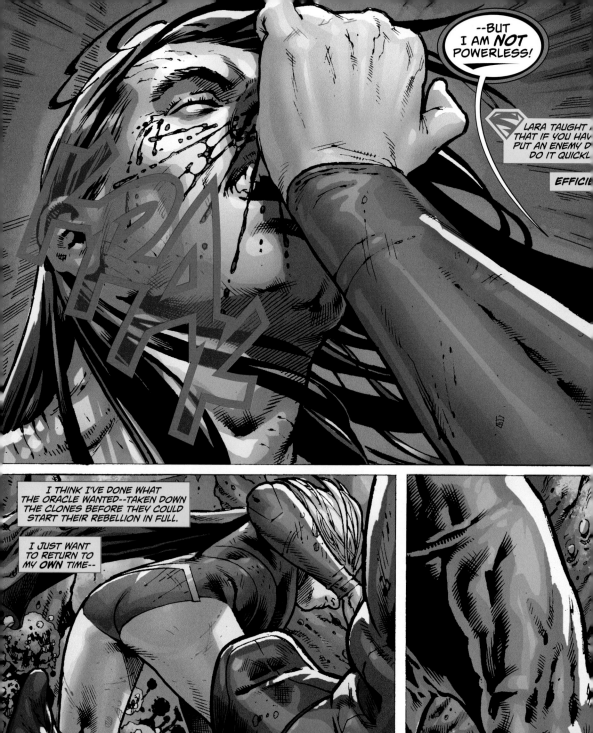

--BUT I AM *NOT* POWERLESS!

LARA TAUGHT
THAT IF YOU HAV
PUT AN ENEMY D
DO IT QUICKL

EFFICIE

I THINK I'VE DONE WHAT THE ORACLE WANTED--TAKEN DOWN THE CLONES BEFORE THEY COULD START THEIR REBELLION IN FULL.

I JUST WANT TO RETURN TO MY *OWN* TIME--

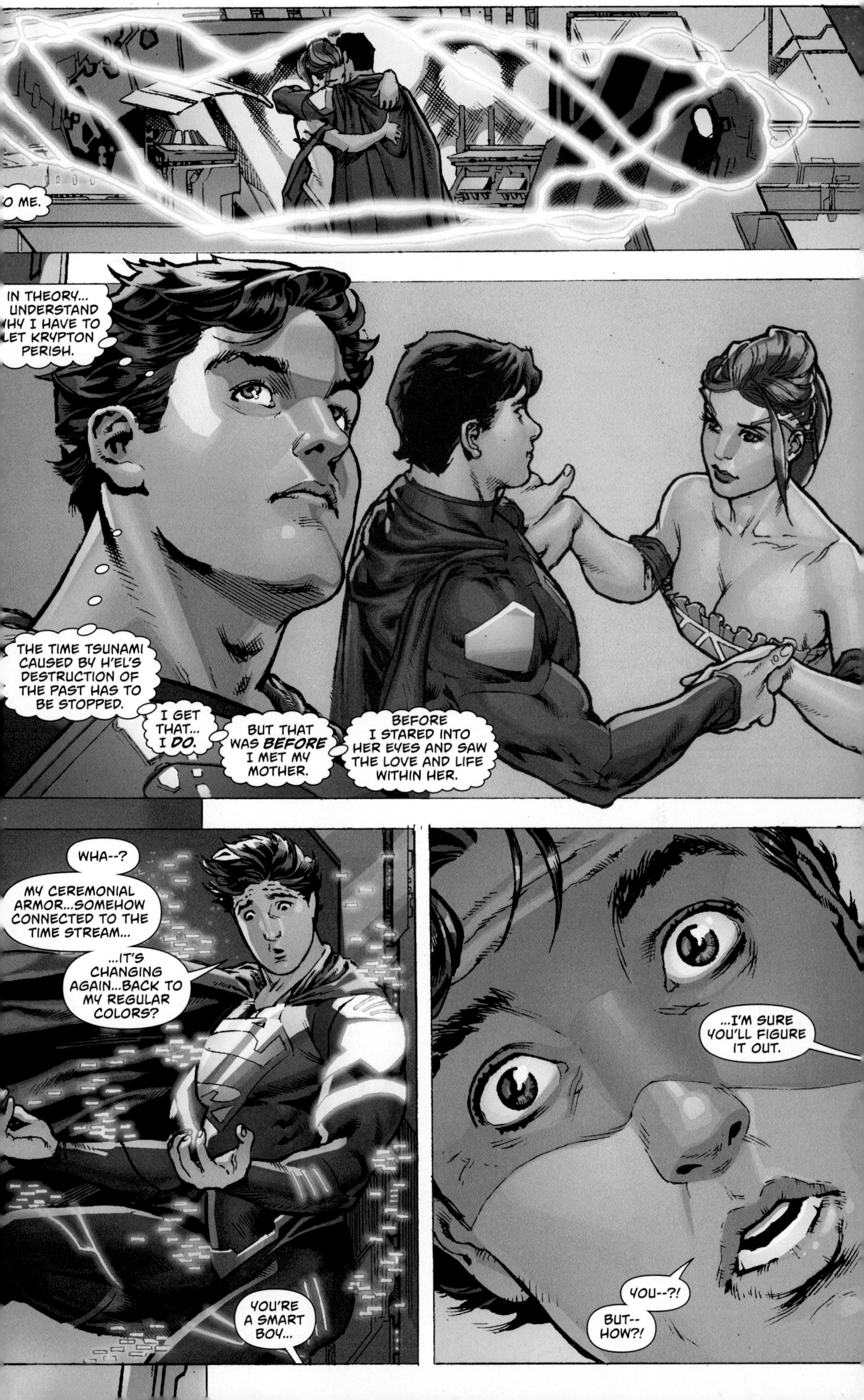
O ME.
IN THEORY... UNDERSTAND HY I HAVE TO LET KRYPTON PERISH.
THE TIME TSUNAMI CAUSED BY H'EL'S DESTRUCTION OF THE PAST HAS TO BE STOPPED.
I GET THAT... I DO.
BUT THAT WAS BEFORE I MET MY MOTHER.
BEFORE I STARED INTO HER EYES AND SAW THE LOVE AND LIFE WITHIN HER.
WHA--?
MY CEREMONIAL ARMOR...SOMEHOW CONNECTED TO THE TIME STREAM...
...IT'S CHANGING AGAIN...BACK TO MY REGULAR COLORS?
YOU'RE A SMART BOY...
...I'M SURE YOU'LL FIGURE IT OUT.
YOU--?!
BUT-- HOW?!

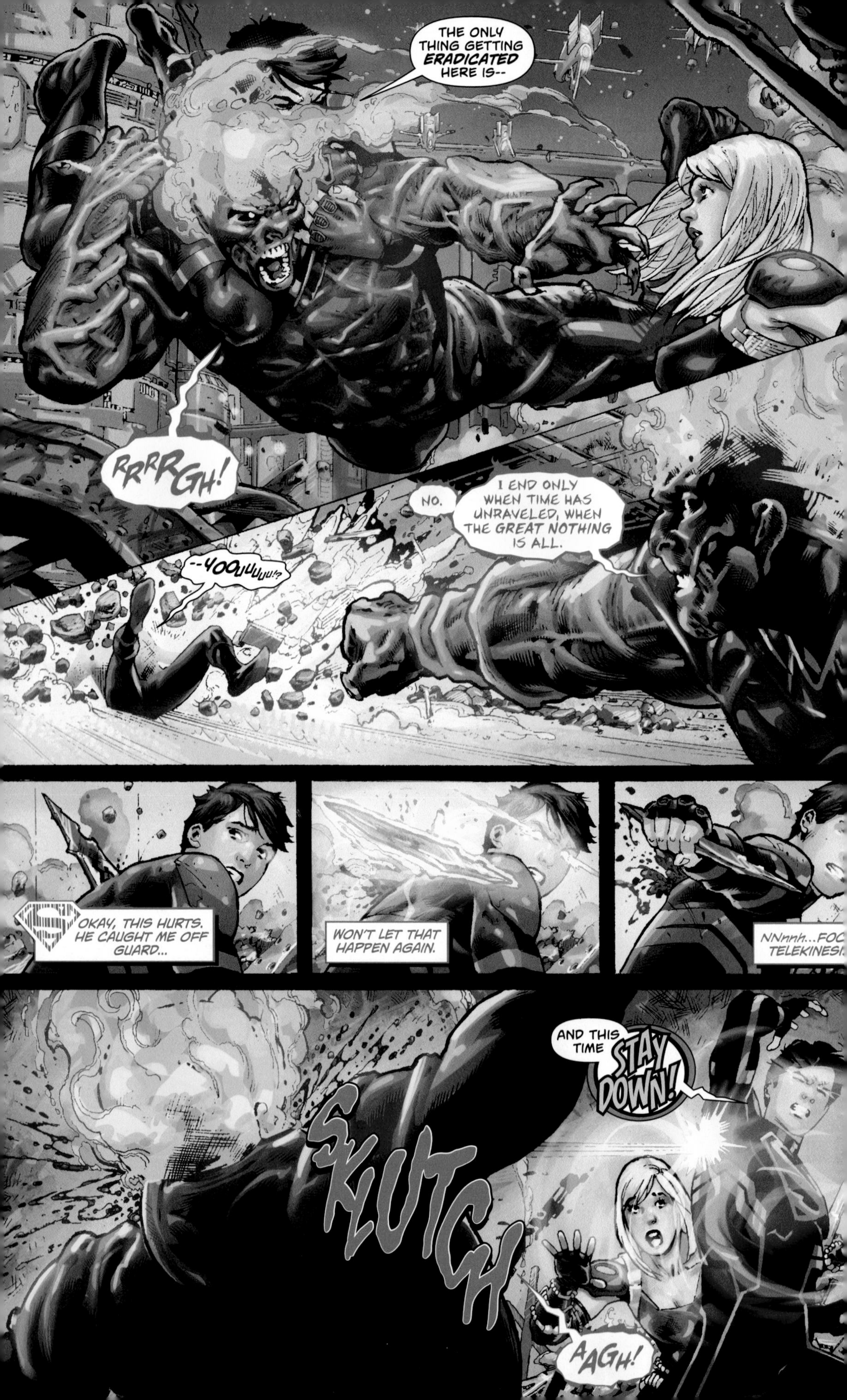
THE ONLY THING GETTING ERADICATED HERE IS--
RRRRGH!
--YOOUUUUU!?
NO.
I END ONLY WHEN TIME HAS UNRAVELED, WHEN THE GREAT NOTHING IS ALL.
OKAY, THIS HURTS. HE CAUGHT ME OFF GUARD...
WON'T LET THAT HAPPEN AGAIN.
NNnnh...FOC
TELEKINESI
AND THIS TIME
STAY DOWN!
SKLUTCH
AAGH!

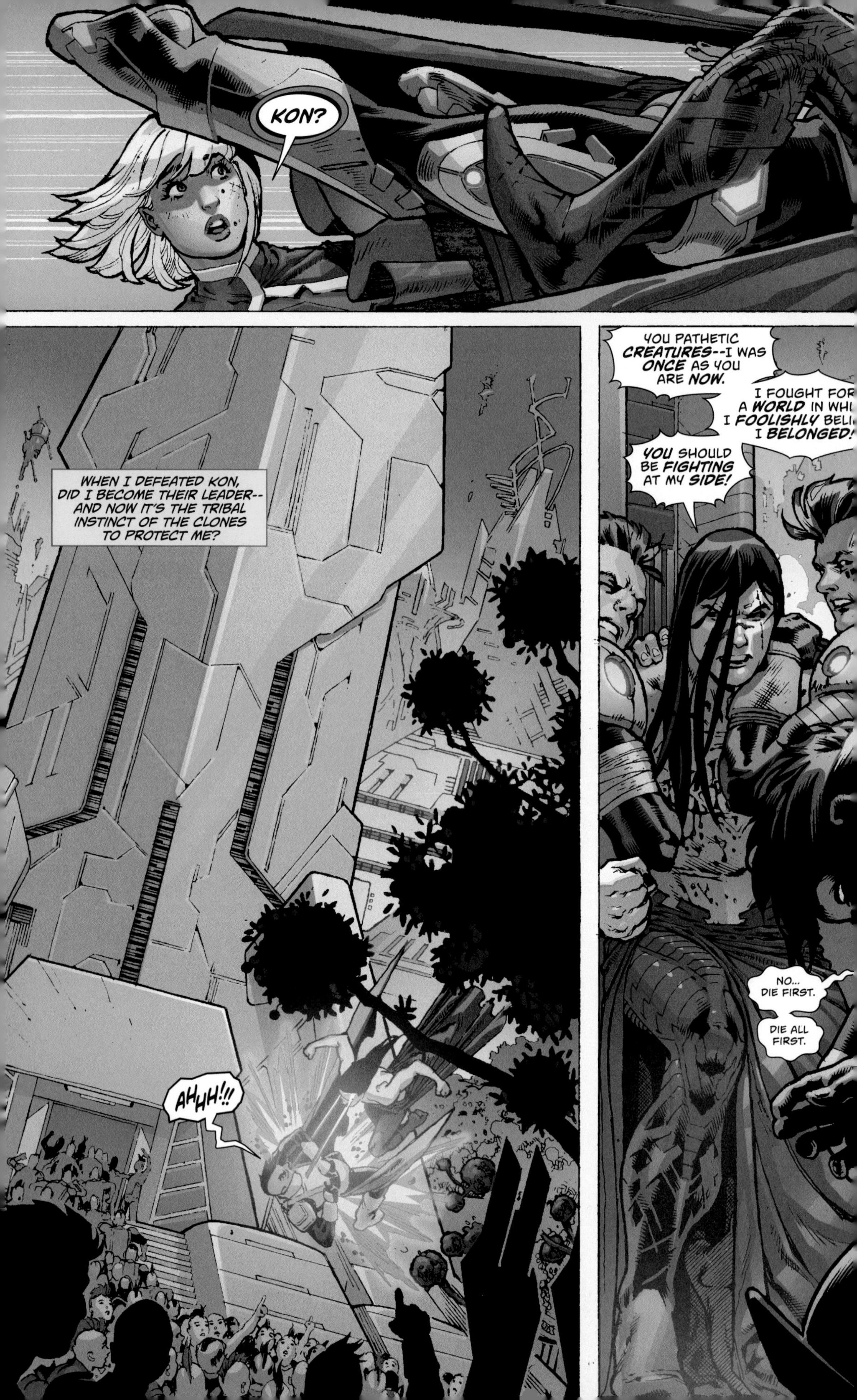
KON?
WHEN I DEFEATED KON, DID I BECOME THEIR LEADER-- AND NOW IT'S THE TRIBAL INSTINCT OF THE CLONES TO PROTECT ME?
AHHH!!!
YOU PATHETIC CREATURES--I WAS ONCE AS YOU ARE NOW.
I FOUGHT FOR A WORLD IN WHI I FOOLISHLY BELI I BELONGED!
YOU SHOULD BE FIGHTING AT MY SIDE!
NO... DIE FIRST.
DIE ALL FIRST.

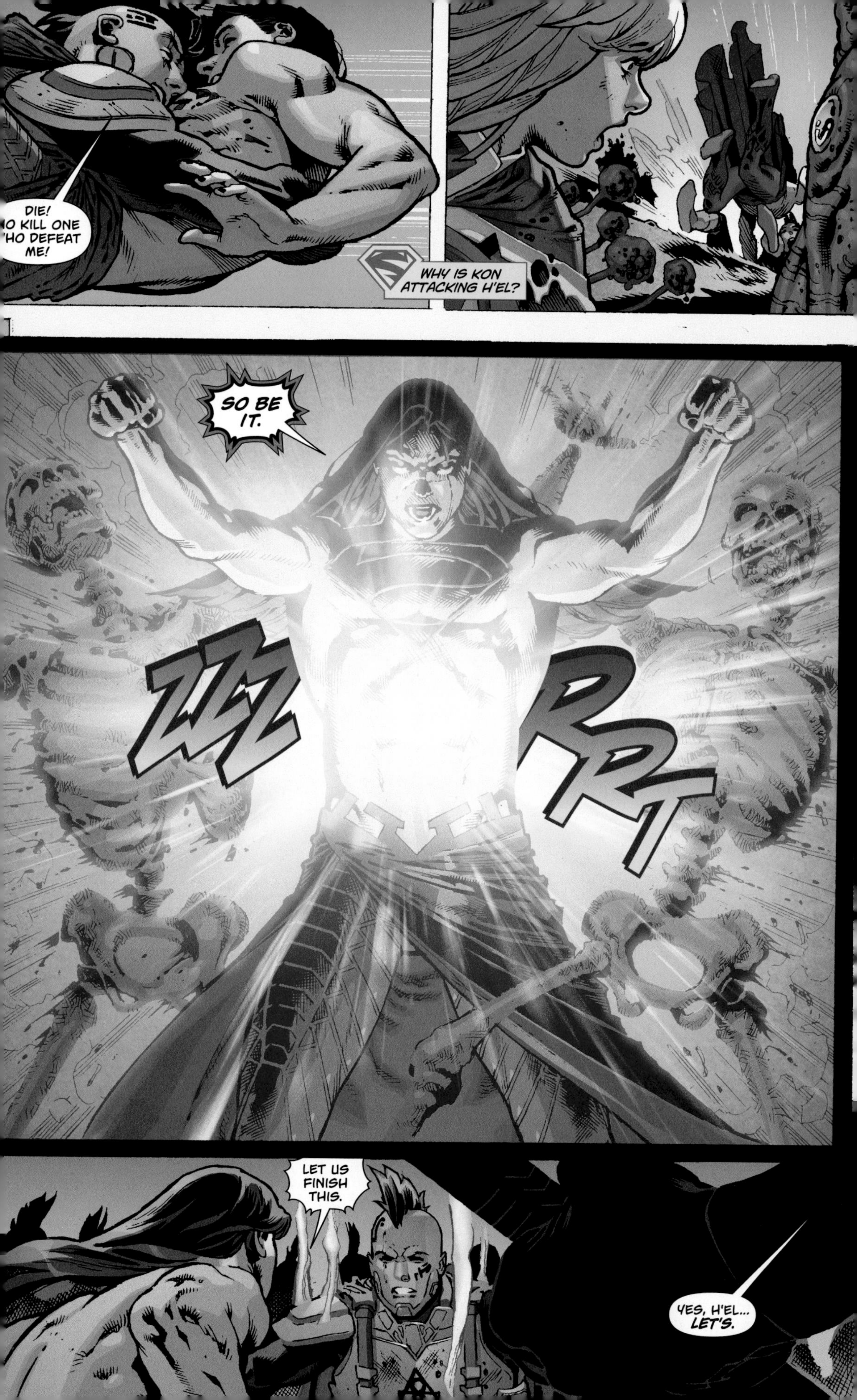
DIE!
O KILL ONE
HO DEFEAT
ME!
WHY IS KON
ATTACKING H'EL?
SO BE
IT.
ZZZ
RRT
LET US
FINISH
THIS.
YES, H'EL...
LET'S.

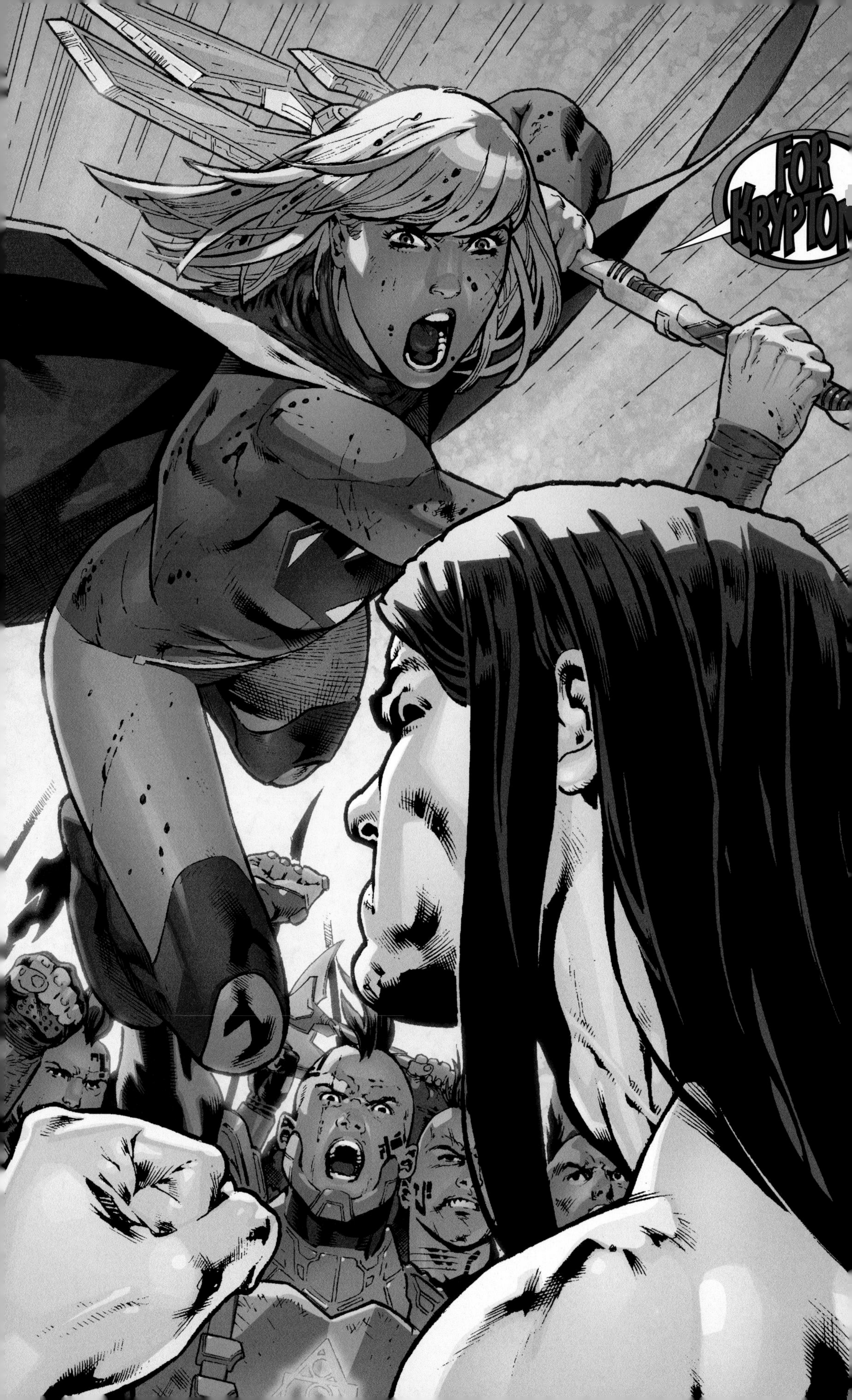
FOR KRYPTON

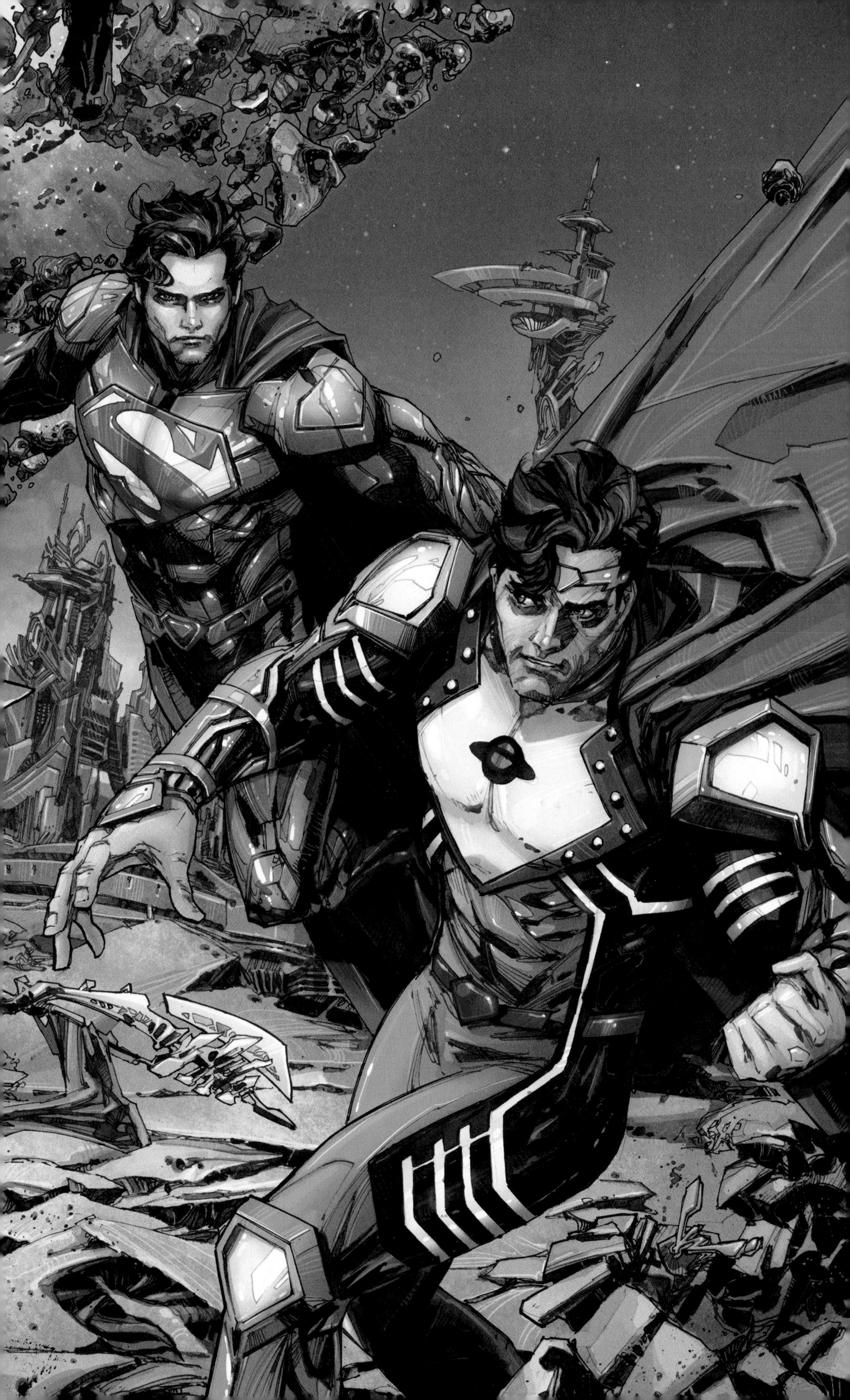

KRYPTON RETURNS PART FOUR

SCOTT LOBDELL writer **KENNETH ROCAFORT** artist **BLOND** colorist
cover art by **KENNETH ROCAFORT**

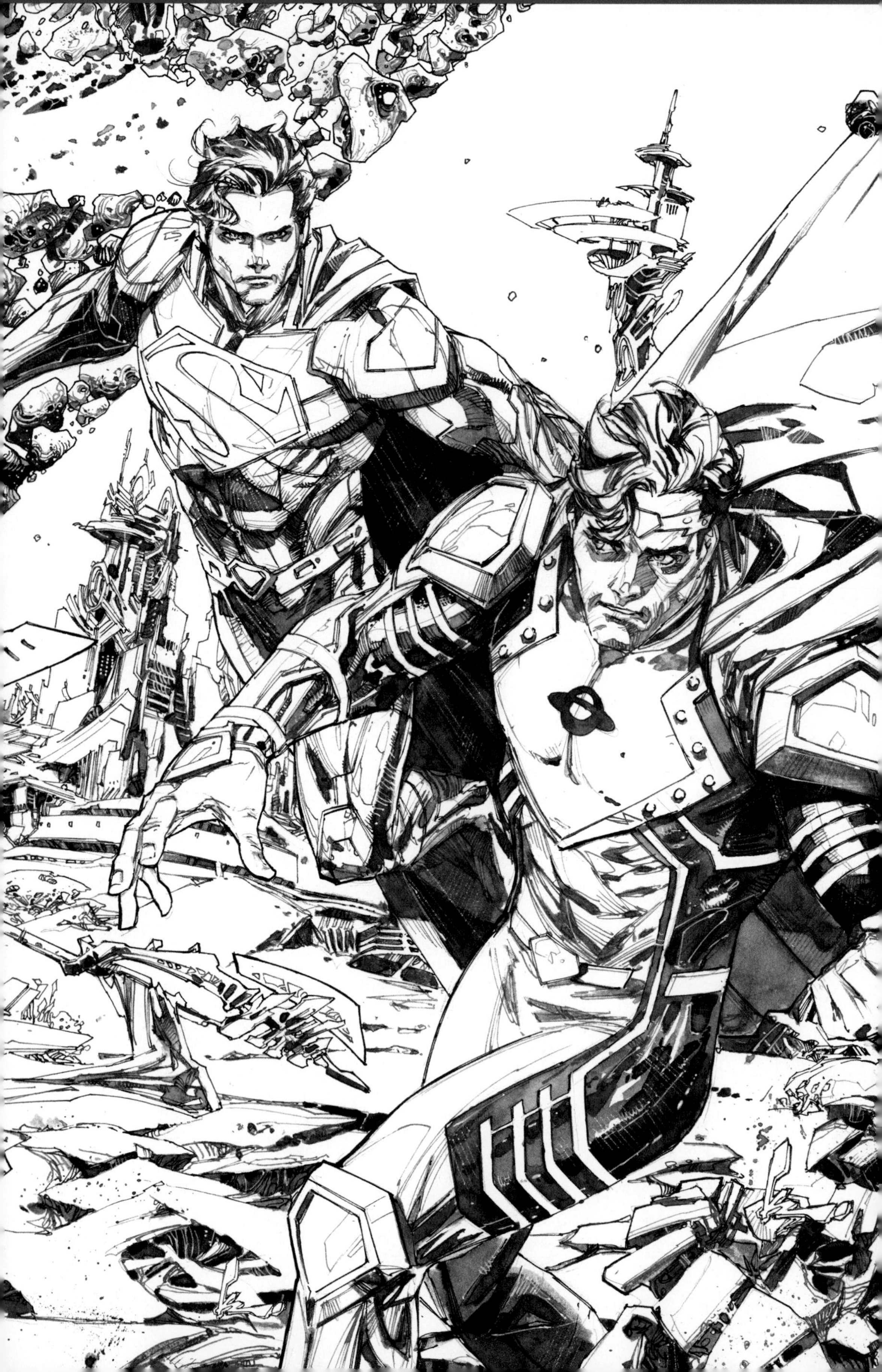

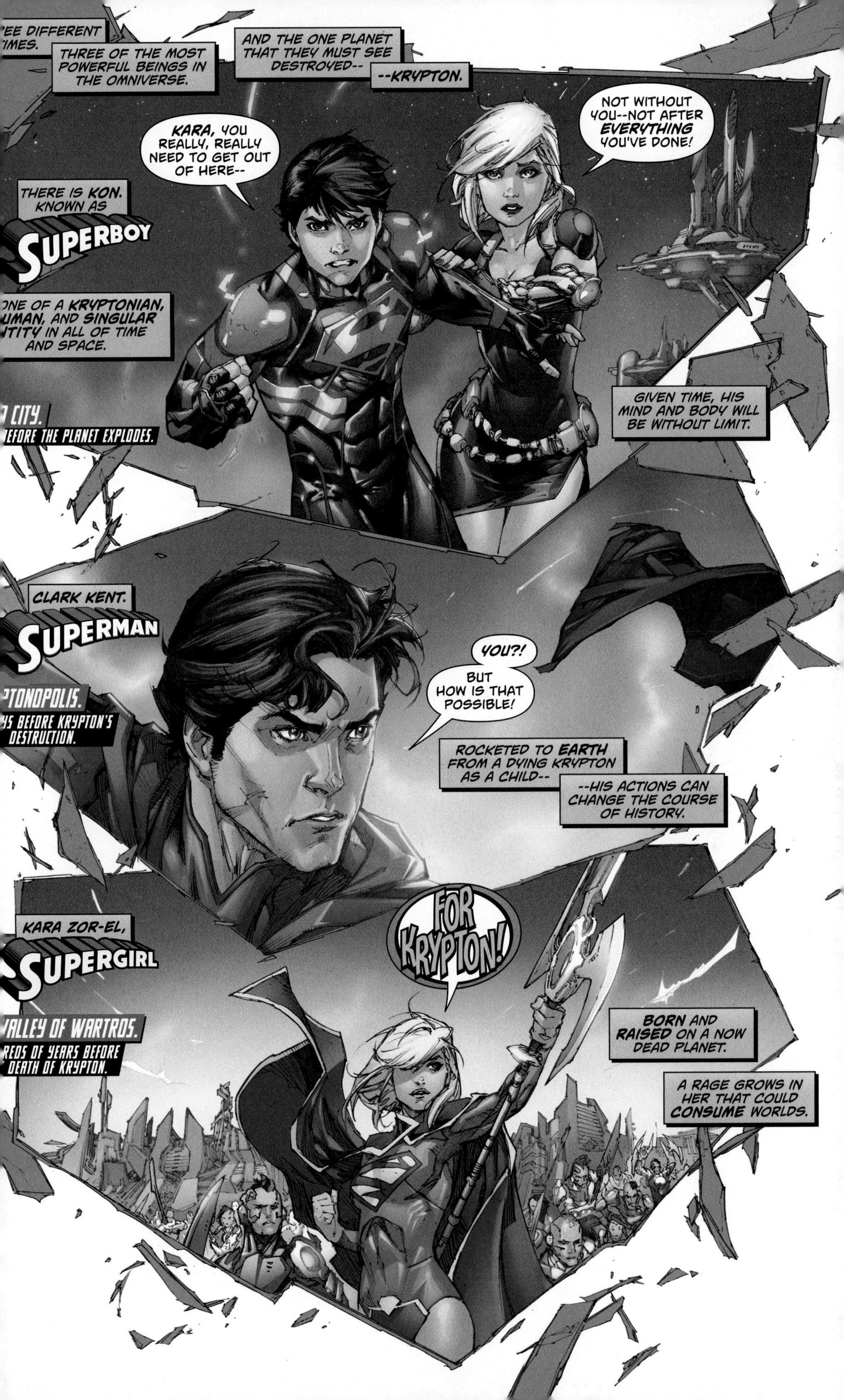
EE DIFFERENT
IMES.
THREE OF THE MOST POWERFUL BEINGS IN THE OMNIVERSE.
AND THE ONE PLANET THAT THEY MUST SEE DESTROYED--
--KRYPTON.
KARA, YOU REALLY, REALLY NEED TO GET OUT OF HERE--
NOT WITHOUT YOU--NOT AFTER EVERYTHING YOU'VE DONE!
THERE IS KON. KNOWN AS
SUPERBOY
ONE OF A KRYPTONIAN, UMAN, AND SINGULAR NTITY IN ALL OF TIME AND SPACE.
CITY.
EFORE THE PLANET EXPLODES.
GIVEN TIME, HIS MIND AND BODY WILL BE WITHOUT LIMIT.
CLARK KENT.
SUPERMAN
PTONOPOLIS.
YS BEFORE KRYPTON'S DESTRUCTION.
YOU?!
BUT HOW IS THAT POSSIBLE!
ROCKETED TO EARTH FROM A DYING KRYPTON AS A CHILD--
--HIS ACTIONS CAN CHANGE THE COURSE OF HISTORY.
KARA ZOR-EL,
SUPERGIRL
FOR KRYPTON!
VALLEY OF WARTROS.
REDS OF YEARS BEFORE DEATH OF KRYPTON.
BORN AND RAISED ON A NOW DEAD PLANET.
A RAGE GROWS IN HER THAT COULD CONSUME WORLDS.

RRUMMBLE

THE QUAKES?

IT FEELS LIKE THE PLANET IS *TEARING* ITSELF APART.

IT'S KRYPTON. THE ERADICATOR WAS RIGHT. THE *END* IS NEAR.

IT'S JUST AS YOUR FATHER AND UNCLE PREDICTED.

THEN *DO* SOMETHING!

I WILL, KARA.

I'M SORRY. I DIDN'T REALIZE YOU NEVER KNEW THE TRUTH ABOUT TONIGHT.

WH-WHAT DO YOU MEAN?

I NEED TO COME BACK HERE AND FIGURE OUT WHAT IS HAPPENING WITH THIS STRUCTURE BENEATH ARGO CITY.

WHEN I SCANNED IT DURING THE BATTLE WITH THE ERADICATOR--

--IT IS CLEARLY SOME KIND OF CITYWIDE *ANTIGRAVITY* EXPERIMENT.

BUT IT'S *NOT* POWERFUL ENOUGH TO ESCAPE KRYPTON'S EXTREME GRAVITY.

WHY WOULD I-- ...

IF THESE PEOPL DON'T GET OFF THE PLANET...

...IT IS N FAULT

MY BATTLE WITH *JON*-- THE "ORIGINAL" VERSION OF ME--WAS LIKE A MASSIVE *INSTRUCTIONAL* ON HOW TO USE MY POWERS.

I AM ABLE TO REACH INTO HER MIND AND MAKE HER *FORGET* EVER HAVING MET ME.

SO THAT... HA.

SO SHE CAN EVENTUALLY MEET ME BACK ON EARTH AND *HATE* ME JUST FOR BEING A CLONE.

I MISSED MY "RIDE BACK HOME" ALREADY. ALL THAT'S LEFT IS TO MAKE SURE YOU'RE SAFE AND TO BE *THE HERO* I ALWAYS SHOULD HAVE BEEN.

FAR INTO KRYPTON'S PAST...
HISTORICALLY, IT WAS CALLED THE KON UPRISING--AFTER ITS RUTHLESS LEADER.
THE LAST STAND OF THE CLONES WHO SOUGHT TO DESTROY THEIR CREATORS.
BUT IT TURNS OUT THE HISTORY BOOKS GOT IT WRONG.
ON THIS DAY THE CLONES RALLIED BEHIND A MYSTERIOUS YOUNG WOMAN--ME--WHO CONVINCED THEM TO BATTLE A THREAT GREATER THAN ANY KRYPTON HAD EVER KNOWN.
WITH JUST A TWIST OF MY LANCE-- I'LL HAVE WON.
BUT...CAN I DO IT?
WHAT ARE YOU WAITING FOR, KARA?
MY "BELOVED."
IT WAS A SIMPLE MATTER TO BETRAY ME ONCE BEFORE.
DON'T PRETEND YOU CARE AT ALL WHAT HAPPENS TO ME.
BY RAO! YOU'RE AN IDIOT.
I LOVED YOU.
EVEN AFTER ALL YOUR LIES...YOUR MANIPULATION.
I UNDERSTOOD WHAT YOU WANTED.
IT WAS WHAT I WANTED WITH ALL MY HEART AND SOUL.
BUT YOU FORCED MY HAND, H'EL.
AND DAMMIT IF YOU'RE NOT GOING TO DO IT AGAIN!

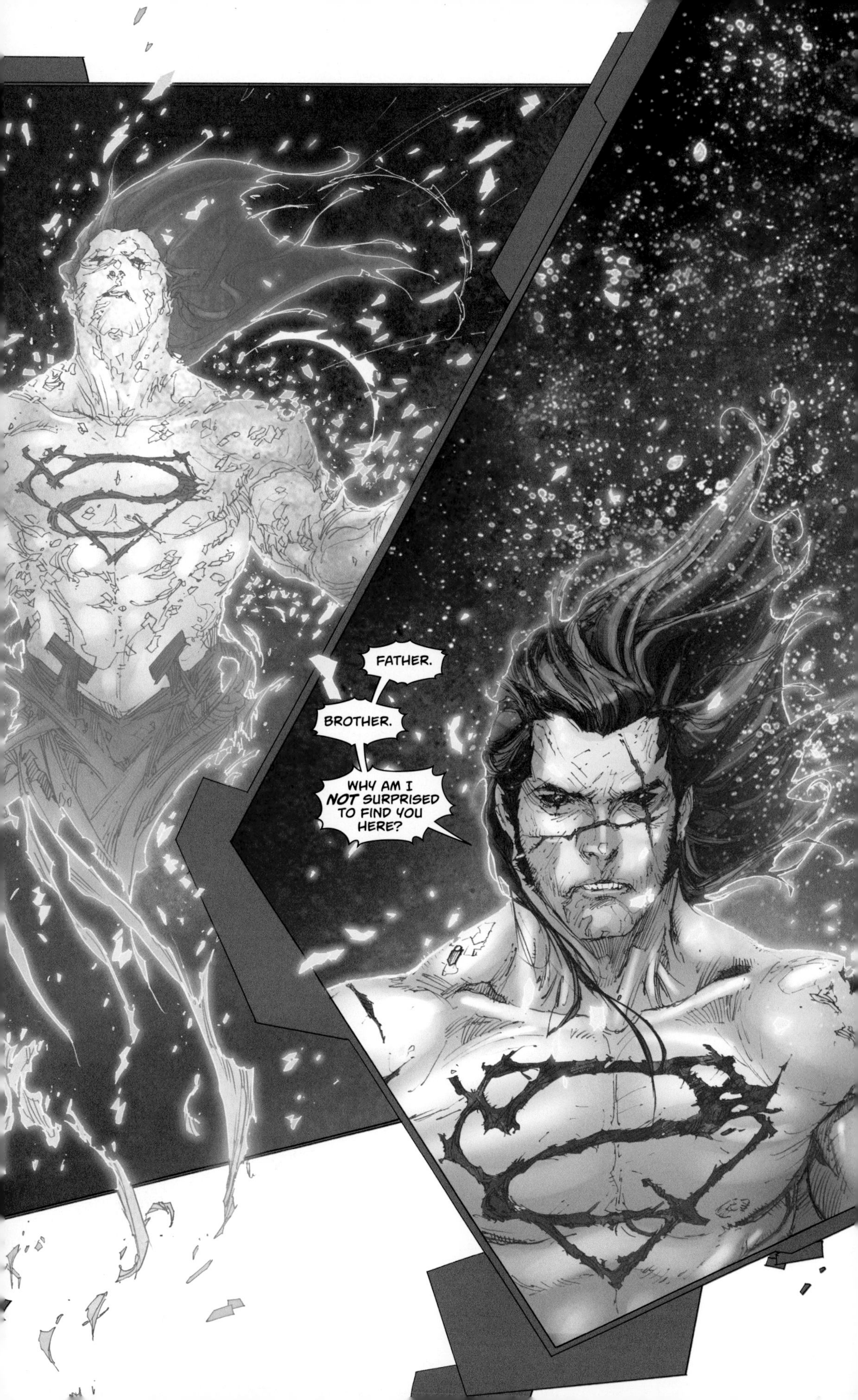
FATHER.
BROTHER.
WHY AM I *NOT* SURPRISED TO FIND YOU HERE?

BUT AS THEY LEAVE...

...SOMETHING UNEXPECTED HAPPENS.

FOR JUST AN INSTANT--

AND FOR AN INSTANT, KAL-EL AND KARA ARE NO LONGER ORPHANS OF THE OMNIVERSE.

AN INSTANT...

--KRYPTON RETURNS.

...OR SOMETHING MORE?

NEVER QUITE...THE END